Changing Ideas in Strategy

Changing Ideas in Strategy

Editor
Arun P. Sinha

Narosa Publishing House
New Delhi   Chennai   Mumbai   Kolkata

Changing Ideas in Strategy
220 pgs. | 24 figs. | 17 tbls.

Editor
Arun P. Sinha
Professor of Management
Indian Institute of Technology Kanpur
Kanpur

N A R O S A P U B L I S H I N G H O U S E P V T. L T D.

22 Delhi Medical Association Road, Daryaganj, New Delhi 110 002
35-36 Greams Road, Thousand Lights, Chennai 600 006
306 Shiv Centre, Sector 17, Vashi, Navi Mumbai 400 703
2F-2G Shivam Chambers, 53 Syed Amir Ali Avenue, Kolkata 700 019

www.narosa.com

Printed from the camera-ready copy provided by the Editor.

ISBN 978-81-8487-100-5

Published by N.K. Mehra for Narosa Publishing House Pvt. Ltd.,
22 Delhi Medical Association Road, Daryaganj, New Delhi 110 002

Printed in India

CONTENTS

Section 1

CHANGING IDEAS IN STRATEGY:
A PROLOGUE

Arun P. Sinha

Professor of Management
Indian Institute of Technology Kanpur

This book is about tracking changes in ideas that are responsible for organizational transformation, that is, changes in ideas of strategy. Change works in both positive and negative ways. The implementation of a strategy is commonly meant to be for benefit of an organization; but it might just as well have a deleterious effect. Either way, this effect of the concept brings new understanding to the actors, who may then proceed to modify the concept itself. Because, strategy, a social concept, is experiential and dynamic; it transforms a social entity, and depending on the nature and quantum of this change, it might lead to a change in itself. When results are beneficial, the idea gets reinforced, else it is modified.

Another point to note is that a strategy can change a system substantially from what it was when the concept was put in action, and one may never re-create the same *initial conditions* in the same or other system. Yet, there are two reasons why it is still useful to track the thinking behind the intervention, as well as the change that resulted from it. Such tracking is useful firstly because it helps us better *understand and archive* what has been a beneficial strategy and what has not been. While this in itself is significant, the tracking is also useful in a futuristic sense; it helps us make at least an *educated guess* about what could be a beneficial strategy for some organizations.

To illustrate how strategy-thought and social reality interact, and how this interaction is at the center of above change, let us look at the history of business and the history of management concepts during the second half of 20th century, particularly in US. The US economy, through a number of high-profile commercial firms, went into the growth mode. They were further encouraged by thought-leaders such as the marketing academic Theodore Levitt (1960), who wished firms would grow *wherever they might satisfy needs of customers*, that is, diversify. Some firms grew well, some did not, therefore the corporate consultants and academics began to explore *what direction of expansion* was more appropriate to suggest to a growth

1

seeking firm (as in Ansoff, 1965). There was also the fact that even well-calibrated diversification led to some casualties, while many industrial firms that stuck to their R&D-oriented field continued to perform well. This led to another sage advice to firms: they might stick to their *core competence* (Prahalad & Hamel, 1992).

On the implementation side, whether strategic moves were of diversification or of core-competence types, the firms have frequently used approaches that turned out to be impractical. The old organizational structures were often the key reason for failure; and this led to thinking about *Strategy-structure linkage* as another important advice of management consulting (Chandler, 1962). Of course, this strategic *fit* introduced an inevitable inflexibility. Some corporations found that they had exhausted the growth potential in their existing buyer segments, and yet, many prospective consumers remained un-served because they could not afford the price. Innovative players reinvented their strategies to escape this bind. They decided to tap the under-consuming low-income segments (as in micro-credit and mobile telephony). *Bottom of the pyramid* thus emerged as another key strategic concept (Prahalad, 2006).

These few concepts have been picked only as an illustration. There are indeed many more conceptual milestones of great significance in the various fields of organizational study. These few concepts are examples to exhibit a sense of the two-way interaction of strategy concepts with the social system. As one retraces the above milestones, of Ansoff-Chandler-Prahalad, it might also appear that the concepts are *determined* directly by respective *environments*. This evolutionary view would be an attractive interpretation, but it also entails a possible leap of logic. Strategic milestones happened not just because of a particular kind of situation but also because of choices that corporate leaders made. The bottom of pyramid concept, for example, could have been as much of a sage advice in 1970's as it is now in the 21st century.

It is important nonetheless to explore how these conceptual milestones happened to come about when they did, and the process of their emergence. No mutual relationship of concept with action in an entire social system can emerge instantaneously. Within each milestone must be incremental happenings. Many organizations may have taken parallel strategic actions that *made a difference*. Instead of vanishing like (unsustainable) blips over time, they were imitated and learnt by other actors and, over time, led to a bulk of such happenings in many organizations, such as to become milestones. *Which of these* strategic actions would have so taken-off that we would consider them to be milestones? This is a question we cannot explore here without more research. Yet, as students of strategy, we might at least take the opportunity to <u>track</u> the major changes that we currently observe in the strategy space, notice them while they occur in at least some of the organizations.

The 11th Annual Convention of Strategic Management Forum, SMF08 at IITKanpur, during 8-11 May 2008, occupied itself with just such a theme. Papers and cases selected from this convention are now introduced to readers of this volume, titled rather expectantly as "Changing Ideas in Strategy".

The first changing ideas in this volume are about new kinds of *missions* that have emerged in commercial organizations as well as those in some socially relevant ones. Substantial new missions have begun through the development of information and communication technologies, and through the wider emergence of a service-dominant society. Examples of these ideas constitute the first section of this volume. The second section deals with emergent *organizational forms*, such as the progressively more relevant *small enterprise*, in commercial and non-commercial domains, the emergent structuring of organizational sub-units that ensures a better fit for the adaptive orientation of the organization, and the strategic necessities of the inter-organizational context.

Furthermore, strategy concepts must now take account of new *resources* that were not earlier in formal reckoning. Innovation is one such resource, which forms the basis for section four. This section also discusses a second emergent resource that occupies the mind of the strategist - its *social capital*. Finally, before the editorial *epilogue* is section five of the volume that begins with a piece on the new *geographic locus* of organizations. With progressive globalization, and with the splintering of value-chains, organizations have begun to cater more-and-more to global markets, and have therefore moved towards networking across borders as a more viable strategy. This section also includes write-ups that deal with the increasingly more significant role of advertising, the role of flexible decision-methods in ever-changing environment and, finally, the aspects of firm growth. The editorial *epilogue* summarizes the key themes that emerge and how they constitute "Changing Ideas."

Thus, the sections of this focused set of writings include both, pieces where authors explore purely on a conceptual basis, as well as writings that bring out concepts from data on actual behavior of organizations. Conceptual pieces keep away from actual data. Empirical studies analyze real organizational processes, and how and which strategic choices appear to make a difference. Many of these are in a *case-format*. Whether analytical paper, or teaching case, these write-ups generate ideas that are *emergent* for strategy; they all have the prospect of becoming *milestones*.

It is also relevant to point out that the ideas here are not specific to a country. Even in the papers or cases where the frames of reference, and the data or case-locations, are Indian, the concepts that emerge are location-free. Not merely that the ideas are applicable to the so-called third world or even emerging nations. They are possible milestones everywhere!

ACKNOWELEDGEMENT

Finally, there is a customary packet of thanks. It would be an utterly selfish thought that by listing of gratitude, one can somehow relieve oneself of the profound debt and often superior contributions of others. One can however be reassured by the expectation that sometime somewhere, it will all *level-off*.

The named authors of papers and cases here, all participants in the convention, and the un-named persons, who helped to organize the convention, deserve grateful thanks. There are three people who must however be individually mentioned. They were most crucial to the making of this volume through their contributions to SMF08. First, Dr. Krishna Kumar, Professor of Strategy at IIM Lucknow, is the social entrepreneur behind Strategic Management Forum. He made SMF08 happen, through push and pull and untiring personal motivating. Bringing this volume to the publisher is again a saga of this same quiet pushing and support, from this same person, affectionately known to many as KK. The other big debt of this volume is to Dr. Runa Sarkar, now Faculty at IIM Kolkata. As convener, she brought vigor and efficiency to the organizing of SMF08. Her seamless combination of practical vision, team-building, and academic management was vital force in the event, and hence for this volume. Finally, one more person made major contribution: improving the structure and readability of many of the selected papers and cases.

Mansi Joshi, a recent graduate of Computer Science from MNNIT Allahabad took this up purely out of personal interest, and transformed many of the originally rough pieces in this volume. Thanks to you all.

It is to you, the reader, that makers of a book owe the most. While it is hoped that readers would excuse the errors and limitations, which inevitably belong to the editor, it is also hoped that readers would send in their critique which is actively solicited.

Arun P. Sinha
Editor
asinha@iitk.ac.in

REFERENCES

1. Ansoff, H. I. (1965) *Corporate Strategy*, New York: McGraw Hill.
2. Chandler, A. D. (1962) *Strategy and Structure: Chapters in the History of Industrial Enterprise, Cambridge*, MA: MIT Press.
3. Levitt, T (1960), "Marketing Myopia", *Harvard Business Review*, July-August 1960: 45-56
4. Prahlad, C. K. and Gary Hamel (1992), Core Competence of the Corporation, *Harvard Business Review*, 68(3): 79-91.
5. Prahlad, C. K. (2006), *The Fortune at the Bottom of the Pyramid*, Upper Saddle River, NJ: Wharton Book Publishing.

Section 2

EMERGENT MISSIONS

EMERGENT MISSIONS

Mission is a concept of major emphasis for the strategist. In Ansoff's (1965) view, mission of an enterprise is the various product *needs* it satisfies, described often as *scope* of the firm. Existence of a *common thread* among all these missions would be desirable for the enterprise. A more overall view of mission of a firm is *the business it is in* (Drucker, 1974). This relates the firm to its overall social purpose, the reason for its existence.

Customers and users are essential to a strategy discourse about mission. Needs of individuals and of organizational customers may however change over time. New missions tend to get formulated, whether through splitting or integration of value-chains or otherwise. It is also useful to see in our present context whether missions that were earlier not so prominent may have now become prominent in the economy.

The paper, by Subhash Sharma, presents a modified view of organizational objectives, a view that is more 'holistic'. He tries to make us move from an *economic concept of business* to a concept of *human actions in business*, which covers aspects like:

- o choice to do business with someone on the basis of likes & dislikes
- o business as a social institution, and
- o business as an institution in interaction with spiritual aspects of people (inside and outside the organization)

The case Northern India Call Center Limited describes a medium sized family-owned firm in the call-center business with emergent implications for industry and society. The third piece is also about the services sector. It describes the unique features of planning for businesses like retail, malls, etcetera, and how flexibility is critical to planning here.

Finally, this section has a case where the missions as well as the form are different from what has been generally seen. There have been changes in the organizational arrangement for socially relevant work sponsored from industrialized nations for the benefit of groups in poorer countries. Many mediating organizations are now in this value-chain. This case is about one such organization, an NGO run by a multilateral agency for social development.

REFERENCES

1. Ansoff, H. I. (1965) *Corporate Strategy*, New York: McGraw Hill.
2. Drucker, P. F. (1974), *Management – Tasks, Responsibilities, Practices*, New York: Harper and Row.

TOWARDS HOLISTIC PERFORMANCE SCORECARD: A NEW STRATEGIC INITIATIVE

Subhash Sharma

Indian Business Academy, Bangalore and Greater Noida

INTRODUCTION

Performance scorecard is an important tool to measure performance of an organization. Earlier scorecards were largely focused on financial performance of the corporation. For example, *Padta* system followed by some Indian organizations was rooted in daily reporting of financial performance, particularly in terms of cash generation. Many monthly and quarterly reporting systems were also focused on financial performance as key determinant of organizational performance.

For any performance measurement system we need a foundational framework. The metaphor of 'Business House' conceptualized in terms of following five key functions represented by SMFPHR, can serve as a conceptual model:

1. **S**: Strategy
2. **M**: Marketing
3. **F**: Finance
4. **P**: Production
5. **HR**: Human Resources

Metaphorically, the roof of such a business house is constituted by the Strategy, Marketing and Finance triangle. Its room represents the production function and its foundation is represented by Human Resources. Such a view of a business house gives us a conceptual basis for designing Business Success Performance Scorecard (BSPSc). Figure-1 represents this perspective to develop such a performance scorecard.

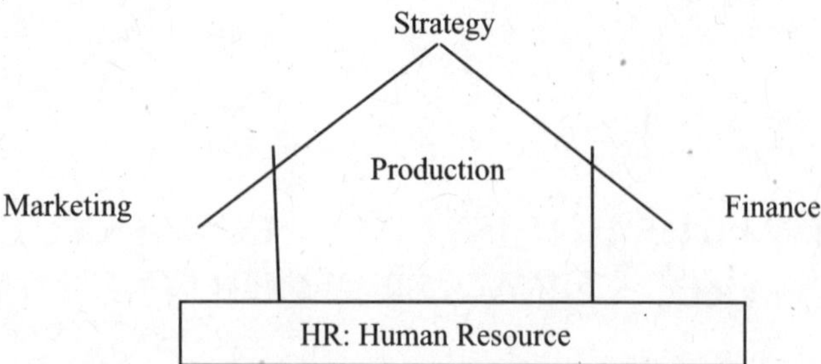

Figure 1: House of Business for Developing Performance Scorecard

When performance scorecard takes into consideration the performance of the entire business house, we obtain a better assessment. The performance scorecard should also consider SWAN analysis with respect to each function as well as the whole organization. The concept of SWAN analysis developed by this author (2007) and expanded in his book Market's Maya (2009) has the following elements:

S: Strengths
W: Weaknesses
A: Achievements
N: Next step/Next initiative

When SWAN analysis is done for each function and for the organization as a whole, it creates a linkage with organization's ViSA (Vision, Strategy and Action plan). This is the essence of the scorecard based on the business house metaphor suggested above.

BALANCED SCORECARD & BEYOND

Kaplan and Norton (1996) took another view and developed the concept of Balanced Scorecard. They suggested that vision and strategy of an organization should be linked with the following four perspectives: Customer Perspective, Financial Perspective, Internal Business Perspective, and Learning & Growth Perspective

They elaborate on these perspectives in terms of following key ideas:
Customer perspective: To achieve our vision, how should we appear to customers?
Financial perspective: To succeed financially, how should we appear to our shareholders?
Internal business process: To satisfy shareholders and customers, what business processes must we excel at?
Learning and growth perspective: To achieve our vision, how will we sustain our ability to change and improve?

They argue that scorecard should focus on a balanced view of the organization in terms of the above indicated four perspectives and these four perspectives should be linked to vision and strategy. They also suggest that each perspective should be analyzed in terms of objectives, measures, targets and initiatives. This would ensure that the strategy is translated into operational terms. Figure 2 presents their model of Balanced Scorecard.

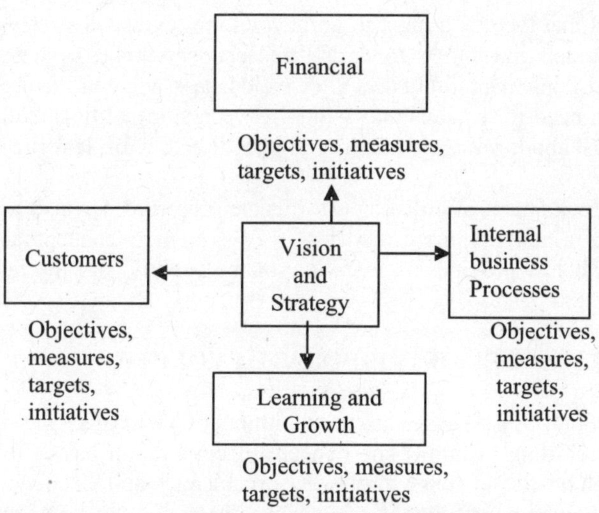

Figure 2: Kaplan & Norton (1996) Conceptual Framework for Balanced Scorecard
(Source: The Balanced Scorecard, Robert S Kaplan, David P Norton, Harvard Business School Press, Boston, Mass., 1996, p.9)

Balanced Scorecard represented a breakthrough, because earlier scorecards were largely restricted to financial performance; they were not directly linked to the strategy of the organization.

It may be observed that the four perspectives suggested by Kaplan and Norton broadly correspond to SMFPHR framework of organizations presented in the form of 'Business House'. Customer perspective is captured in performance scorecard of the marketing function. Financial perspective is captured through the finance function. Internal business process to a large extent is captured by performance scorecard of the production and operations function of the organization. Learning and growth perspective is captured through performance scorecard of the Human Resource Development function. Thus, there is broad correspondence between the two frameworks. Managers of the 'Business House' are also interested in knowing how the house appears to customers, shareholders as well as other stakeholders. In their framework, Kaplan & Norton focus largely on customers and shareholders. When we use the metaphor of 'Business House', we get a better conceptual foundation as now the focus is on how the house appears not only to customers and shareholders but also to other stakeholders as well as society at large. Is this house creating pollution? Is it environmentally sound? Such questions are not answered by Kaplan and Norton's Balanced Scorecard. Hence, in true sense it is not properly balanced. In addition, their framework does not include concerns such as corporate social responsibility, ethical performance of the corporation. Thus, there is need to develop a new approach to scorecards wherein these dimensions are also taken into consideration while assessing the performance of the corporate. It implies a holistic view of performance and thereby we need to develop Holistic Performance Scorecard (HPSc). Thus, Business Success Performance Scorecard (BSPSc) as well as Balanced Scorecard should be expanded to measure performance on holistic basis.

It may be indicated that Michael Porter and Mark Kramer (2006) have expanded the traditional view of strategy by suggesting interdependency between business and society and thereby between society and strategy. However, Gustavsson

(2007) suggests that there is a need to go beyond the 'extended strategy' concept of Porter and Kramer and move towards 'transcendent strategy' wherein strategy formulation and implementation takes a 'consciousness' view of the organization, so he points to the need for establishing a link between spirituality and strategy. These expanded views about strategy take us in the direction of Holistic Performance Scorecard.

For development of holistic performance scorecard, we also need to look at the evolution of a new corporate model as well as its new conceptual foundations. The discussion below provides an overview of the evolutionary journey of the new corporate model.

FOUR STAGES MODEL OF CORPORATE EVOLUTION

Ackoff (1981) provides us an evolutionary view of changing concept of corporation. According to him, "The concept of corporation has evolved from one that was mechanistic to one that was organismic and from organismic to organization. Viewed as machine it was taken to have no purpose of its own, but an instrument for use by its owners in pursuit of their profit objective. Viewed as organism the corporation was taken to have survival and growth as it principal purpose…Viewed as an organization the corporation was seen to have responsibility to all its stakeholders and to society, the larger system of which it is a part" (pp. 48-49. Ackoff further suggests that corporations should contribute to improve the quality of life of others. He suggests the need for developing measurement systems for the same. This is a pointer towards the idea of Holistic Performance Measurement Systems (HPMS).

Drawing on Ackoff and others, Sharma (2005, 2007) identifies four stages of evolutionary journey of corporations. These are as follows:

Stage I: Corporations and Shareholders: The primary objective of the corporate was to maximize the wealth of shareholders. Competition, efficiency and profit provided the basic foundation for this model.

Stage II: Corporations and Stakeholders: There are many stakeholders and there should be a proper balance between the interests of various stakeholders. For example, corporations can maximize the wealth of shareholders by polluting the rivers. Social movements have now put pressure on corporations to prevent this.

Stage III: Corporations and Society- Citizenship model: In this stage of their evolution, corporations have been conceptualized as corporate citizens. Hence, expectations on ethics and environmental concerns have gained importance. Corporations are expected to follow 'principles of ethical business' and not merely, 'principles of business'.

Stage IV: Corporations and Sustainable development- Corporations as social institutions: In this conceptualization, corporations are viewed as social institutions with dominant influence on society. Hence, there is need for a symbiotic relationship between society and the corporations. They are expected to contribute towards sustainable development of society. Their linkage with sustainable and holistic development needs strengthening. As social institutions corporations should achieve synergy between efficiency, social equity, ethics and environmental concerns.

While Stage I model was largely an efficiency model, in stage II model, social equity concerns were incorporated to some extent, and in stage III model, ethics were also considered important for conduct of business. Now in their stage IV evolution as social institutions, corporations are expected to achieve appropriate balance between efficiency, social equity and ethics and also be concerned with transcendental values of environment, women's equity, psycho-spiritual advancement etc. This is a new age model wherein corporations are viewed as social institutions and not merely business entities, that is, in addition to the bottom line concerns, they have a social purpose, and they should be guided by sustainable and holistic development. Fig. 3 presents the above discussed evolutionary perspective of the corporate model.

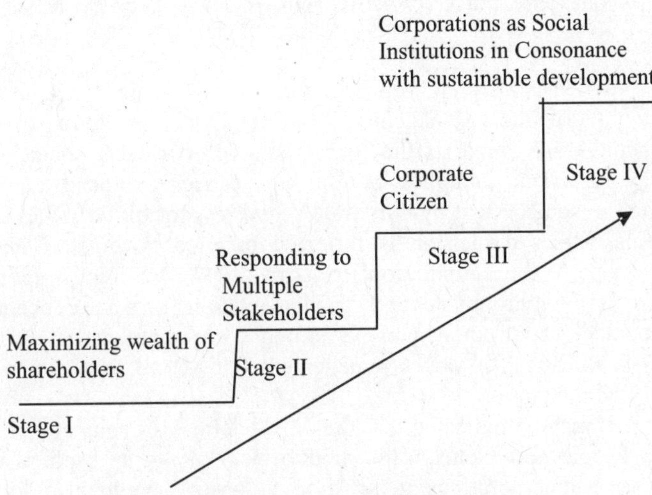

Figure 3: Four Stages Model of Corporate Evolution

CONCEPTUAL FOUNDATIONS OF NEW CORPORATE MODEL: 4 Es FRAMEWORK

Evolution of the new corporate model is also linked to new paradigms of development thinking. Evolution of development thinking from economic development to new paradigms of sustainable development and integrative holistic development has influenced the corporate world. Sharma (1996) suggested the 4 Es model of holistic development and management emphasizing the need for achieving a proper balance between following four Es:

1. Efficiency
2. Equity
3. Ethics
4. Ecology

Figure 4 presents this framework as a synergy model of development. In this model the 4 Es are in dynamic interaction and they are in proper harmony thereby synergy is created in society.

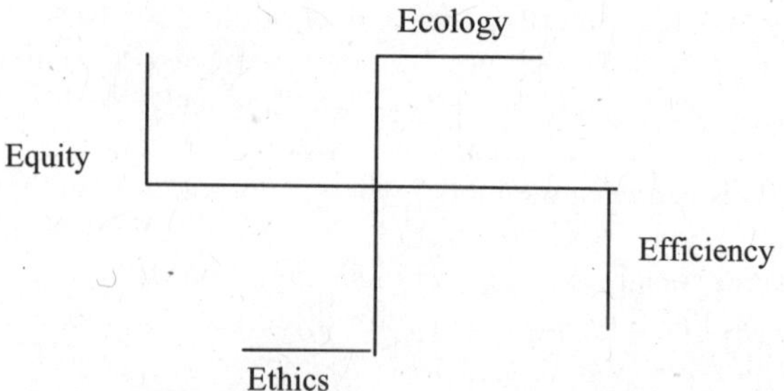

Figure 4: 4 Es Framework for New Corporate Model
(Source: Management in New Age: Western Windows Eastern Doors, Subhash Sharma, 1996, p. 92).

When applied in corporate context, this model leads us to the concept of Holistic Corporate Management (HCM), wherein foundations of corporate management are based on the four pillars of efficiency, social equity, ethics and ecology. Efficiency implies bottom-line concerns. Social equity dimension is reflected to some extent by corporate social responsibility (CSR) and neighborhood concerns. Ethics dimension is reflected in good governance and the 'Character Competence of the Corporation' (Sharma, 2002). Ecology is reflected in terms of concern for environment and implementation of the concept of sustainable development in corporate context through 'environmental management systems'. Thus, in Holistic Corporate Management (HCM) all four dimensions of the 4 E model find integration.

It may be indicated that the 4E model has an equivalence in 3 Ps model of Profit, People and Planet. This model, also known as triple bottom line model, suggests that corporations in addition to profit, should also focus on CSR and environmental concerns captured through the imaginative phrases, people and planet. In fact, corporate social responsibility, environmental concerns and good governance have become new strategic imperatives as well as "new mantras" for the corporate world. We can hear their echoes in the Board rooms and corporate corridors.

Prahlad and Hamel (1992) suggested the concept of Core Competence. This concept originated from the efficiency model of the corporates. However, for Holistic Corporate Management (HCM), we need to include 4Es framework.. Hence, corporations as social institutions should focus on the following:
1. Core competence and similar other strategic management tools in consonance with efficiency and competitive advantage paradigms.
2. Corporate Social responsibility (CSR) to meet social expectations of social equity paradigm.
3. Concern for environmental issues
4. Character competence of the corporation in consonance with ethics and good governance requirements.

These four ideas constitute a new conceptual foundation for designing Holistic Performance Scorecard.

FROM PEST TO STEPS: SPIRITUALITY AND STRATEGY LINK

Philosophical foundations of the new corporate model can also be traced to some well known Indian concepts such as Gandhi's Trusteeship model, concept of *loksangraha* (welfare of the society/stakeholders) and the concept of *shubh-labh*. Gandhi's trusteeship model is finding its expression in multiple stakeholders concept of the corporates. The concept of *loksangraha* is expressed in the idea of Corporate Social Responsibility (CSR) and the concept of shubh-labh is finding its expression in ethical concerns as well as 'moral sentiments' of business as advocated by Adam Smith. In fact, the shubh-labh concept takes us beyond Adam Smith's 'moral sentiments' as it also suggests the need for a spiritual touch to business activities. . It may be indicated that in the expression *shubh-labh, shubh* is indicative of the sacred dimension and *labh* is indicative of the economic dimension. Thus this concept has a linkage with the concept of "sacro-economic" view of business activities. Charles Drekmeier (1962) mentions the phrase 'sacro-economic' in his seminal work, 'Kingship and Community in Early India' providing us an insight that the concept of sacro-economic view has been in existence in Indian civilization since ages. Chakraverti (2000) observes that, "The expression (Shubh-labh) which translates roughly into 'auspicious profit' implies that ancients had unearthed the morality of the market and found its effect- wealth generation through profit- beneficial to society". While the idea of 'sacro-economic' has been in existence, its application in the field of management and in the corporate context is new. In corporate context it implies that corporate is not merely an economic entity but should be viewed as 'sacro-economic' entity. Conventional literature on strategy is based on competitive advantage framework and ignores the 'moral sentiments' as well as 'sacro-economic' view of enterprises. Even, Kaplan and Norton's Balanced Scorecard does not care for Adam Smith's 'moral sentiments'. Above stated three ideas viz. Trusteeship (from Gandhi), loksangraha (from Gita) and shubh-labh (from Indian business tradition) provide us a new conceptual foundation for the new corporate model wherein corporates are considered social institutions and not merely profit making machines at the cost of environment and social disruption. This framework can be referred to as 'House of Shubhlabh' and is sacro-economic in its strategic architecture. This is the essence of the 'sacro-economic' model of corporates.

New conceptual foundations suggested in our discussions require a shift from PEST analysis to STEPS analysis to incorporate the nature of spiritual environment in which organizations are functioning. Spiritual environment includes the ethical context of business. In PEST analysis, ethical dimension is not given due consideration. STEPS model suggested by this author (2001) in the context of a nation's development vision has following dimensions:

S: Social
T: Technological
E: Economic
P: Political
S: Spiritual

When applied in the context of environmental analysis and to the field of strategic management, it suggests a link between spirituality and strategy. It may be indicated that PEST is not a very positive metaphor. In contrast, STEPS is a positive metaphor. It may also be indicated that link between spirituality and strategy has not been explored. As indicated earlier, recent work by Gustavsson (2007) provides a broad indication for a need to explore this linkage. In general an indirect linkage has been highlighted by many through the need for ethical concerns in the activities of the corporation. It may be observed that traditionally strategy literature was rooted in the competitive advantage framework and maximization of shareholders' wealth. However we do come across people who refuse to add certain types of business activities to their portfolio because of environmental, social, ethical and spiritual concerns. For example, many vegetarian business persons refuse to enter non-vegetarian businesses even though it may add to their competitive advantage. The recent concept of Socially Responsible Investments (SRI) is also an indicator in this direction. Ethical and spiritual concerns are also considered critical for good governance.

Drawing from Porter's 'extended strategy' and Gustavsson's 'transcendent strategy' concepts we arrive at the **SSS** (Spirituality-Society-Strategy) model wherein strategy formulation and implementation is driven by spiritual values and spiritual concerns including ethical concerns as well as social responsibility requirements. Essence of **SSS** model is as follows:

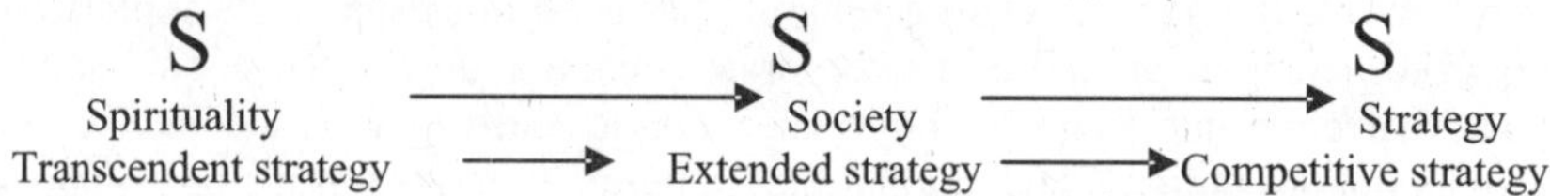

IMPLICATIONS FOR PERFORMANCE SCORECARD: FROM BALANCED SCORECARD TO HOLISTIC PERFORMANCE SCORECARD

It was earlier indicated that Balanced Scorecard represented a breakthrough in performance measurement as it expanded the earlier concept of performance measurement from its narrow focus on financial performance. However, our discussion indicates that balanced scorecard has its own limitations as its view is limited to organization as an economic entity/ business entity. Issues such as ethical performance, environmental performance, social responsibility and spiritual concerns are not included in its domain. There is a need to base performance measurement system in the concept of corporate as social institution. While business entity concept led us to Balanced Scorecard, social institution concept leads us to Holistic Performance Scorecard. Using the framework of Business House presented earlier and incorporating the 4 E's framework as well as STEPS framework, we arrive at a new conceptual foundation for holistic performance scorecard. This conceptual foundation is presented in Figure 5. Using this framework we can develop specific metric for its various elements on the basis of SWAN analysis for each performance area. In fact SWAN analysis can be combined with OMTAI (Objectives, Measures, Targets, Achievements, and Initiatives) for each performance area including CSR and Good governance. It may be indicated that a comparison of Targets and Achievements identifies the performance gap and initiatives indicate how this gap will be bridged. Thus, TAI (Targets, Achievements, Initiatives) when combined with Objectives and Measures (OM), gives a comprehensive view of performance.

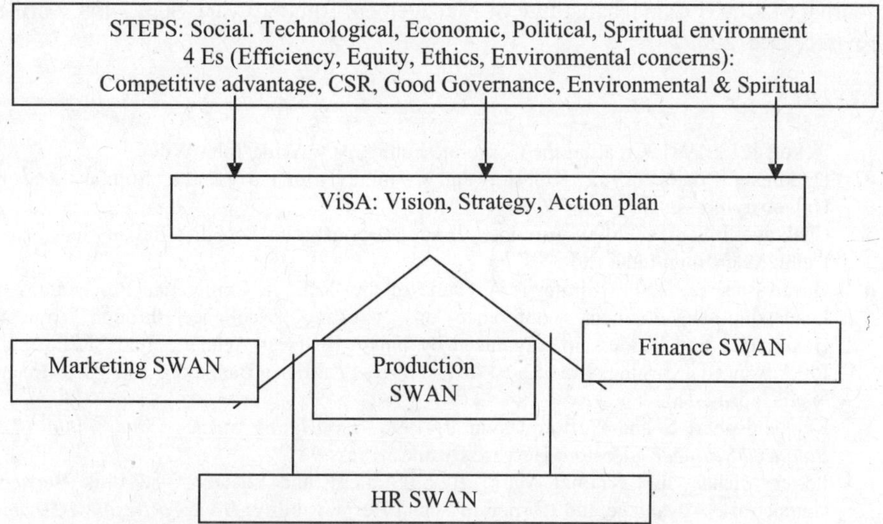

**Figure 5: From Business Entity to Social Institution: Foundational
Framework for Holistic Performance Scorecard**

This framework presented above suggests that 'strategic vistas' of an organization should give due considerations to efficiency / competitive advantage, social equity/ social responsibility, ethics/ good governance and spiritual environment. Earlier performance scorecards were largely based on efficiency paradigm / competitive advantage paradigm of treating corporate as merely a business entity. This philosophy is also reflected in Balanced Scorecard developed by Kaplan and Norton. Our discussion indicates that this paradigm is undergoing a change and corporations are emerging as social institutions as a result of pressure from environment and many other social and spiritual movements. Therefore, need for Holistic Performance Scorecard to reflect the contribution of the corporate world towards environmental concerns, social concerns, good governance and betterment of spiritual environment. This implies that time has come to move beyond the Balance Scorecard (BSc) to Holistic Performance Scorecard (HPSc) to achieve a better symbiosis between corporate world, society and individuals.

CONCLUDING REMARKS

Are there organizations that follow the ideas presented above? Balanced Scorecard has been in use in the corporate world and corporate world also recognizes the importance of CSR and good governance. Many corporations include a brief write up on their CSR activities and initiatives for Good governance in their balance sheet. This implies they are moving in the direction of Holistic Performance Scorecard (HPSc). This indicates that it is possible to have performance card that is in consonance with holistic perspective of organizations. In future more corporations may adopt this approach as a result of pressures from social movements, environmental movements and spiritual movements.

NOTE: An earlier version of this paper was published in Vilakshan, Journal of XIMB (Xavier Institute of Management Bhubneswar), Sept 2008. Further revised, Dec. 2009.

REFERENCES

1. Ackoff R.L., 1981. Creating the Corporate Future, New York, John Wiley.
2. Drekmeier Charles, 1962. Kingship and Community in Early India, Bombay: Oxford University Press.
3. Chakraverti Sauvik, 2000. Antidote: Essays Against The Socialist Indian State, New Delhi: MacMillan India Ltd.:
4. Gustavsson, B., 2007. 'Strategy- A Game of the Past', in Conference Proceedings of Leadership Development Conference on, 'Creating Excellence through Strategy, Governance and Leadership' organized by Indian Business Academy and SMT Centre for Advanced Learning, Mar 13-14 and Mar 16-17 at IBA Bangalore and IBA Greater Noida, pp. 12-18.
5. Kaplan Robert S and Norton David P, 1996. *Translating Strategy into Action: The Balanced Scorecard*, Boston: Harvard Business Press.
6. Porter Michael and Kramer Mark, 2006. Strategy and Society: The Link Between Competitive Advantage and Corporate Social Responsibility, *Harvard Business Review*, 84(12): 79-91.
7. Prahlad, C. K. and Gary Hamel, 1992, Core Competence of the Corporation, *Harvard Business Review*, 68(3): 79-91.
8. Sharma, Subhash, 1996. *Management in New Age: Western Windows Eastern Doors*, New Age International Publishers, New Delhi.
9. Sharma, Subhash, 2000. 'Forward Engineering for Strategic Gearing: A Conceptual Framework', *Indian Journal of Public Administration*, Oct –Dec., Vol. XLVI:4, pp. 667-674.
10. Sharma, Subhash, 2001. 'Development STEPS' in *Vision Karnataka 2025: Strategies and Action Plan for Sustainable Development*, (ed) Jeevan Kumar D and Susheela Subramanya, Sothern Economist, Bangalore, 295-298
11. Sharma, Subhash, 2002. 'Character Competence of the Corporation', *Journal of Human Values*, 8(2):107-118.
12. Sharma, Subhash, 2005. 'A Model for Corporate Development: A Holistic Approach', *Vilakshan, XIMB Journal of Management*, II (2): 71-78.
13. Sharma, Subhash, 2007. 'Ethical Foundations of New Corporate Model: Implications for Strategy and Leadership', in Proceedings of 10th International Annual Convention on *Strategic Management for Firms in Developing Countries*, (ed) Atanu Ghosh and Gargi Banerjee, Allied Publishers Pvt Ltd., New Delhi, 242-245.
14. Sharma, Subhash Sharma, 2007. 'Corporate SWAN: SWAN Model for Strategic Analysis, A Concept Note', SS/IBA/Sept. 2007, Indian Business Academy (IBA), Bangalore & Greater Noida.
15. Sharma, Subhash, 2007. *New Mantras in Corporate Corridors: From Ancient Roots to Global Routes,* New Age International Publishers, New Delhi.
16. Sharma, Subhash, 2009. *Market's Maya: Lotus Millionaires from New Madhushala*, IBA Publications, Bangalore.

NORTHERN INDIA CALL CENTER LTD.

Arun P. Sinha[1]
Himanshi Vij[2]

[1]Professor of Management, Indian Institute of Technology Kanpur
[2]Final Year BTech student, Punjab University, Chandigarh

THE CASE

Northern India Call Center Ltd. (NICCL) is a medium sized enterprise owned by Ramesh Kapoor, Chairman, and run by him with the help of his daughter Saloni Kapoor, the CEO and Vice Chairman. It has call-centers in three cities. NICCL currently has the option to enter into a deal with Sisodia Telecom for 150 seats of inbound calls over North India which would give a major boost to the revenues of NICCL. Instead of serving twenty odd clients, the firm might even consolidate on three major ones. But Sisodia had strict conditions.

They will appoint the Delhi branch of the American consulting company, Burst & Old to audit performance. Unlike the usual audit, this will be more elaborate and strict. The contract will include financial penalties for shortfall in audited performance. A second requirement of Sisodia is to get things on stream in two months, by 1 December 2007.

The Operations Manager was quick to remind his boss, "Sir, I do not know whether this is possible. We took six months to set up the Noida center when Air Communication Ltd gave us a new circle. Sisodia needs three times that many seats!" To which RK queried, "Look Manjeet, last year you suggested increasing seats in the Chandigarh centre instead of starting the new one at Mohali. And it took us barely one month to increase seats. Can we not do the same for our Noida centre?"

Rekha, the HR Manager seemed uncomfortable with this. Some of the Customer Care Executives (CCE's) were already complaining about the lack of physical space. They feel it is too cramped, and they lose concentration.

Saloni Kapoor (SK) was concerned about another issue – recruiting sufficient CCE's. They would now have calls from Barmer and Basti which could be a problem as most of their employees are Punjabi Speaking.

It did not seem like an open and shut case to SK. Competition in the market was increasing; large software players were expected to enter NICCL's market, and this was a major worry. She suggested doing homework on the issue. And soon began to review NICCL through files on her desk.

NICCL

NICCL was set up as an IT-training franchise in 1999 for multimedia training. It set up operations at a central location in Chandigarh. Great Multimedia, the franchisor, supplied learning material. In 2002, this business was transformed into a BPO (call-centre). Turmeric Telecom, a licensee for mobile telephony in Punjab-Haryana, was beginning to upgrade customer care. With guidance from Turmeric's general manager, phones and other equipment were added. Starting with a 40-seat BPO to handle *inbound* calls, NICCL's business was now very prosperous.

CURRENT LOCATIONS AND CAPACITY

The company made gross sales of around Rs. 25 Crore in 2006-07 through its three centers - Chandigarh, Noida, and Jaipur. A fourth center is planned to be set up in Mohali. The center in Jaipur is important for back-up support, just in case local problems disturb another center's operation. According to the HR manager, supply of manpower is also easier in Jaipur, which has no big employers. Table-1 below gives a recent month's comparison of the three centers.

Table-1
The Three Centres of NICCL

	Chandigarh	Noida	Jaipur
Number of Seats	300	400	450
Agents	310	500	400
Percent Uptime	97.5	95	90
Service Level (for inbound process)	95	95	85

Noida is the company's most recent call centre. It is close to Delhi and Gurgaon, and a booming IT hub. Trained manpower is easy to find, due to rampant job-hopping. The region has a concentration of young people from the upper middle class, who are fluent in English and also IT-savvy.

Chandigarh, though a Tier-II city, has exhibited fast growth in the IT sector. It now has a Technology Park with development centers of companies like Infosys, the Quark City in Mohali, and prominent BPO enterprises like Convergys, Wipro, and EDC.

SERVICES OFFERED BY NICCL

NICCL caters mainly to domestic Telecom companies. It offers 'processes' of both kinds – Inbound Calls, and Outbound Calls. All its inbound processes work 24x7.

Both inbound and outbound calls are handled at each of the three centers of NICCL, which caters to Punjab, Haryana, Chandigarh, Delhi and Rajasthan. The centers are kept independent for operational purposes. All the processes that NICCL runs at these centers are either in Hindi or in Punjabi.

Distribution of seats, and agents, to inbound and outbound calls is very fluid. It depends on the contracts that are currently on. Currently, around 210 of the 300 seats in Chandigarh are being used, though the center has over 310 agents. Its inbound process uses 50 seats each shift, and 160 seats are used for outbound work.

THE MARKET

NICCL is a key *partner* of ACL for Punjab circle since 2004. This is one of the 25 circles where ACL operates. In Punjab circle, ACL is one of the three players licensed to operate mobile telephone service. ACL has tied up with partners to provide various parts of the value-chain. Since 2004, NICCL has contributed to ACL's customer care helpline, and various outbound services in marketing and promotion.

ACL parcels out the helpline and other outsourced services to multiple partners. It grades the partners into A, B, & C categories. NICCL and a few other call-centers are graded as 'B' level partners. Two MNCs are graded at the 'A' level, while a large number of centers of less than 50 seats each are at 'C' level.

NICCL claims to maintain a service level of over 95% for most processes, that is, over 95% calls of the process are answered. "This is far higher than the MNCs which operate at around 50% level", says the CEO and Vice Chairman Saloni Kapoor. She finds it strange that despite 'better' service, and despite bidding lower, they are not perceived in the same class as large BPOs and MNCs.

She also believes that, compared to large companies, her BPO is more flexible; they are able to expand capacity almost overnight to meet a sudden need. An MNC will not do that. They will also not approach the telco on their own, whereas for NICCL it is normal practice. "We know who in the client company to contact; we ourselves assess their process requirements because we make it a practice to talk to the relevant managers. Sometimes we get business because of what we have pointed out to the manager in the telco."

COMPETITION

Call-centers for India's domestic market are a large industry growing at a rapid pace. Captive centers dominate the business, though third-party centers account for almost a quarter (see below). Daksh, Convergys, IBM, Dell are some key third party players. With easy availability of technology, small centers were also started by local entrepreneurs in Tier II and III cities and also in metros. These cater to clients having limited or regional requirement. They use mostly the local language, and are able to avoid problems related to long-distance connectivity. Some of these, like NICCL, have grown to medium scale of 200-2000 seats, and to multiple locations.

THE CALL CENTER INDUSTRY

The Call Center industry is part of a worldwide phenomenon of business process outsourcing. Their activities are mainly of inbound calls (helplines) and outbound calls.

In case of **inbound call** service, Customer Care Executives (CCEs), known also as agents, take calls related to a particular process. 'Process' refers to the set of aspects that an outsourcing company wants the helpline to deal with, and how the responses are to be given. There is wide variety in what the helplines deal with. It may relate to customer service and queries, technical support, sales support, order taking, and so on. Except for some processes limited to normal office hours and days, others are 24x7, for which, agents are online all the time, receiving and responding to calls.

Outbound Calls are made by agents to promote a product or service or scheme, or to get feedback. The process may focus on customer service & customer retention service, database marketing, lead generation/qualification, market research, registrations, renewals or sales including up-sale, cross-sale, and continuities. These services have fixed (daytime) hours. A customer care executive might spend 8-9 hours a day for an outbound service.

India is one of the most prominent suppliers of call center service. The global outsourcing industry was estimated to be worth US$ 233 bn in 2006 (Rachael King, The Outsourcing Upstarts, The Business Week, July 31, 2007).

. According to a report based on a study by Dataquest (Domestic call center revenues to exceed Rs 8500 cr in FY-08, 12 Feb, 2008, Indiatimes News Network), the domestic call-center industry in India did business worth Rs. 6200 Crore in 2006-07, and is expected to grow 65% in 2007-08, compared to 42% in the previous year. The study also estimates the following break-up of the business for 2006-07:

$$\begin{array}{ll} \text{Captive call-centers ----- Rs. 3598 Cr} \\ \text{Third Party vendors -----} \quad \underline{1602\ Cr} \\ \qquad\qquad\qquad\qquad\qquad 6200\ Cr \end{array}$$

Of the third party vendors, the study estimated the revenues of 'organized' players at 1097 Cr and the 'unorganized' ones at 505 Cr. In this, the companies that employed more than 200 people were classified as 'organized'. Parallel estimates by IDC, for the domestic ITeS sector in India, are 6650 Cr for 2006 and 11970 Cr for 2007 (http://bpo-service.blogspot.com/2008/01/bpos-talk-local-for-expansion.html). The study also forecast a growth of 19.7% CAGR during next four years, versus 17.4% for India's IT/ITes export market.

The Dataquest study gives the following estimate of employment in India's domestic outsourcing sector, as of December 2007:

$$\begin{array}{ll} \text{Captive call-centers ----- 130,000 agents} \\ \text{Third Party vendors ----- } \underline{150,000\ agents} \\ \qquad\qquad \text{TOTAL} \quad 280,000\ agents \end{array}$$

Remuneration for call-center agents in India varies widely across locations. Table-2 below gives the range of remuneration for both fresh as well as experienced personnel in 2006 at call centers in three cities in India.

Table-2
Range of Remuneration at Call Centers in India (in Rupees/month)

	Fresh Agents	Experienced Agents	Supervisors
Mumbai	8000 - 15000	10000 - 15000	17000
Bangalore -small center -big name firm	5000 – 7000 8000 - 12000	5500 - 14500	
Kolkata -small center	4500	8500	8500

(Source: http://www.ecommercetimes.com/story/43967.html?welcome=1205508457)

TECHNOLOGY & EQUIPMENT

Equipment used in NICCL has been sourced from suppliers in UK. This, the company claims, is comparable to any big or international firm in the industry. Key brands, systems, and equipment include -- Predictive Dialer: Concerto; Automatic Call Distribution: Nortel/Ericsson/Corel; Multiplexes: Nortel; Servers: HP/IBM; Connectivity: TDM/MPSL, ATM/FR; Redundancy: 2 Level (On Ring Topology); Mode of Connectivity: Optical Fiber End-to-End; Power Backup: Online UPS and Generators.

Additional features include: automatic call distribution, call blending, caller ID customization, dialed number identification service (DNIS), digital recording, full automated scripting, interactive voice service (IVR), predictive dialing, preview dialing, knowledge based routing, report customization, remote monitoring third party transfer.

ORGANIZATION STRUCTURE

There are four departments in the organization - Operations, Finance, HRD, and Technical. The structure is described in Exhibit 1. The **Operations** team is the largest in number. It includes, at the lowest level, all the agents who take or make the calls. There are a number of 'floors' at each center and each floor has a floor incharge (FI) who coordinates the agents on that floor. Sometimes, two 'floors' are segregated only by a glass partition. A team leader (TL) heads a group of FI's, and a group of TL's are headed by a Supervisor. All supervisors report to the Assistant Manager (Operations) who reports to the Manager (Operations).

The proportions of employees at the four levels of hierarchy in operation at NICCL are something like the following:

- For every 15-20 calling agents, there is one FI,
- For every 3 FIs there is one Team Leader and
- For every 3 TLs there is one Supervisor.

The Technical department takes care of the management of infrastructure, the calling processes, the network security and the databases.

Finance is handled by Chartered Accountants and others who do the accounting and financial analysis, budgeting, financial planning and taxation functions of the company.

HRD is run by HR Manager, under the direction of SK. This department looks after:

- Management of Personnel, their compensation, and other conditions of work
- Recruitment
- Training
- Performance appraisal and improvement

Training at NICCL is focused on agents, and is mostly done in-house. New agents inducted into the company are trained according to the requirements of the process they are hired for. For example, the ACL inbound process requires a 23 day induction program. There are five regular trainers in NICCL. To get more trainers, the company often looks within. An Internal Job Placement notice is circulated. Contenders first make presentations to NICCL, and are then evaluated by the client, say the Performance Management Group of ACL.

HR still has the status of being peripheral to the business. In the words of someone in the firm's HR department, *'We are the wives (!) of the family. All the money that the husbands earn from operations - callings, different business processes and so much of hard work - we spend it on training, recruitment, welfare of the employees and the like. But still, it is all in a positive spirit and for welfare of the organization as a whole.'*

DECISION MAKING

The company is governed by a board headed by the chairman (Ramesh Kapoor), along with Saloni Kapoor, and three other directors. Apart from being CEO and Vice Chairman, SK heads Corporate Affairs and is also Director (Finance), and Director (HR). Her married sister is notionally head of the 'international office' in New Zealand.

During its early days with Turmeric, NICCL was a small business, run single-handedly by RK. With growth, SK joined and acquired an almost total hold over the Chandigarh centre. Though major decisions are taken jointly by RK and SK, the Chandigarh operations are handled mostly by SK, who is in constant telephonic touch with her supervisors.

Noida and Jaipur operations are looked after by center-managers. Routine decisions like granting leave, employing new calling agents, their training and examination, contacting clients for a particular process are handled by the center-managers. Financial and strategic decisions -- like incrementing salaries, giving bonuses, introducing new policies – are taken only by the Kapoors. Ramesh Kapoor pays frequent visits to these offices to supervise operations, or is in continuous telephonic contact.

ACTIVITIES FOR A NEW CONTRACT

When a BPO signs-up a **Process,** that is, a new contract for a client, it has to do the following activities – Planning, Implementation, and Control.

Planning:

This refers to the planning of a new process, its requirements, infrastructure, manpower, and finance. It includes the following.

Script and Delivery: This is the actual operation, in both inbound and outbound calls. Each call has an *Opening of Script* when the call begins and *Closing of Script* when the call ends. The entire transaction is recorded by the call center, for evaluation of agent and for training.

Training

Customer Care and Sales Training: For every new process or agent, technical training has to be provided – about the script and its technology. Sales training, given for outbound calls, is about interacting with the customer to introduce new schemes, sell goods or obtain feedback.

Soft skills and behavioral training: Soft skills and behavioral training refers to improving the communication skills of the agent, preparing them to talk fluently in the relevant language, talking politely to the customer, being patient and tolerant with them, and so on.

Implementation:

Mock Calling: Mock calling refers to the calls made by the agent inside the center, so as to test them on their skill and to make them comfortable with the whole process.

Customer Feedback: The call-center must compile customer satisfaction data – on answers they got, on agent's behavior, on efficiency of agent, quality of answer etc.

Test Audits: These are designed to assess agent's performance. The audit contains the time they were on their systems, number of calls they took or made, how they handled the calls, customer's response etc.

Agent Performance Review: The performance of agent must be reviewed by HR manager along parameters like the feedback of Floor In charge, Team Leader, Supervisor, customer, and sometimes Team members.

Control:

Updating Script and Delivery: Whenever a new development takes place or an unusual question is raised by the customer, or any growth happens, the script is updated accordingly and so is the delivery process.

Performance Check: The various parameters of agent performance mentioned above as well as overall process parameters like work flow management, productivity, and achieving service goals are determined.

AUDITING OF AGENTS

Auditing is done in NICCL as an evaluation of the employee, the financial system, the process and the entire project. Auditing the agents is most critical.

Internal Audit

NICCL has internal auditors (1 for 30 agents) for each process. The auditors have one-on-one interaction sessions with the agents where they discuss the agent's performance, career chart, and feedback regarding the process and the organization.

Auditors are also needed to keep a check on the activities of the calls made by the agents. Quality Audit Feedback Reports are filled in to file details of work, concerns about agents, and activities of a random subset of the calling agents (Exhibit 2).

The two types of internal audit- Quality Audit Feedback Report (Exhibit 2) and Audit Daily Work Record (Exhibit 3) are separate. One is a monthly report of the process done randomly; the other is a daily report on all agents. Daily audit is submitted to and examined by the Team Leader or Floor Incharge of calling agent, to check their daily performance about the calls made, received , queries solved , problems faced and so on. The Audit Daily Work Record is compiled and submitted to the top management to review performance and give incentives if any.

For further control, the agents in NICCL are required to record their log-in / log-out, idle time, terminal time, as well as their break time.

Client-Certified Audit

Client-audit for manpower is performed by certified auditors, who have to clear specific internal examinations and tests, before becoming an auditor. These tests consist of a written test, followed by an interview and examination. These auditors are not direct employees of NICCL; they are assigned by the client company (like ACL or Sisodia Telecom) whose process is being handled by NICCL.

The auditors test the performance of agents, primarily by using *voice loggers*, which record all the conversation between the agent and customer 24x7. These voice loggers begin with opening of script. The auditor checks for the following-- handling the call well, being polite and empathetic to customer, providing entire knowledge or detail requested by customer, and cordially closing the script. The voice loggers are confidential to the client. Besides, auditors may also drop in at the center for surprise check.

In case of unsatisfactory performance, an agent is verbally reprimanded. After three such occasions, the person is given a written warning. If such a warning fails to have effect, another written warning and a monetary penalty are given. If the agent again fails to come up to expectation, the employment is terminated.

PERFORMANCE APPRAISAL

Performance appraisal of employees in NICCL occurs annually or as the need arises. The HR department handles this. Agents for *Inbound call service* are assessed by the Call Quality (CQ), Call Audit (CA), the number of interactions from the customers and at times the customer feedback. *Outbound call service* agents are assessed by the number of sales made, the quality of sales, targets achieved in a set period of time, and the regularity at work. The agent's floor in charge (FI) and supervisor are also asked to comment on the agent's performance. An annual increment is given if the appraisal is satisfactory.

REWARDS AND MORALE AT NICCL

NICCL gives a Certificate of Appreciation to select employees for motivating them. Besides, there are a number of cash awards. There is a monthly award for the Best Floor In charge, and the Best Calling Agent. This is given on the basis of number of hours worked, the amount of output delivered, the attendance and regularity, targets achieved, and the team-spirit. HR personnel observe employees and decide on the basis of their data.

Another important reward is promotion. NICCL often uses Internal Job Placement to fill up positions. These give opportunities for growth to employees. Internal job placement is also sought after by agents, because it gives the opportunity to interact with more clients from wider geographical locations and to experience more than one telecom client.

Saloni, who is 27 years old, believes in 'Work hard-party harder' culture and encourages the same for employees. She has set up a dress code for NICCL employees – formals on Monday to Thursday, casuals on Friday to Sunday. Every Saturday, the centre organizes 'fun' activities like antakshri, dumb charades, interactive games, informal talks with seniors in the organization. They also celebrate birthday parties of employees and have *best dressed* competitions every weekend.

One employee, in an interview however, pointed to 'politics' inside the company – which leads to promotion of less deserving person. This employee also felt aggrieved by some outsider being hired for a senior position instead of promoting internally. This, according to the employe, "is the major reason why employees leave NICCL."

ATTRITION AND RECRUITMENT

SK is happy with the low level of attrition (3%) among agents. Yet, because NICCL often takes in students doing part time jobs or working in vacations, who work temporarily and leave when institutions re-open, the center sometimes faces severe shortage of people.

According to SK, the market for agents is governed by external factors. New, bigger BPOs come up, or an existing one gets affiliated to an mnc that offers a higher package, or creates a cosmopolitan environment, or has a more established brand name. People are attracted to these names and sometimes move away in groups, leaving a void in the center.

SK resents that many agents do not view their job as a long term commitment, and are also susceptible to poaching. NICCL itself has to play the same card – an employee visits another company, drops in a word about better options at NICCL, like salary, work environment, flexible timings etc. The word spreads!

COMPARISON WITH BIGGER BPOs AND INTERNATIONAL BRAND NAMES

"A very obvious question in the fast changing call-center environment is," asked a case writer, "When BPOs like Dell, Infosys, Quark, Tech Mahindra etc are present in Chandigarh, is it not tough to survive? Aren't your competitors having an edge over you? Don't you think that your trained calling agents will be eager to shift to these places?"

SK responded with an emphatic 'no'. We have a kind of family environment, and the personal attention each employee gets here, which is just not possible in a large BPO. The ambience is cordial and people work as if living in one big family. That, according to her, is the advantage of a family-run business. She attributes this to the 'family atmosphere' that she believes NICCL has. Almost all agents are known to her by name.

The whole process of working is transparent here, political issues amongst employees do not really creep in, and there is justice and fairness for all employees at all levels. Also, "we match the salaries offered to agents at the big brand centers. In fact, NICCL gives them special bonuses on Diwali, New Year, on their birthdays etc. This 'personal touch' is missing in the huge BPOs."

However, when agent Manoj, on the verge of moving to a center with an international brand name, was separately interviewed about this issue, he said the brand name makes all the difference. His new company's name is well known all over the world for its work culture, its environment and its projects, whereas NICCL is known only in Chandigarh. The bigger international BPOs offer their employees an opportunity to work in a cosmopolitan environment, to interact with customers abroad and have a platform where one can professionally grow very fast.

This calling agent wanted to be trained by trainers of international repute who could teach him more than what he learnt here, he wanted a place where he could improve his personality and language skills, get the exposure of an MNC and the ways of the Americans or the British. His point was that if the salary offered, and technology used are both the same at these places, then why not opt for the bigger and famous one. Regarding the issue of being in a family environment, he commented that he has one family at home, which is great for him. He is out here to work and does not need any 'so-called family atmosphere'.

DILEMMA OF THE CHAIRMAN

Ramesh Kapoor did not know what to do. They had put all their heart into getting this offer from Sisodia Telecom. He was confident that the new system-vendors in Delhi could put up a center within the deadline. It was the large requirement of agents that worried him. He was worried how they would get and train such a large number, because the in-house training capability was also limited. A stricter audit could also be a problem for his agents, because they may not be too highly skilled and trained. On the other hand, if the large contract was dropped, he would not know what to do with the upcoming 1000 seats center.

COST

Estimates in 2007 indicated prices for floor space to be Rs. 3000 per sq ft in both Chandigarh and Jaipur, while it was Rs. 5000 in Noida. Other capital costs, including hardware, software, furniture & fixture, networking and communication equipment (all based on a high-end software venture) amount to Rs.2 lakhs per seat for a 250 seat floor.

TO SISODIA OR NOT

With this background, it was perhaps reasonable, thought Saloni before the (Final) meeting that they might take up Sisodia's offer. As they all filed in to the meeting room the HR manager mentioned to Saloni that Manoj, their star agent at Chandigarh, had sent in his resignation.

This upset Ramesh Kapoor. He wondered why agents kept leaving. Were they not paid enough? Or, maybe the agent in question could have been made a Floor Incharge.

Saloni intervened to say that Manoj had a tiff with an auditor, because he was performing much faster than anybody could imagine. The auditor even suspected that Manoj was manipulating the customer with false information.

Meanwhile, as the meeting started, Ramesh made another disclosure. India's major IT company Jamshed Software had, rather unexpectedly, entered the domestic call-center business, and had grabbed the all India customer care service for European Phone, which took over 15 circles of Cottonea Telecom earlier. Anyway, let us look at the question of Sisodia's offer.

The Finance manager was more prepared than last time. He used some numbers from his calculation to suggest, "We can use the existing center at Noida for an additional 300 seats that we require." To which the HR manager countered, "We have hardly 22,000 sq ft, wall to wall. Your suggestion would make it even more cramped."

"Why not acquire some floor near our Jaipur center," asked Ramesh Kapoor. The finance manager replied: "We can buy, or even take it on rent. Current monthly rentals are around Rs. 6.50 per sq ft in Jaipur and 8.70 in some parts of Noida."

With all this data, and the events in the background, SK was getting unsure of her earlier thinking to accept Sisodia. "We might have to look at long term implications", she said. "We are already committed to the space in Mohali, and the large space (to come up in due course) at Noida. If the export players move into domestic market, we may be in trouble."

"But, we have the experience of domestic business. We have always been very efficient. Can we not capitalize on that?" asked the Chairman. "And is it necessary to look like an international company?"

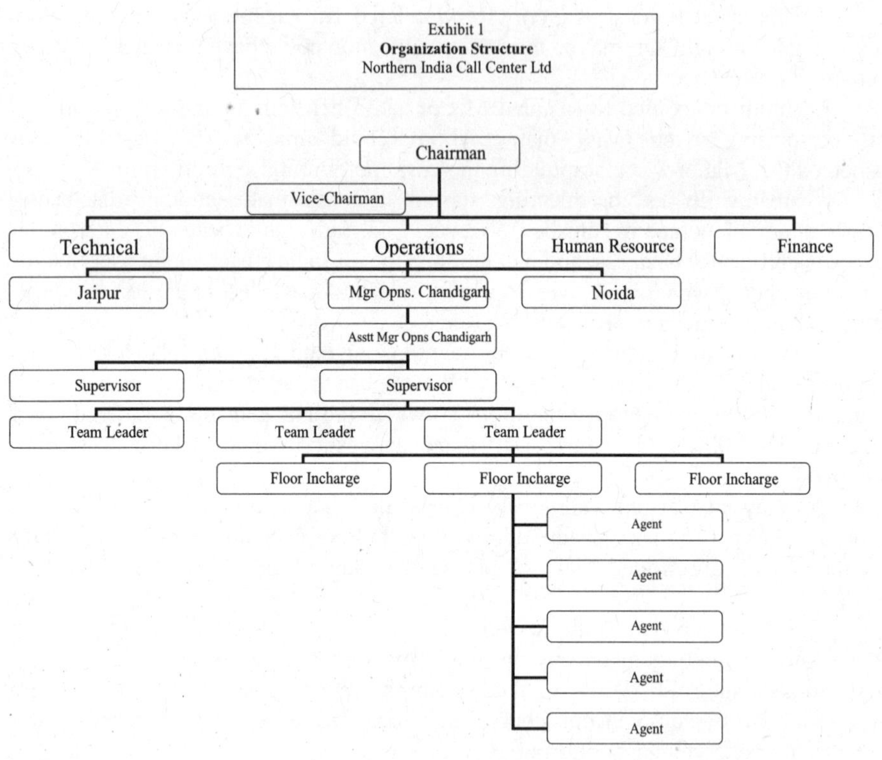

Exhibit 1
Organization Structure
Northern India Call Center Ltd
Chairman
Vice-Chairman
Technical
Operations
Human Resource
Finance
Jaipur
Mgr Opns. Chandigarh
Noida
Asstt Mgr Opns Chandigarh
Supervisor
Supervisor
Team Leader
Team Leader
Team Leader
Floor Incharge
Floor Incharge
Floor Incharge
Agent
Agent
Agent
Agent
Agent

Exhibit 2
Quality Audit Feedback Report

Exhibit 2 - Northern India Call Center Ltd
Chandigarh
Quality Audit Feedback Report

Name of Process	PUNJAB XXXXXX
Date of Feedback	June'07
Name of the Auditor	Sarika Garg
Shift Timings	9 AM To 6 PM

S.NO.	AGENT	FI (floor incharge)	CONCERNS	SCORE	AGENT'S SIGN.	FI'S SIGN.
1						
2						
3						
4						
5						
6						
7						
8						
9						
10						
11						
12						
13						
14						
15						
16						
17						
18						
19						
20						

AUDITOR		AVERAGE SCORE ON	#DIV/0!

SIGNATURE OF THE AMO

Exhibit 3
Audit Daily Work Record

Audit Meter -1 31		69															
	Sarika Garg																
Total Avge			89%	93%	93%	93%		93%									
Total Count		0	17	12	17	9	0	14	69								
Sl. No.	Names	FI	1-Jun	2-Jun	3-Jun	4-Jun	5-Jun	6-Jun	7-Jun	Count of 1st week	Avge of 1st week	8- Jun	…..	15-Jun	Count of 2nd week		
			Sarika	Sarika	Sarika	Sarika	Sarika	Sarika	Sarika			Narehs Sarika		Narehs Sarika			
1	Apurva	Gupta															
2	Arpana	Joshi															
3	Avtar	Singh															
4	Bhagwan	Gupta															
5	Davinder	Joshi															
6	Deepika	Singh															
7	Gaj	Gupta															
8	Gurpreet	Singh															
9	Handa	Gupta															
10	Jasdeep	Joshi															

IWM PROJECT BY IOCW: A CASE STUDY ON FAILURE OF A SUCCESSFUL PROJECT

Shubham Kumar
Doctoral Student, Pennsylvania State University
Erica Hagen
Graduate Student, SIPA, Columbia University

"So, Ms. Alyssa, apart from your internal evaluation reports do we have any other evaluations to substantiate the opinion- that the Intelligent Water Management (IWM) project is beneficial for the populace and is working on the ground?" asked Ms. A. P. Buch, the Secretary[1], Ministry of Rural Development, Government of India (GoI).

"Yes, positive evaluation work by WHO[2] Geneva, a perception study on water reuse by DFID[3] and the creation of a guidance manual on IWM by ERI[4] resulted in state government interest in the program in 2006 and a technical proposal by the PHED[5]. By the end of 2006 the program was the subject of an International Learning Exchange (ILE) program and was visited by international experts of the Middle East, Africa and Europe. And all of them gave favorable reports." replied Alyssa.

"Well, that looks impressive, what is your own opinion about the project? Should it be upscaled throughout India?"

After a drawn out thoughtful pause, "Yes, I think it should definitely be".

BACKGROUND

International Organization for Children and Women (IOCW), with its headquarters in Geneva, is one of the largest multilateral organizations supported and respected by most countries throughout the world. It has projects on alleviation of poverty, health issues and basic human rights spread all over Africa and Asia. Its donors are basically USA, Japan and the European Union.

Dr. Harry Hamilton joined IOCW in 2004 as an Associate Officer after completing his doctorate in Environmental Sciences from the University of Nottingham. With a plethora of research papers behind him, Dr. Harry was highly respected in his field. After working for a year in the WES[6] division of Somalia, he was promoted and sent to India. His area of operation included Madhya Pradesh in Central India.

Central India with all the complexities[7] of India duly in place was a water scarce area. Its rural populace was one of the poorest in the World and performed badly on most of the indicators of Human Development Index (HDI) [8].

Dr. Harry after a month long tour of the region realized that solving water problem was one of the most essential steps before any improvement in the living conditions took place. He had a solution in mind that involved Water reuse and rainwater harvesting. With the help of ERI he developed a technically robust system. For this he first wanted to start implementing this system in the ashrams[9] of Madhya Pradesh (Figure 4).

After approval of his plan of action, from the superiors, the first few pilots were tested and evaluated in tribal areas of Madhya Pradesh, with the support of the State Government. Within a few months the pilot said to be high successful could be seen as being replicated in the rest of Central India by the Government itself (Figure 1). Within IOCW it was projected as a model project implementation. IOCW pushed Government to make it part of the programs for national water policy implementation (see Appendix A.2). Both the state and the Central Government were keen to promote such a successful project which had emerged in a small span of time. Dr. Harry, called the rising star of the organization, was expected to be promoted to a senior position in one of the fastest promotions in IOCW history[10].

Along with that, IOCW, decided to document the progress of the successful IWM project by calling in temporary consultants from Massachusetts Institute of technology (MIT), under the supervision of Dr. Harry himself.

These two development management Doctorate students, Alyssa and Manya, working as short term consultants came across surprising facts about Intelligent Water Management (IWM) (see Appendix A.3) project which was said to be highly successful. Their foremost task was to document the stages through which the project progressed so that it can be shown as a model for future project implementations by IOCW and sister organizations.

ORGANIZATIONAL STRUCTURE

IOCW, India, with its central office in New Delhi worked through its field offices in 15 states of India. New Delhi office directly reported to Geneva Headquarters. New Delhi office was headed by an Executive Director.

The whole organization worked through its two main service systems- the core services and the supporting services. The core services (grade C officers) worked through seven verticals: Child Protection, Reproductive &Child Health, Nutrition, Education, HIV/AIDS and WES (Water Environment and Sanitation). The supporting services (grade S officers) were divided into five verticals: Administration, Finance, Communication, Information Systems and Procurement.

IOCW recruited employees through international selection procedure. Generally specialists with 1-2 years of relevant work experience joined at the Associate Level (C4 and S4 level) at Field Offices. They reported directly to the Officer (C3 and S3 level) of their vertical. For example, Associate WES Officer reported to the WES Officer. Each vertical also had general services staff hired on temporary basis to assist these permanent officers. Apart from these experienced specialists were hired to act as consultant for specific projects.

At the state level, the C3 Officer, had to coordinate all activities with his counterparts from the supporting verticals. These coordination activities were supported by a Programme Officer (a C3 officer) who reported also to Chief, field (figure 3). The level 3 Officers reported to the Chief, field Office and also to the Chief of their vertical sitting at the Central Office. All projects originating at the level 4 had to pass through both the Chiefs. At the central level the coordination activities were supported by Chief, Administration. The rest of the structure at the Central level reflected the structure at the state level.

The core services were the verticals based on the development goals the organization wanted to fulfill through its Country Program[11]. There could be certain overlaps in work profile in some states and depending on local projects the duties varied from state to state.

Duties of WES Officer, Bhopal were.

WES Officer: To contribute to designing and implementing the scaling up of the WES projects in Schools and Total Sanitation Campaign (TSC) and IWM activities in Madhya Pradesh. To the extent possible, interventions are to be informed by evidence of people's knowledge, attitudes and practices relating to water supply, sanitation and hygiene, especially of women, children and the poor. Interventions are to be designed to promote social inclusion and reinforce IOCW-supported initiatives in other sectors.

The profiles of the major supporting verticals are:

Programme Manager: To coordinate the operational aspects of the programme for efficient and effective programme implementation; leverage the coordination of convergent districts and presence of the District Facilitators to give better results for women and children

Communication Officer: Responsible for facilitating and influencing the State Government's policy, planning, implementation, monitoring and evaluation, for an assigned programme or specific projects within one State in India.

Finance Officer: Responsible for approval and sanction of funds for program implementation by each core vertical while conducting timely audits for the utilization of the same. The approval for extra funds apart from the budget provided had to come from Chief, Finance and Chief, WES.

Procurement Officer: Responsible for procuring the equipments and other necessary materials after getting requirement from the WES Officer and sanction of funds by Finance Officer from the WES account.

After level 3, the promotion could take any of the 2 tracks. The officer could try to get promoted to executive management side by being the Chief, Field

Office (track 1) or could try for the Chief, Vertical (track 2). In track 2 he would finally get posting for level 1 in Geneva for that vertical. While in track 1, he could get the post of Executive Director. Generally track 1 promotion was considered more prestigious than track 2.

Annual evaluation of each officer is done by his superior to whom he reports. At level 3 the evaluation is done by Chief, field office and the level 2 officer of that vertical. The evaluation is done mainly based on 3 parameters:

1. Personal Development: Highly subjective evaluation based on general skill development. Interpersonal

skills, etc.

2. Junior staff development: Highly subjective evaluation based on general skill development. Interpersonal

skills, trainings provided, etc.

3. Country Program Development: A few general metrics are

a. Status of Old projects and how much upscaling has been done

b. Number and status of new projects started

c. Promotion of projects through government intervention, etc.

IOCW followed the equivalent Human Resource structure as followed by ICSC (International Civil Service Commission) for the UN Organizations. For each higher post there were heavy increases in base pay. While, "Within-grade increments are awarded on the basis of satisfactory service" (UNCS, 2006)

Brief Country Program Implementation Structure

The regular work of IOCW country program was a collection of sector specific projects. Some projects were state specific while some were upscaled to National Level. The upscaling was done on the basis of favorable reports of the state project. Annually some fund was earmarked for Research & Development, which was used by C3 (and above) officers to try out new projects. These projects were transferred to sector specific general budget heads after their efficacy was established. But the upscaling was done with the help of the Government of India (GoI) and the funds for national projects provided by IOCW were primarily to streamline the transfer of projects from IOCW to the government. This scenario was different from most countries in which IOCW was working. The thinking at Geneva level was India was emerging as an economic powerhouse and hence needed only ideas to improve the situation of children and women. This meant the primary goal of IOCW, India, was to try out new projects and after their ability was established, to upscale these at a national level with major funds sourced from GoI. After that it was slowly transferred into GoI hands. Upscaling of a state project to the national project was considered a highly prestigious achievement by most officers because of India being a major developing country.

General Project Life cycle (from idea to national program)

There were several essential steps through which a concept travelled before it was recommended by IOCW for policy incorporation in the Indian government system or for being upscaled as a national project (Figure 5). The first phase was concept development, which started by partnering with reputed research institutes for technical modeling. Proposals and suggestions for construction and management were developed with the help of partner NGOs who understood the local conditions and had a grassroots presence. Along with this, advocacy for the project took off simultaneously with the senior state and central government officials.

The second phase, which was the evaluation phase, consisted of field testing at sites meeting certain selection criteria. The evaluation was mostly done by officers of IOCW. Special care was taken that no one from the same vertical was the evaluator for the project.

After the successful development of the pilot project, the concept travelled through two simultaneous paths of policy and program. At the one end efforts were generally made to include all the parts of the concept in the policy framework. At the other end, efforts were made to upscale the pilot to a national level program. These two developments went hand in hand, so that the policy inclusion facilitated the actual implementation of a large-scale program on the ground. In order to achieve this goal, the agency first determined the key individuals in the government system to influence the adoption of both program and policy, and provided them with the appropriate advocacy material & technical reports from the evaluation phase.

People and organizations:

Dr. Genessa Giorgi was the present Executive Director of IOCW, India. Dr. Rachel Rosenheck was the chief, WES. Dr. Umaru Obasanjo was the Chief, Bhopal Field Office. Mr. K. G. Saxena was the head of NGO – Madhya Pradesh child and women upliftment organization (MPCWUO). He was a retired IAS Officer of Madhya Pradesh Cadre. 17 small NGOs from all over the state of Madhya Pradesh worked under the aegis of MPCWUO which acted like an umbrella[12] NGO. The board of directors and management of MPCWUO consisted of retired senior IAS officers and some renowned academicians. Most of the present incumbents in the MP Administrative circles were former colleagues of these people.

History of the program:

Water scarcity problems especially affect the rural population, which is 73.33% of the total population in MP (Census, 2001), raising the burden of diseases and mortality. The effect is harshest on those that are already poor and often excluded from the rest of the community such as Scheduled Tribes (ST), Scheduled Castes (SC), and Other Backward Castes (OBC). The tribal and SC population together cover 35% of the Madhya Pradesh total population. A large percentage of these tribes are concentrated in western MP, especially in the districts Dhar and Jhabua, which both have a tribal population higher than 50% (GoMP, 2002). Amongst these the tribes, Bhils and Bhilalas are the dominant groups along with Pateliyas (Russell, 1975).

The IWM program was developed (Figure 6) by IOCW, Bhopal, in conjunction with ERI in 2005 in order to reduce fluoride contamination and water scarcity within marginalized communities and promote sanitation and health issues. Thus the initial target of providing safe drinking water and increased ground water availability through IWM were ashrams.

The main components of IWM are greywater reuse and rainwater harvesting. Greywater reuse describes the process by which bathwater is treated through a simple filtering system, and then reused for flushing of toilets and irrigation purposes. Rainwater harvesting is the collection of rainwater from a flat clean rooftop into a water storage tank in order to dilute fluoride-contaminated drinking water.

Additional expected impacts include reaching the most excluded parts of the community, raising awareness about water conservation, improving educational indicators, and demonstrating that IOCW is able to leverage government funds (figure 3) for innovative concepts.

To target these impacts the concept requires funding, equipment, training, staff and labor as inputs. The subsequent implementation of IWM in selected ashram schools includes training sessions for different stakeholders, approval from the stakeholders, the actual construction of the physical structures, the creation of a Water Safety Club (WSC) among the students, continuous Information, Education and Communication (IEC) activities, system maintenance and monitoring. All of these activities are supported by a partner NGO on the ground.

Findings:

When for their first meeting with Dr. Harry they were ushered inside his room, they found the walls plastered with cuttings from national and regional dailies talking about him and his project, which was definitely impressive for a newcomer. As for Dr. Harry himself, in the words of Alyssa, "He seemed quite young yet dynamic for his job profile. Comparable to any current Hollywood actor, more than 6 feet tall, blonde hair, blue eyes, aquiline features with a permanent smile fixed on his face. He had that persona where the person facing him would naturally assume that this guy knows what he is talking about. He had that aura of being a leader. He would agree to most negative things anybody said, remolded it according to his opinions and threw it back as if that is what the offender meant. Unlike his colleagues he looked more like a top corporate management guy."

Dr. Harry began with, "This project is close to my heart. Not because it is my baby. Not because it has brought respite to the poorest of the poor. But because I have seen how this project has fulfilled in a wholesome way the implementation objectives we stand for, i.e. participatory approach, enhancing social inclusion and thus bringing the maximum social impact in a sustainable way[13]."

He continued, "As you know, IOCW closely resembles the functioning and objectives of UNICEF and we are proud of it, since we are achieving that with lesser bureaucratic set up. And, for the matter of you starting the work, I propose you meet some of the top state officials who know about the program. You would get a nice overview. I shall arrange the meetings."

The next important meeting was with Engineer-in-chief[14], PHED. On the topic of IWM he started with, "I think water problem is one of the most important problems being faced by this country. Especially the marginalized communities and this is one of the most important steps in resolving that problem."

Manya asked, "Do you think it is more important that the government sets up drinking water supply and not try to resolve the crises by these other smaller impact projects."

"No, we are achieving whatever targets we are provided with. But whatever is being provided gets wasted. We have to stop this. And IWM is the savior for the community. This has been a success for PHED which has now plans of implementing this in all the schools of the state. I have also been invited by Dr.Harry to Geneva to present in a conference how we can achieve success in water conservation using these. You waste water and government provided water is not the solution."

Similar views were expressed by Mr. Baidya, Tribal Commissioner[15], Bhopal region. "When I first went with Dr. Harry to the school where IWM was implemented I was pleasantly surprised to see the faces of happy tribal children. Immediately I realized that something revolutionary was taking place which was also established by the reports from ERI, our most prominent research institute, that how water was being saved.. I have instructed my tribal department to help IOCW in all its pilots and as quickly as possible start implementing this in all ashrams. I have even been invited by Dr. Harry to present this innovative project in the conference on development issues being faced by Asia Pacific region in Malaysia."

Over the next 2-3 weeks they met various senior district and regional officials. The opinion invariably was positive. They started their first field trip with district of Jabalpur in the western MP. Their first interaction was with Assistant Commissioner, Tribal Welfare Department, Mrs. Kumudini Srivastava. She was all praise for the program following the same line as her boss Mr. Baidya.

After the interview a few wardens of the ashrams from the Jabalpur region came to meet her. While they were waiting for her, Alyssa introduced herself as a researcher and just as a matter of fact asked them what their opinion was of the IWM system. This interaction was an eye opening experience. One of the wardens replied, "It is a failed project. IOCW people don't know what the current situation on the ground is. Have they asked for opinion of parents of the children? The children are supposed to clean the system. Whose parents are going to let their children clean the system?"

Another warden continued, "Even if we provide a cleaner probably the IOCW people don't know the social habits of the people over here. Most of the boys in India pee in the bathrooms while taking a bath. Do you think anybody would carry this water for flushing when it has just been cleaned by a mesh of stones? The girls even use the bathroom as a urinal otherwise. How feasible it is to change the habits of the children."

The third warden added, "And you know the caste problem in India how can you expect children of some other caste to use that supposedly cleaned water of the other castes. Even if we provide flushes at certain places, still the children are hesitant to even touch that flush system. I am not saying the system is not good but without much effort it is being put. It would take a generation to change such habits and inculcate a different social behavior. The government is also implementing this at such a fast pace without consulting us."

Although a bit taken aback, the assistant commissioner still smiled and intervened, "See all this is off the record. You know it very well; we get circulars from the top and just implement it. If the top bosses are so sure, who are we to put up problems? The problem is- the system and methodology needs continuous improvement. There was one a solar cooker project by IOCW. Thousands of solar cookers were installed by IOCW in hundreds of ashrams by us on the basis of a few pilots by IOCW and after getting us to spend crores the project was left for us by them. The system got lost in the daily routine of our department and ashrams. You need to continually advise us and the stakeholders involved when the baby was yours. It is not your resume where you keep on increasing the points by adding upscaled projects to your kitty. You are coming with development objective and this is not development in my view. Anyway this is for the top officials to decide."

Alyssa being shocked by this development could only ask, "Do IOCW officials know about this and still do such a thing?"

Mrs. Srivastava replied, "Some of their officials know yet ignore the signs. Some don't even know. They have such a long chain when the program actually reaches the ground. So much is at stake for so many. The NGOs have their money, government officials have their foreign jaunts and IOCW officials have their personal interests. And to control there is no external audit and surprise checks. A foreign person going to a ashram and watching the ashram already spruced up by NGOs is not the way to check. Here these wardens told you some truth otherwise many wardens have their motive of hiding this fact because they also get funds in the name of new projects and get to meet senior officials. Who would deny such an opportunity? Ultimately it is the responsibility of IOCW to develop some mechanism to get the actual situation on the ground."

After this different kind of meeting, the two consultants decided that Manya who knew Hindi would get away from the group whenever inspecting the schools and talk to villagers and local people to get the real situation.

Excerpts from the report submitted to Chief, field office Bhopal

In our field visits to our utter surprise we found many of the ashrams where IWM was reported complete were still not complete or broke. This was truer for the government implementations and luckily not in IOCW implementations (which are less than dozen ashrams. The future for the program does not look good as having its own implementations in sound condition and of the government not in good condition doesn't bode well for the program. A rethink should be done before suggesting it for further upscaling.

Upscaling to all schools:
Participation during the design phase: This was only found in IOCW/NGO implementations. However, in many new ashram implementations performed by the PHED in the Jabalpur area, the wardens, students and parents had not been informed about what was being implemented until it was already under construction. IEC (Information, Education and Communication) in these places was supposed to happen after construction.

However, even for IOCW implementations we are also concerned that this level of attention will decline beyond the pilot phase when visits to schools are at a maximum. There is already a difference in the level of participation between the first implementations and those that followed.

IEC for children in relation to IWM has shown to be very successful, but there is still a lack in proper IEC for adults. This IEC should be directed towards awareness and knowledge about the need for water conservation in the future. All stakeholders should receive IEC that is designed specifically for them. This means: more technical IEC for engineers and more basic education for villagers. Many officials seemed only partially sure of the benefits of the program and had no reports, evaluations, or documents at hand.

Reaching the most excluded: IWM has so far been implemented primarily in well-functioning ashrams close to the district centers or main roads. During the pilot phase, this was in order to establish demonstration schools that can be used for exposure visits. IOCW's implementation ashrams were found to be in good condition, clean, and tightly managed, with strong leadership by the warden and functioning parent-teacher associations (PTAs). Interior ashrams (non-implementation) located far away from main roads were found in poor condition, in need of repairs, reliable staff, boundary walls, sanitation facilities and water sources. Because the program is supposed to cover 100% of ashrams in some districts, such as Jhabua, IWM is intended to eventually reach the distant ashrams.

There will be challenges in reaching this goal. Some wardens in the more remote areas of Jhabua stated that their first priority was fences around the ashram and toilets, which will be needed before IWM. Also, according to NGO members and government officials, there is resistance to providing the interior regions with services. Officials rarely visit these remote areas, and any assignment in the tribal region is itself widely known as a "punishment posting" for an official. NGO members also may be unwilling or unable to travel for hours on dirt roads to get to these ashrams, and initially some were reluctant to accompany the team members to conduct this research. There are also risks of violence and robbery in remote tribal regions of MP. However, these regions are truly the most vulnerable and must be included in the upscaling plan in a way, that IWM can properly function and bring the impact needed.

Reaching the most excluded is not an easy task, and it should be carefully considered before inclusion as a top priority. The goal should not be to implement IWM in every ashram in every state, but focus on the ashrams where it would really benefit those that need it the most. It should also be taken into consideration that the people that need it the most might not be able to able to benefit from it before other needs are targeted.

Social exclusion among tribes and castes: During upscaling, IWM will likely encounter social tensions among castes. Some implementation areas of eastern MP already must confront such issues. Wardens in Jabalpur said that upper-caste parents will refuse to allow their children to clean the system because that work is meant for the lower castes. Also, different castes often use different water sources in rural India. While all ashrams are SC and OBC designated, within these groups there are still divisions into higher and lower caste. An aggressive IEC campaign for parents as well as students will be necessary to combat these prejudices even if cleaning tasks are reduced among students in the future. Wardens must also create mixed-caste groups of students and make sure the WSC is mixed-caste. New implementations in these areas should be closely monitored for discrimination along caste lines and a social evaluation performed in mixed-caste schools.

<u>Upscaling to Household implementations</u>

Reaching the most excluded: A household greywater reuse system can be built for 845 rupees, which for a landless Bhil laborer is equal to about half a month's salary. Therefore it would not be possible for most of these families to have it in their home. The private household implementations are not affordable to the poorest and most excluded in the community. Social exclusion among tribes and castes: In the hometowns of the students and community surrounding the ashram there is a bigger distinction between tribes, and the children would not play or speak with other tribes. Household interviews showed that this tribal distinction was very visible among adult villagers. Bhils, for example, are considered to be subordinate to Pateliyas and Bhilalas. Furthermore they are considered by others (and to some extent even by themselves) to be less clean, illiterate, non-veg and more likely to drink alcohol. In the village context the selection of who gets financial support for the individual household reuse system may exacerbate social tensions and forms of jealousy. Care should also be taken to select grassroots motivators and other workers (laborers, etc) from different tribes and different status.

<u>Sustainability</u>

Water scarcity must reach a level critical enough to make users feel a demand for water reuse in order for the system to remain in use. In one ashram, the greywater was simply being washed out into the "garden" which consisted of some trees near a lake, because they had actually no need and demand for the implementation. This ashram seemed to have ample water supply already. We also encountered an ashram where they planned to turn the system on only during water scarce months of the year and otherwise leave it off, because they often had regular tap water supply. While this might be a practical way to use the system, it is not intended to be used this way and this would preclude the possibility of groundwater recharge through water saving throughout the year. In another ashram some staff members stated that the system was only turned on when visitors came.

However, with too little available water in the ashram, reuse becomes unfeasible: younger students may be bathing at a local hand pump instead of at one ashram like in Jhabua. The same is true for the potential of greywater reuse in private households. Families who have so little water at home that they go to the nearest water body to wash and clean do not produce sufficient greywater at their houses to keep the reuse system running.

Need should be established within both a lower and an upper boundary for water availability, a range in which the usage of the system becomes most likely. This will prevent using resources on implementing systems that will not or cannot be used.

After this report submission, Dr. Harry called an emergency meeting with them; "You people don't know what you have done. At least the final report should have been given only after consultation with me. Chief is from the other vertical you should have understood that. Thankfully the relations of Obasanjo were good relations with Rosenheck. See a lot is on stake in this project. You guys also know how much your future assignments with IOCW and sister organizations would depend on your current level of work. Please redraft the report based on your correct perception"

This meeting left them wondering what should be their response in the meeting with the senior government officials in New Delhi.

<u>**Appendix A**</u>

A.1: Excerpt from the proposal

"The proposal has been prepared as per the discussions held in the chamber of the Engineer-in-chief, Public Health Engineering Department, M.P. Bhopal, Dr. Harry Hamilton, Project Officer, WES, IOCW Bhopal, and Executive Engineers from all over the state were present during the discussion. The scheme would be implemented in the list of hostels (Ashrams) provided by the Assistant Commissioners, Tribal Department."

A.2: News excerpt from a prominent regional daily (May 15th, 2007)

Bhopal: IOCW Regional Director (South Asia) David Johnson made a courtesy call on Madhya Pradesh Chief Minister here on Friday. The Chief Minister told the IOCW delegation that several schemes are being implemented in Madhya Pradesh to encourage institutionalized delivery. David Johnson informed him that IOCW is willing to extend help to Madhya Pradesh Government in its schemes for the children and women's development. Special cooperation is being made by IOCW in the schemes being run for small children at Guna and Shivpuri.

The Chief Minister in turn informed the IOCW team about the projects being conducted in the state for women's empowerment and children's development, including the IWM scheme being run with the help of IOCW. He also gave away presents to the delegates as mementos on behalf of Madhya Pradesh government.

Those present on the occasion included IOCW (India) director Dr. Genessa Giorgi, IOCW's Madhya Pradesh representative Dr. Umaru Obasanjo and Chief Minister's Secretary.

A.3: IWM program

The IWM program of IOCW is meant to cater to the primary need for safe and sufficient water supply, while being fully in consonance with the objectives laid out in the policies16 of the government. The main components of WWM are greywater reuse and rainwater harvesting. Greywater reuse describes the process by which bathwater is treated through a simple filtering system, and then reused for flushing of toilets and irrigation purposes. Rainwater harvesting is the collection of rainwater from a flat clean rooftop into a water storage tank in order to dilute fluoride-contaminated drinking water.

According to the particular system design, several additional components can be used to address the specific needs of an ashram. These components are: greywater treatment system, greywater reuse, rainwater harvesting, fluoride dilution, groundwater recharge, water safety plan, play-pump and hand washing units (Figure 4).

A.4: The main pillars of participatory approach, social inclusion and sustainability according to IOCW are (these excerpts have been taken from various IOCW documents which have based on UN and other international definitions):

Participation is one of UNICEF's values, which they define as follows:

[Participation is] the process of sharing decisions which affect one's life and the life of the community in which one lives. It is the means by which democracy is built and it is the standard against which democracies should be measured. . . . [it is] the "right" of all children to have their opinions taken into account when decisions are being made that affect them. (SOWC, 2003).

A participatory process is, in brief, the transfer of information from one who knows (insider, local) to one who does not know (outsider, expert) (UNICEF presentation, 2005). In development programs, a participatory approach helps to create sustainable change at the grassroots level and is considered good practice. When used right it can create ownership, build capacity, make sure a project is relevant and empower the people involved. Many development scholars argue that top-down policy, meaning planning from outsiders without input from the community, rarely meets the needs of the targeted people and is regarded to be weak in revealing local complexities. (Gosling and Edwards, 2006).

In the context of the IWM program, it has been argued that participation means the inclusion of all relevant stakeholders from the beginning and in every step of the process. As the primary stakeholders, students and ashram staff should have the chance that their voices are heard before any major decision concerning a IWM project is taken. This includes input on construction, design, and throughout the implementation process.

Social inclusion is a major aspect of UNICEF's policy under the new country program for India 2008- 2012:

Social Inclusion is one of UNICEF's central areas of work. […] [UNICEF must ensure] that all our policy and program actions are fully informed of the dynamics of social inclusion that result in persistently unequal outcomes for different groups disadvantaged by caste, tribal, religious and other identities, as well as by geography and other circumstantial factors. (UNICEF India Country Director, 2006)

The concept of social exclusion exists widely within Indian society; SC, ST and OBC are defined as excluded groups and are regarded as most vulnerable. Within each of these groups, children, and especially the girl child are particularly vulnerable.

Analyzing social inclusion in the context of IOCW's IWM program, means examining on a district level whether the most excluded or vulnerable ashram are receiving the benefits of the program. At the ashram level, the differences among tribes and between tribal and non-tribal students should be assessed whether the IWM system exacerbates any social tensions within the ashram. To ensure a maximum social benefit, IOCW's IWM program should support the most vulnerable elements of society and lead to more equity within the society.

Because the program is supposed to spread from ashram children to their families and communities, aspects of household implementations and of ashram-community relationships should be kept in mind.

Sustainability: There are several indicators that can be used to measure the sustainability of a project over the long-term. The indicators for the sustainability of the IWM program are based on the World Bank's evaluation indicators (OED Online). While this is in no way an exhaustive study of sustainability, these criteria will be essential for the proper functioning of the system during the upscaling period and into the foreseeable future: Demand and need should be high; social acceptability should be sufficient; responsibility for the operations and maintenance of the system should be clearly defined and duly followed; responsibility for regular monitoring should be clearly defined and allocated to the competent authorities and departments; and the program should show resilience to institutional shifts and stakeholder turnover.

REFERENCES

1. Bayly, S. (1999) "Caste, Society and Politics in India from the Eighteenth century to the Modern Age", Cambridge University Press.
2. Census (2001), [Online]. Available: www.censusindia.net
3. GoMP (2002), Government of Madhya Pradesh Report Dynamic Ground Water resource report for MP.
4. Gosling, L. and Edwards, M. (2006) A Practical Guide to Planning, Monitoring, Evaluation and Impact Assessment - Development Manual. Save the Children
5. HDR (2005), Human Development Report, United Nations Development Programme.
6. IWM (2006), Internal Proposal on Intelligent Water Management in Madhya Pradesh, IOCW
7. Jha, J. and Jhingran, D. (2002) "Elementary Education for the Poorest and other Deprived Groups: The Real Challenge of Universalization", Centre for Policy Research
8. OED. Operations Evaluations Department. www.worldbank.org/ieg/cae_methodology.html.
9. Russell R. V. (1975) The Tribes and Castes of the Central Provinces of India, Cosmo Publications
10. SOWC (2003), State of the worlds children. Child participation
11. UNCS, (2006) United Nations Common System of Salaries, Allowances and Benefits, International Civil Service Commission.
12. UNICEF Presentation (2005) Victor P. Karunan, Adolescent Development and Participation, Programme
13. Division. UNICEF-HQ NY. http://www.unicef.org.tn/medias/violence/victor_karunan.pdf

---

1 Secretary, GoI is one of the senior most Indian Administrative Services (IAS) Officers. The IAS is the most important administrative service of India, both at the central and state level, where these officers hold all strategic administrative positions. Those dealing with India have the opinion that the power of the IAS officers in the Indian polity is huge.

2 World Health Organization.

3 Department for International Development, United Kingdom

4 Environmental Research Institute is one the premier research institutes promoted by the GoI.

5 The major activity of the Public Health Engineering Department, Madhya Pradesh, is survey, investigation, preparation and execution of water supply and sanitation schemes throughout the state. See Appendix A.1

6 Water, Environment and Sanitation

7 The Caste system is the biggest complexity in India. "Defined by many specialists as a system of elaborately stratified social hierarchy…much the same significance in social, political and academic debate as race in US, class in Britain and faction in

Italy...Nevertheless, if one is to do justice to India's complex history, and to its contemporary culture and politics, caste must be neither disregarded nor downplayed - its power has simply been too compelling and enduring" (Bayly, 1999).

8 With HDI of 0.619, India ranked 128th out of 177 countries mentioned in the Human Development Report (HDR, 2005)

9 Ashram schools are residential schools for tribal children. Ashram schools generally provide admission to children from habitations at least 6-8 km. away from the school. If children from nearby villages are admitted, they are not provided with boarding. The curriculum of Ashram schools includes agriculture and other life skills in addition to general subjects. Many parents in Jharkhand, Orissa and Gujarat preferred Ashram schools as they provided free food, clothing and boarding. Some parents said that education of their wards in Ashram schools was not obstructed, when parents migrated for work. (Jha & Jhingran, 2002).

10 Based on informal interviews with other IOCW officials.

11 Country Program is a period plan (5 Years for IOCW) where certain development goals need to be fulfilled by the present organization in that country in the manner specified in the period plan. International Organizations with country programs don't necessarily have permanent organizational presence and can wind up the operations in that country if they feel their presence won't help in its larger goals or the host country.

12 This structure helped these NGOs to take up their matters with the state government and other international agencies in a coordinated way.

13 See Appendix A.4

14 Engineer-in-Chief is the senior most technical officer of Public Health Engineering Department of the state. All implementations take place with his permission

15 Madhya Pradesh is divided into 5 administrative regions. Tribal Commissioner of a particular region is the senior most bureaucratic person for a particular department and all ashrams function under him and all schemes are implemented in ashrams with his consent.

16 The National Water Policy 2001 of GoI states that, "Special efforts should be made to investigate and formulate projects either in, or for the benefit of, areas inhabited by tribal or specially disadvantaged groups such as socially weak, Scheduled Castes and Scheduled Tribes."

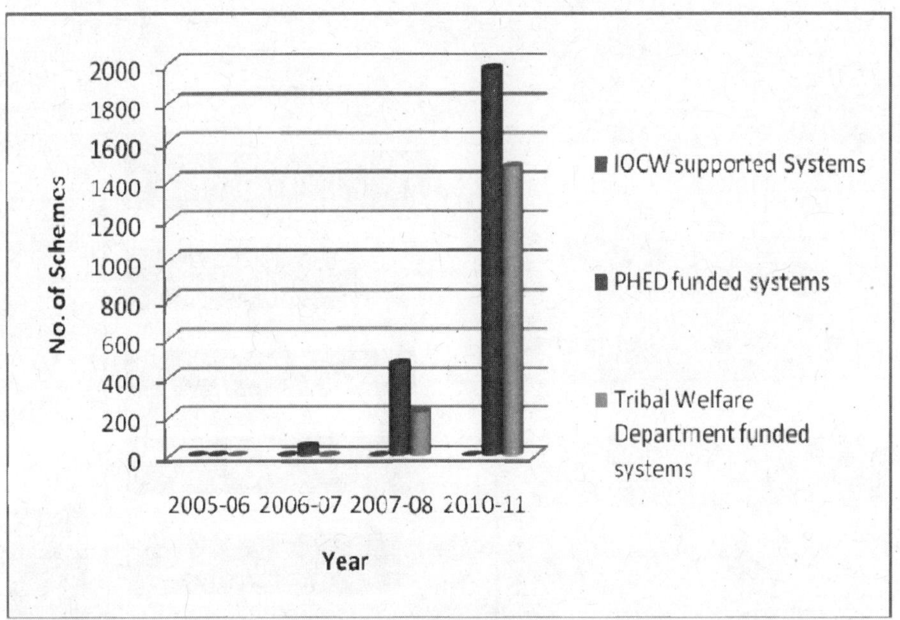

Figure 1: **Number of intelligent Water Management schemes (present and future) (IWM, 2006)**

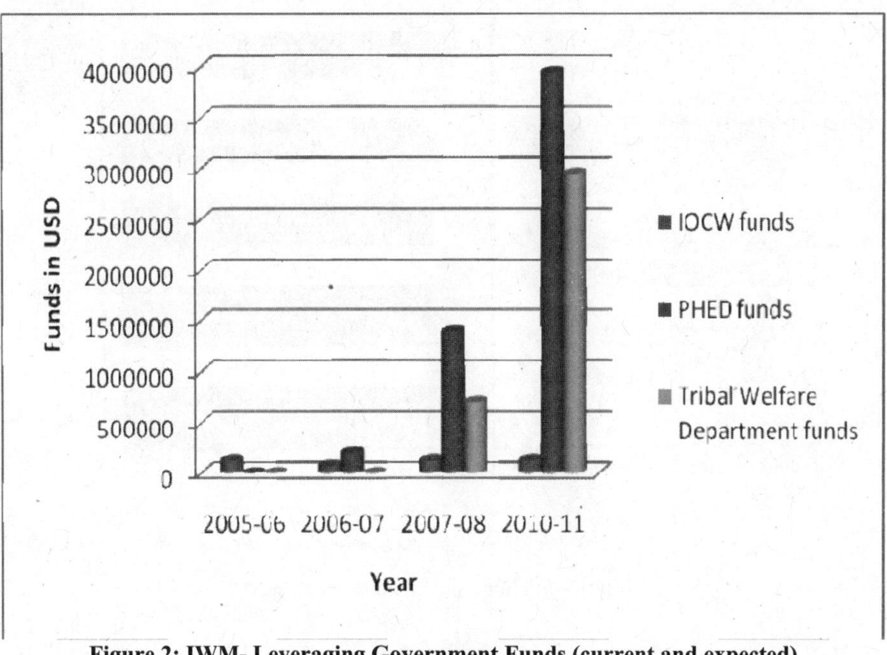

Figure 2: **IWM- Leveraging Government Funds (current and expected) (IWM, 2006)**

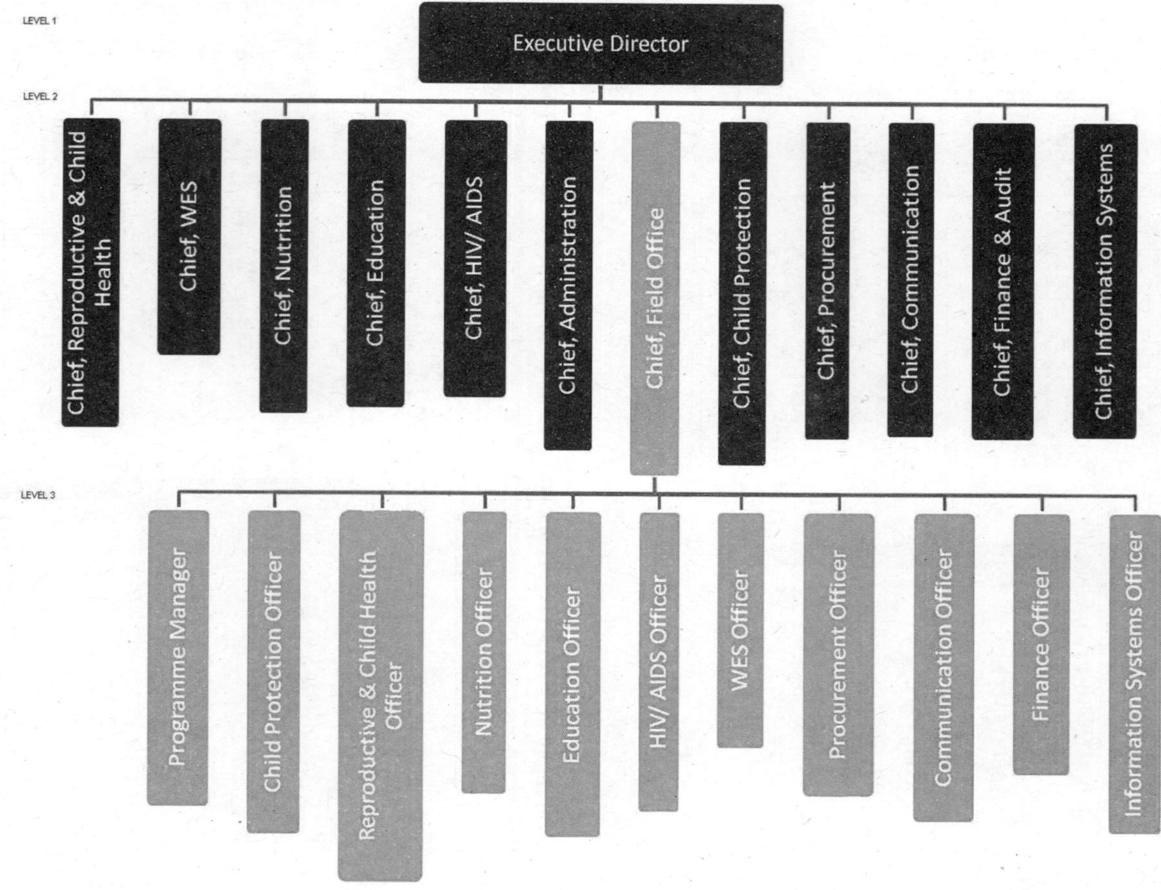

Figure 3: **Hierarchical Relationships**

Figure 4: Intelligent Water Management System

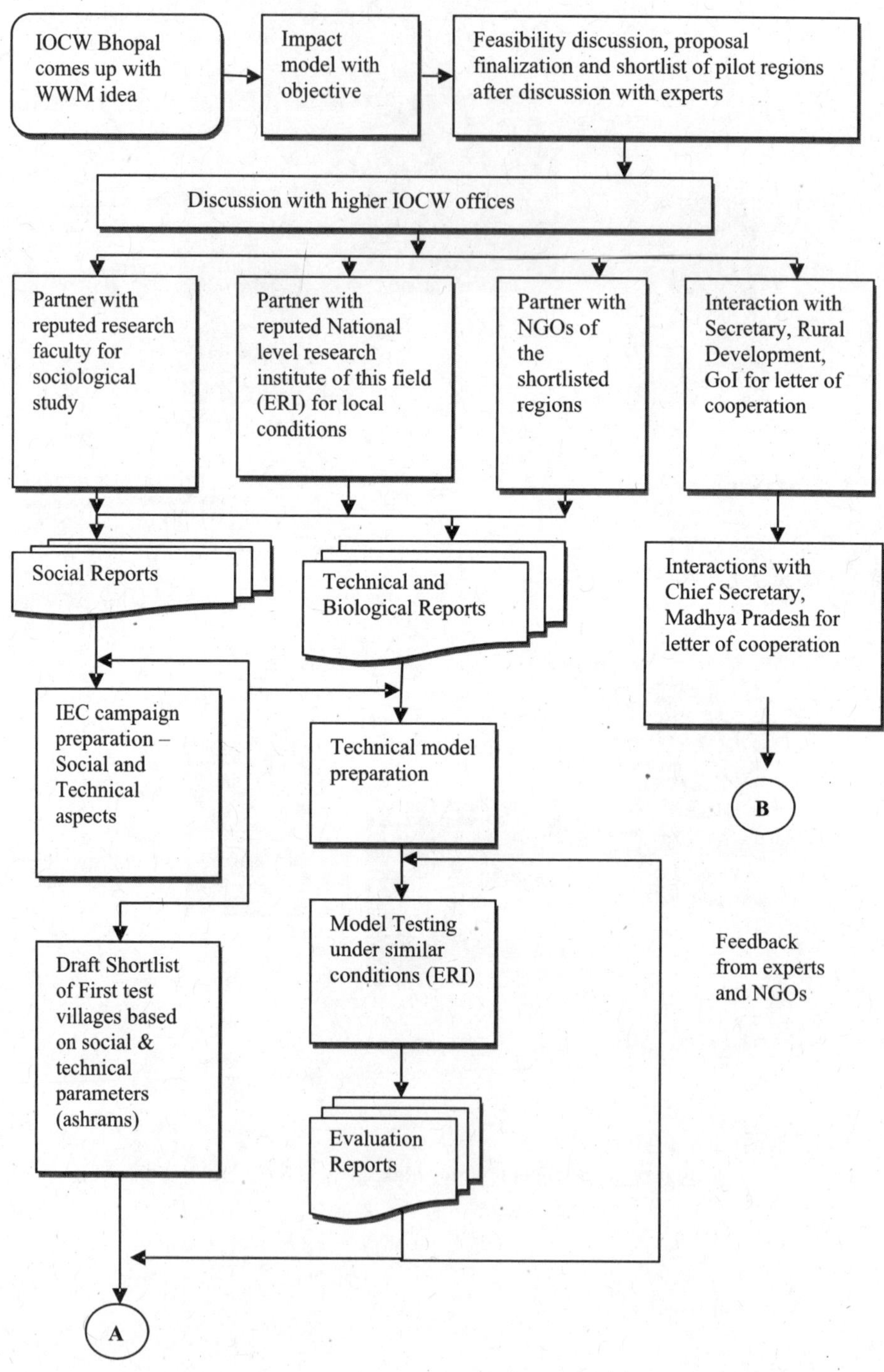

Figure 5: IWM as an example of General Project Implementation.
(From idea to evaluation)

Figure 5 (Contd.)

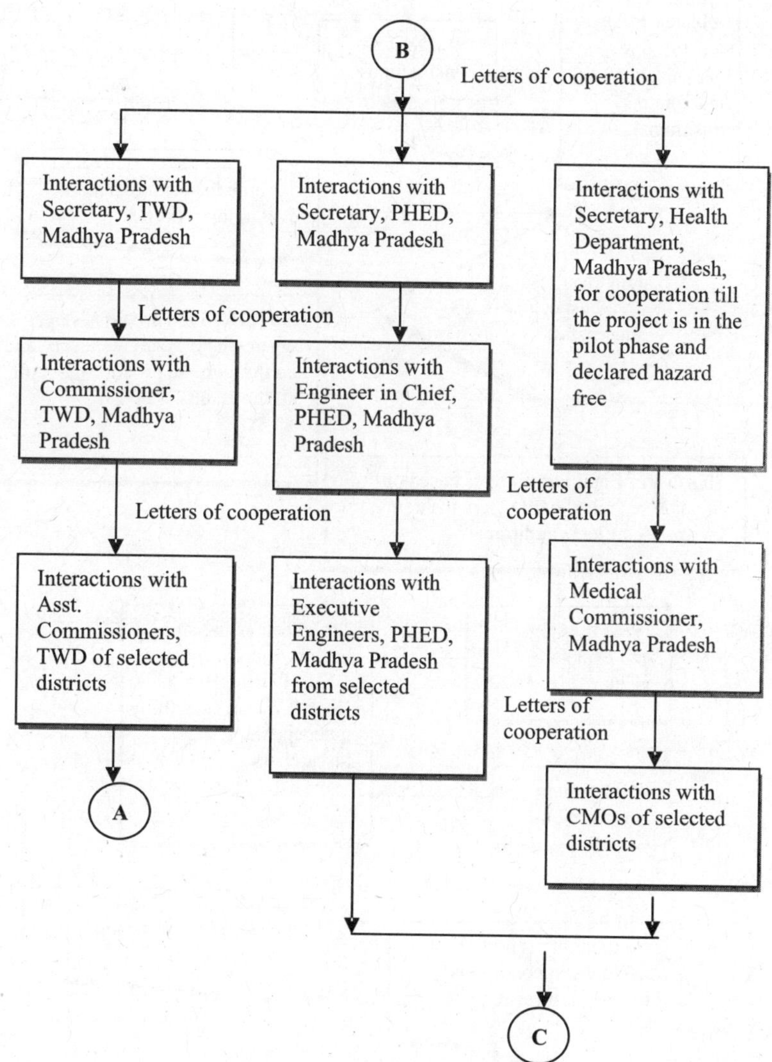
B
Letters of cooperation
Interactions with Secretary, TWD, Madhya Pradesh
Interactions with Secretary, PHED, Madhya Pradesh
Interactions with Secretary, Health Department, Madhya Pradesh, for cooperation till the project is in the pilot phase and declared hazard free
Letters of cooperation
Interactions with Commissioner, TWD, Madhya Pradesh
Interactions with Engineer in Chief, PHED, Madhya Pradesh
Letters of cooperation
Letters of cooperation
Interactions with Asst. Commissioners, TWD of selected districts
Interactions with Executive Engineers, PHED, Madhya Pradesh from selected districts
Interactions with Medical Commissioner, Madhya Pradesh
A
Letters of cooperation
Interactions with CMOs of selected districts
C

Figure 5 (Contd.)

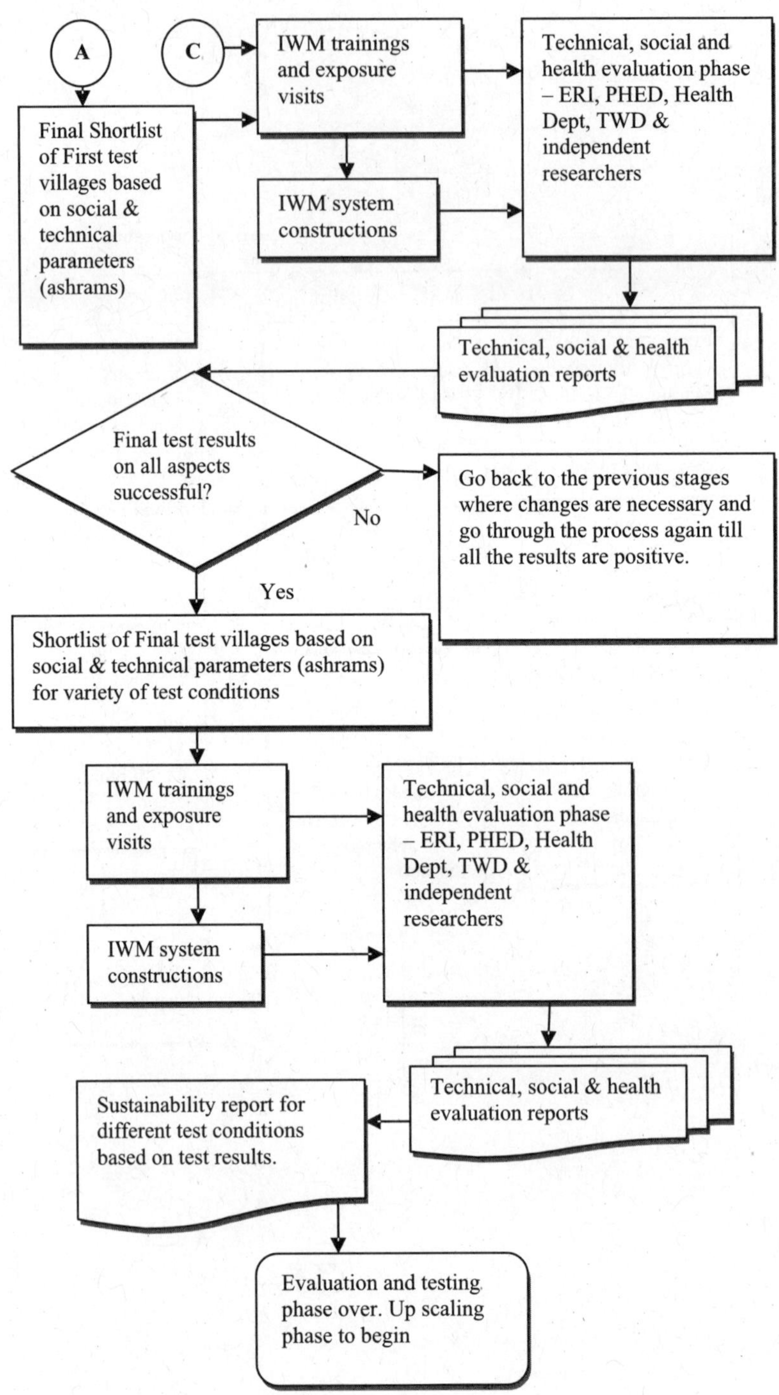
A
C
IWM trainings and exposure visits
Technical, social and health evaluation phase – ERI, PHED, Health Dept, TWD & independent researchers
Final Shortlist of First test villages based on social & technical parameters (ashrams)
IWM system constructions
Technical, social & health evaluation reports
Final test results on all aspects successful?
No
Go back to the previous stages where changes are necessary and go through the process again till all the results are positive.
Yes
Shortlist of Final test villages based on social & technical parameters (ashrams) for variety of test conditions
IWM trainings and exposure visits
Technical, social and health evaluation phase – ERI, PHED, Health Dept, TWD & independent researchers
IWM system constructions
Sustainability report for different test conditions based on test results.
Technical, social & health evaluation reports
Evaluation and testing phase over. Up scaling phase to begin

<u>**Figure 6**</u>: **Intended impact model of IOCW's IWM program**

<u>**ISSUE:**</u>	Solving water scarcity; safely and sanitation in marginalized communities
<u>**STRATEGY:**</u>	Greywater reuse and rainwater harvesting
<u>**ORGANIZATION:**</u>	TWD, IOCW, PHED and local NGOs
<u>**ENVIRONMENT:**</u>	Macro: Districts with > 50% SC/ST population | Micro: Ashram school for tribal children and individual households

INPUTS

Equipment (play pump, filter material)

Trainers for all levels (ashram, community, govt, NGO, masons)

Funding for materials, training, labor, repairs)

Staff and labor (every stakeholder)

Labor to clean and maintain

↓↓

IMPLEMENTATION

Selection of target ashrams, effected NGO

Trainings at different levels (students, ashram staff, engineers, laborers, NGO members)

Approval from all stakeholders

Construction of the physical structures

Creation of WSC

Ongoing IEC

Ongoing maintenance

Monitoring of water quality

↓↓

SHORT RUN OUTPUTS

Children with better hygiene behaviour

Increase of toilet use of ashram

increase in available water quantity

Reduction in fluoride level of drinking water

LONG RUN OUTPUTS
Increase in ground water level
Knowledge diffusion to parents leading to numerous household implementations
Communities with better health status
Increase in school attendance, literacy rate

EFFECTS, IMPACTS
Awareness and demand of water safety and quantity
Better hygiene/ sanitation (decrease in disease, mortality rates) higher life quality at ashrams
Higher school retention (gender ration, attendance, literacy rate)
Better education of marginalized communities
Increase in social inclusion
increase in ground water level availability
leverage of govt. funds

SUSTAINABILITY, EFFICIENCY
Knowledge diffusion between generations
Assured funding beyond pilots
changes in stakeholders do not effect the impact
water quality assured by adequate monitoring
sensitivity to feedback and improvement
time, labor, material and cost efficient
high likelihood of O & M

EXTERNALITIES
Weather (annual rainfall, storm, damage)
Poor maintenance
Improper implementation by NGO or Govt.
Problems in supply chain equipment and staff
Problem of collaboration between stakeholders

Section 3

ORGANIZATIONAL FORMS

The consequences and transformations of organizational form are ubiquitous to business history, and extensively researched in business literature. Large firms have dominated markets in many senses, and have therefore drawn attention to the small one. In recent history, there is however a discernible trend towards significance of the smaller organization. With the revolution in communication technology, and with the institutionalizing of entrepreneurship that is globally spread out, small entities have *found their place*. Somewhat related is the trend towards multi-organizational relationships in the pursuit of satisfying human need. It is such relationships that impart much of the efficiencies in the smaller and widely distributed organizations. In this section, SME firms' strategic issues are the focus for the first paper. This is followed by two cases and another paper. The paper is about the *sub*-organizational form. It explores a specific functional area of manufacturing organizations, and how the structure within this unit varies with the firm's orientation towards long term adaptation.

Both cases grapple with the *multi*-organizational situation, and how this affects strategy. Both relate to the government controlled sector, and bring out features of relationships among different arms of the same (public) owner. The case 'Is small beautiful' is about a small academic institution set up by the government. It looks into dependencies of the institution, and what lies in store for its strategizing.

"Smuggling brought on track", the other case, is remarkable one about dys-functionalities in the *multi*-organizational situation. It relates to the government controlled sector, and brings out features of relationships among different arms of the same (public) owner.

STRATEGIC ISSUES IN SMEs

Keerti Prajapati

Fellow Student, Institute of Rural Management Anand

INTRODUCTION

SMEs are an important sector of Indian industry. SMEs account for 40% of the industrial production and 35% of the total manufactured exports of the country (www.laghu-udyog.com). There are several advantages of being SMEs irrespective of their critique. These are: the potential for controlling rising Unemployment, regional imbalance, effective utilization of resources, promoting innovation, rapid and effective internal communication, shorter decision chains, capability for fast learning and adapting routine and strategy, flexibility and fast reaction to changing market requirement as compared to large firms, and entrepreneurial advancement (Das, 1996). Besides, there are several disadvantages inherent in small firms; they cannot enter national market, there are complaints of quality from customers, lack of management skills, fear of taxation, financing problems, isolated location, passive in product range, skill, marketing, raising skill (Weijland, 1999; Das, 1996). Globalization makes it worse in terms of free trade, tariffs, quantitative restriction (QRs), foreign direct investment (FDI), standards, accreditation and certification, regional trading blocs and preferences for green products and process (environment, health, safety) (Industry, www.smallscaleindustry.com). It forces small firms to improve productivity and efficiency in the allocation of resources, consumer demand for enhanced value in terms of cost and quality, and consumer tastes and preferences shifting perceptibly in favour of environment friendly products. By looking at this fact, it is very difficult for SMEs in the race for survival of the fittest.

In order to survive and grow in this competitive environment, comparative advantage is emerging as a strategic option. A firm gets comparative advantage through its technical, entrepreneurial and managerial capability. It can be made possible by focusing on strategic issues. Strategic issues are important for the development of SMEs. Some major strategic issues identified here for this sector are institutional support environment issues, strategic entrepreneurship development, social capital, cluster development and innovation.

SMALL & MEDIUM ENTERPRISE (SME)

There has been always a debate on the definitional issues of SMEs. According to the Reserve Bank of India (RBI), SME as a small scale industrial unit is an undertaking in which investment in plant and machinery, does not exceed Rs.1 crore, except in respect of certain specified items under hosiery, hand tools, drugs and pharmaceuticals, stationery items and sports goods, where this investment limit has been enhanced to Rs. 5 crore. SMEs are established in almost all major sectors such as agriculture, food processing, chemical and pharmaceutical, sports goods, leather and leather goods, plastic products, computer software, and engineering, electronic and electronics, etc (Sampath, 2006) (www.rbi.org).

They are characterized by low scale economies, less capital investment, mostly family-owned enterprise, easy entry and exit, use of indigenous resources and technology which are basically labour intensive technology, and high percentage of migrant labour, high dependence, financial crisis, borrowing mostly from non-banking and local money lender (Varma, 2002), cater localized as well international markets, and insufficient division of labour (Saith, 2001), greater operational flexibility, high propensity to adapt technology, high capacity to innovate, export, high employment orientation, utilization of locally available human & material resources, and having a role in reduction of regional imbalance (www.smeindia.com)

Why SMEs

From past several years and decades, the dwindling agriculture sector has created drastic changes in Indian economy which caused a shift in economy from farm sector to nonfarm sector to service sector (Rangarajan, 2005; Prasad, Mathur and Chatterjee, 2007; Purrushotham, and Rao, 1993; Rao, 2000; Sury, Mathur and Bhasin, 2006). Industry sector plays a significant role in economic development because of its potential to absorb excess labour through generating new employment opportunities, create new skills, and promote entrepreneurship by exploiting available resources.

Major contribution to GDP

SMEs are one of the significant segments of the Indian economy. The Indian SME segment's current production value is almost Rs 816,000 crore (www.indiastat.com). It manufactures more than 8,000 diverse products, ranging from low-technology items to technologically advanced products. The SMEs sector targets both domestic as well global markets. The sector is recognized as the engine of growth, accounting for about 70% of employment and contributes a significant amount for the growth of GDP. Globally, 99.7% of all enterprises in the world are SME.s, and remain 0.3% is large-scale enterprises. By contrast, the SMEs sector in India accounts for 95% of all industrial units. According to the Ministry of Small Scale Industries, the number of registered SMEs units in India has increased from 11 million units in 2002–03 to 11.4 million units in 2003–04, up 3.6 per cent. The production of SMEs units in India increased from Rs.311, 993 crore in 2002–03 to Rs.357, 733 crore in 2003–04. The industry groups - with a large share in the total production of SMEs such as textile products, wood, furniture, paper, printing, and metal products - have recorded high growth rates. Decline in the number of sick units has been reported over the period 1999 to 2003. The Number of sick SMEs units in the country has come down from 3, 06,221 as at the end of March 1999 to 1, 67,980 as at the end of March 2003(www.indiastat.com).

International Market and Domestic Market

SMEs contribute to around 40% of industrial production & exports. The exports grew at a faster rate than production in 2002–03. While production at current prices grew by about 10.53 per cent and exports rose by 20.7 per cent from Rs. 71,244 crore to Rs. 86,013 crore between 2001-02 and 2002-03. The industry groups with a large share in exports are hosiery and garments (29.0%), food products (21.4%) and, leather products (18%). The SSI units continue to create employment. There is huge potential for SMEs especially those are in sector of textile clothing, and other labour intensive products if advanced industrial countries open up their markets.

Employment

The greatest advantage that SMEs have is that they are major employment provider. The share of agriculture in total employment has come down from 61.67 per cent in 1993-94 to 58.54 per cent in 1999-2000, and further to 54.19 percent in 2004-05 (Prasad, Mathur and Chatterjee, 2007). India has employment growth of 1.7 percent annum as against a labour force growth of 1.8 percent annum (OECD Economic Surveys: India, 2007). The number of people employed in the SMEs sector went up from 260.13 lakh in 2002-03 to 271.36 lakh in 2003-04. This sector is next only to agriculture in employment. The proportion of workers in the secondary, tertiary and total non-farm sectors has witnessed a steady increase, for instance from 16.8% in 1972–73 to 25.5% in 1987–88 and to 28.6% in 1999–00 for all non-agricultural sectors.

STRATEGIC ISSUES IN SMEs

Globalization has opened up a new window of opportunities for SMEs such as WTO regime, bilateral and multilateral trade agreements; enhanced credit support, support for technology up-gradation, and comprehensive support for cluster development, marketing assistance, export promotion support and growing domestic and international markets. Besides opportunities, it also poses threats for SMEs such as dumping from developed countries, distrust between SMEs and financial institutions, poor incentive structure for entrepreneurs, virtual absence of enterprise education, non-traffic barriers from developed countries and slow improvement in quality to meet the international standards. To capture opportunities SMEs need to focus on strategic issues (Sampath, 2006).

India's manufacturing firms are not able to fully exploit their comparative advantage of low labour costs and have remained extraordinarily small in scale (OECD Economic Surveys: India, 2007). Manufacturing industrial production is continuously declining from the year 1999-2000. In the year 1990-91 index of industrial production was 9 where, in the year 2001-02 it reduce to 2.3 only except a good growth in the year 1995-96 (Verma, 2000).

Although government support small scale firms in terms of entrepreneurial training, technological up-gradation, financial assistance, market provider, raw material supplier etc, but these are all at micro level with limited effectiveness. There are two reasons; first is high administrative cost, lack of managerial and executive capacity and second is policy mostly favors large firms (Schmitz and Musyck, 1994). Implementation of these programs is unstructured, vague, and they are not delivering intended result. SMEs are facing problems because of inadequate and/or weak linkages. Some of the problems identified by the Government of India report on SSIs are as follows:

- Inadequacy of working capital, delay in sanction of working capital and time gap between sanction of term loan and working capital
- Poor and obsolete technology
- Problem related to availability of raw material.
- Inadequate demand and other marketing problems
- Erratic power supply
- Labor problems
- Infrastructural constraints
- Poor Management
- Inadequate attention to Research and Development
- Diversion of resources
- Inability of the units to face growing competition due to liberalization and globalization

Being small in size brings disadvantage for small and medium enterprises, it increases their dependence on large firms for market, upgrade technology, finance, and unable to achieve economies of scale. Small and medium-sized firms need to **cooperate** in order to survive. Strategic issues emanating from cooperation are like cooperation among the small firms to raise social capital, encourage entrepreneurs to establish their firm in the cluster, able to get support from government and non governmental agencies. Five major strategic issues are identified in this write-up: institutional issues, strategic entrepreneurship development, social capital, cluster development, innovation, and e-commerce. These are depicted in **Figure-1**. Other main strategic issues come under the umbrella of institutional supportive environment.

Strategic issues are interrelated to each other like social capital in terms of business networks helps in developing cluster and promote innovation. But, the use of social capital ultimately depends upon entrepreneur strategic choices.

Institutional Issues

Government's development strategy for SME sector includes protective discrimination e.g. reservation, minority sector lending, etc, integration between large and small e.g. subcontractimg, ancillarisation and vendor development and institutional support through a network of testing centres, tool rooms, entrepreneurship development institutes etc. For proper implementation of policies or any strategy there should be an appropriate distribution of responsibilities among the different institutions. Institutional supportive environment consists of government, research institutions, profit and non-profit organizations, financial institutions, etc. Recognizing the role of innovation in competitive advantage, the Government of India has established research and development or technology support centres for SMEs in India. Problem lies in that they are not able to think in terms of sustainability and competitive advantage.

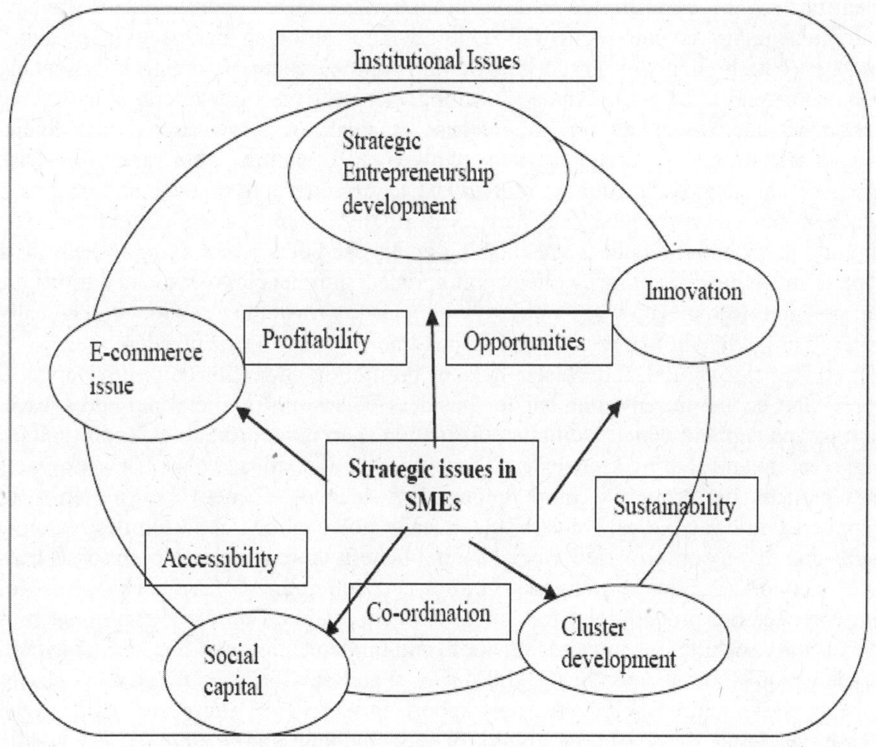

Figure 1: Framework for strategic issues in SME's

To provide them competitive advantage, government has been focusing on cluster development, and has formulated cluster development policy in the Tenth Five Year Plan. United Nations Industrial Development Organization (UNIDO) is playing a leading role in development of clusters in India. Its main focus is on development of networks for enterprises. The stress is on creating competitive rivalries among the cluster partners in terms of innovation, collaboration, cooperation and other differentiators not through the conventional, unhealthy under-bidding among the firms in the cluster (www.unido.org). Other organizations which are working in the field of cluster development are: Central Government, Development Commissioner (SSI), Ministry of Small Scale Industries, Khadi Village Industry Commission (KVIC), Coir Board, Small Industry Development Bank of

India (SIDBI), National Bank for Agriculture and Rural Development (NABARD), Reserve Bank of India (RBI), Small Industries Development Organization (SIDO).

Strategic Entrepreneurship Development

In general the production function consists of land, labour, and capital but, there is a fourth important element that is enterprise. Entrepreneurship is the process of establishing an enterprise by an entrepreneur. Entrepreneurship entails identification of opportunities and exploitation of these opportunities. Strategic entrepreneurship is entrepreneurial action with a strategic perspective. In short, strategic entrepreneurship is the integration of entrepreneurial (opportunity-seeking behaviour) and strategic (advantage seeking) perspectives in developing and taking action designed to create wealth. Because of small size, low capital investment, simple technology requirements, and involvement of family labor, and lower risk involved in business, it attracts individuals to become entrepreneur and acts as a seedbed for entrepreneurship. There is a myth that providing entrepreneurship training helps entrepreneur in establishing enterprise but it is not going to help for a long term. Rather it requires strategic entrepreneurship development which trains the entrepreneur to focus on niche markets which large firms either cannot economically enter or are reluctant to enter because of unattractive risk-return considerations.

Social capital and cluster help in promoting SMEs through developing a social and economic environment for business consisting of social networks, trust, norms, and demand which facilitate information sharing, coordination, opportunities, and creating and sharing knowledge (Durlauf, and Fafchamps, 2004). Cluster attracts entrepreneur by providing more choices of linkages or networks in terms of suppliers, intermediaries, buyers etc means to capture opportunities through accessing diverse information. Social capital benefit entrepreneur in both forms trust and networks. Social networks influence entrepreneur at each stage of entrepreneurship process. Networks help at every stage of entrepreneurship such as opportunity seeking, resources acquisition, and implementation of business or market organization (Casson, and Giusta, 2007). Greve and Salaff (2003) found three phases of entrepreneurship where networks support entrepreneur. These are motivational phase, planning phase (classify into two developing and maintain) and finally establishment phase (split into establishment, and taking over a firm). Trust enables entrepreneur to minimize searching cost, enforcement of contracts, reduction of monitoring cost, facilitating the circulation of reliable information about technology and market opportunities, as well as in the blacklisting of unreliable agents.

Innovation

Generally innovation means creating something new especially a new product or new technology. But, it is just one facet of innovation. Innovation can also be the creation of new resources or combining existing resources in new ways to develop and commercialize new products, move into new markets, and/or services, and to acquire new customers (Swedberg, 2000). Innovation provides entrepreneur a chance to become a first mover, by which the entrepreneur can gain monopoly profit until a competitor imitates its new product or finds a substitute. Innovation cannot be studied in isolation. It should be seen as a system or a process which comprises of actors, institutions and their interaction, as depicted in Figure 2.

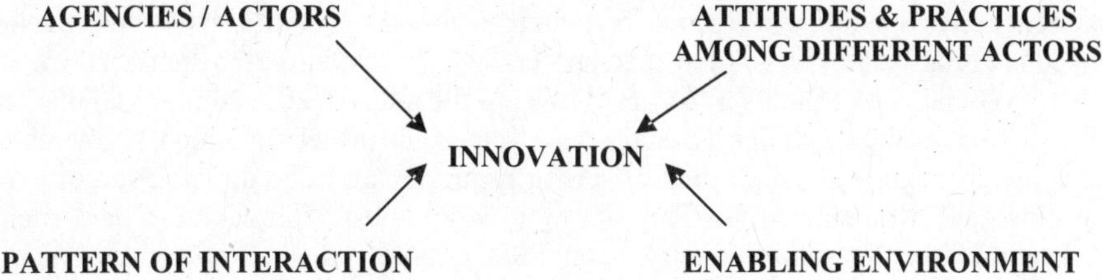

Figure 2: Innovation as a system

Government's policy for innovation in SME has concentrated on technology transfer for better utilization of local resources and for achievement of local self-sufficiency, rather than assistance for R&D. Because of this approach, SMEs suffer in regard to inputs of technology because of lack of resources for investment in R&D for invention, innovation, improvement and development of their processes and products and extending the range of their activities (Khan, and Ghani, 2004). There are some influential factors for innovation in SMEs. These are classified into two categories, namely, internal and external. Internal factors are self-motivation, technical education, and work experience. External factors include customer touch, subcontracting relationship with a large firm, research institute interaction, and government promoted SME support organization, competition and technology change. Thus, innovation provides a competitive edge to the enterprise in the local as well as global markets. Those enterprises, which are innovative, will be able to withstand the competitive pressure and penetrate new markets across industries, regions and times. Size, focus, and personal contact with customers make SMEs an ideal seed bed for innovation (Subrahmanya, 2006).

Social Capital

Social capital has been getting increasing importance because it is the major source of access to information, resources, and markets and even, at times, technologies for the firm. It includes networking with NGOs, government and other development institutions, research institutions, non-profit and for-profit organizations. Social networks mainly consist of vertical or bridging and horizontal or bonding networks. Networks provide credit, access to distant market, lower the risk involved in business, lower the transaction cost, and provide competitive advantage to firms (Iyer and Toh, 2005). Social capital generates and increases trust which reduces transaction cost which entrepreneurs face in searching and accessing information, bargaining, policing and enforcement costs by facilitating cooperation among them (Maèerinskas, and Pakalnienë, 2004). This trustworthiness environment helps to overcome problems of asymmetric information, monitoring and enforcement so that no one can behave opportunistically (Torsvik, 2000; Sjoerd and Schaik, 2003; Beugelsdijk, and Smulders, 2004). Globalization creates an imperative for firms to consider participating in networks and to reflect upon the strategic importance of social networks for the firm. Networks have become crucial to the competitive success of SMEs in the fast-changing and highly competitive global markets. The ability of SMEs to own or control assets or resources is normally more restricted than large firms. More than ever, many of the skills and resources essential to SME's prosperity lie outside the firm's boundaries; for that, SMEs have to develop embedded relationship with these stakeholders who are essential for their survival.

Social capital helps a firm in analyzing the attractiveness of a given market, i.e., where to compete, but it is much more important to decide which segments of the value chain of a given product or sets of produces are to be downplayed or even subcontracted altogether. Whether a firm is a low-cost manufacturer or a niche marketer within the same industry is, at least radical a distinction, with as many implications, as whether the firm is competing in a given market, or another similar to it - concentrating on the same activities of the value chain. Shaping the value chain is really shaping the firm. This can be achieving through strategic networks. Thus, the realization of the importance of networking, and the understanding of the skills involved in making it succeed, are two of the most important entrepreneurial skills that can be taught and developed through strategic entrepreneurship development. Success of any business is contingent on the firm's contacts or what we called networks.

Cluster Development

The idea of cluster development is old but this old idea is getting value because of increasing competitive environment. The idea is that by creating sectarian and geographical concentration of these SMEs, which have the same problems and opportunities, they will be able to face the external competition effectively. India presently has more than 400 modern and around 2000 old clusters (Das, 2005). Some of the popular clusters are the knitwear cluster in Ludhiana, gems and jewelry cluster in Surat and the leather products cluster in Agra, etc.

Broadly, cluster is a geographic concentration of interconnected companies and institutions in a particular field, encompassing linked industries and other entities important for competition (Porter, 1998). Cluster represents a special case of networked firms that are geographically co-located. By enhancing the capacity of specialized firms, clusters result in enhancing regional competitiveness. Furthermore clusters can play a vital role in the cluster firm's ability to innovate. Cluster firms tend to be specialized, thereby gaining from scale economies. Cluster firms thus benefit from their access to the high levels of productivity and responsiveness of other specialized firms, and also from reduced inventory levels, and transportation costs.

One of the greatest advantages of cluster is that it provides competitive advantage under today's fierce competition. Cluster can provide competitive advantage to the firms by affecting competition in three ways: productivity (better access to employees and supplier, access to specialized information, complementarities, access to institutions and public goods, better motivation and measurement), innovation (provide window for customer, make companies learn about technology component, machinery availability, service and marketing concepts, provide capacity and flexibility), and finally formation of new business firms (concentrated customer based, individuals working within a cluster can more easily perceive gaps in products or service around which they can build business, resource availability and stimulate networking among firms) (Porter, 2000).

A cluster must consist of groups of associated and interconnected firms that are linked vertically and/or horizontally through their commonalities and complementariness in products, services, inputs, technologies or outputs activities. In that case there is commonality in inputs purchased, technology, infrastructure, buyers, channel, and production process. Besides, proximity among firms promotes services like transportation, warehouse, communication etc. Thus, this commonality leads towards interrelationships. These commonalities may be source of information about competitor behaviour, new technology developments, and other industry trends. This information is critical for future decisions regarding cooperation for product development and commercialization (Walker, Kogut and Shan 2001). When these SMEs are in a cluster form it adds to their benefit because small firm can enhance its capability and gain competitive advantage only when not as alone but in group. Cluster helps in developing skills in labour so sometime labour obtained a position of privilege; they are given priority in allocation of jobs and are paid higher wages (Smyth, 1992).

Cluster can provide a large number of customers, service and raw materials available readily at reasonable prices, fragmented by orders suppliers to small firms (Das, 1996). Clusters account for a significant percentage of employment and output generated in the manufacturing sector. Their contribution to exports is very impressive. According to a UNIDO study, clusters accounted for nearly 60 per cent of manufacturing exports. Increase Cooperation/Collective Efficiency, Technology and Knowledge Spillover (learning region), Flexibilities, Specific benefits to Small and large firms.

E-Commerce Issues

The potential of E-commerce to enhance business competitiveness in both domestic and international markets has been widely recognized. Some major obstacles to E-commerce development by SMEs are lack of awareness, unsecured products ordering processes, unsecured payment systems, lack of an effective legal framework, poor telecommunication infrastructure, absence of a certification authority, language problem etcetera (Wu, 2001). The benefits of E-commerce most often cited are cost reduction particularly in transaction costs, efficiency rises, and changes in management and production processes of business.

E-commerce also holds out opportunities for SMEs to reach and penetrate global markets, since it allows firms and their customers to conduct real-time, remote transactions via website, without limitations posed by time and geography. E-commerce is therefore, perceived as on unconventional tool which can potentially expand SMEs outreach. E-commerce is defined as "sale or purchase of goods or services, whether between business, households, individual and government and other public or private organization, conducted over computer-mediated networks" (Kansititorn, Poopparadai and Smutkput, 2005). Figure 3 depicts the e-commerce applications for enterprise, which include: electronic transaction such as e-auctions and on-line ordering, virtual mall, e-procurement etc.

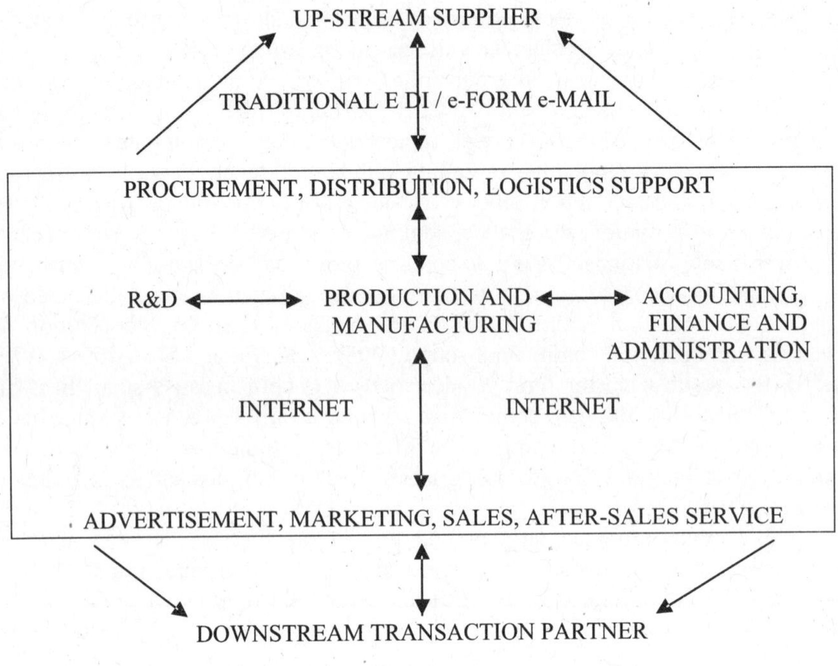

Figure 3: E-commerce Application for Enterprise (Source: Wu, 2001)

CONCLUSION

Firm success depends largely on the extent to which the firm responds to opportunities and threats in the global marketplace. Basically, SMEs target niche-markets that are not covered by large firms; which means that firms encounter diverse consumer needs and competitors' offerings, as well as varying economic and technology conditions. Being responsive to globalization may be particularly important to the success of the SMEs. Diverse linkages of a firm are a long term solution towards success of firms. These linkages act as a strategy for entrepreneur. Although, Industrial development cluster approach is not new but, by looking at competitive environment, now days, it attracts interest of many researchers especially for the development of SMEs in rural and urban areas. Policies and programs should be structured to set up clusters to source new technology and innovation. Cluster helps in creating social capital of an entrepreneur, sharing knowledge among different firms in cluster promote innovation; ultimately it all works as a strategic resource for an entrepreneur to run a successful business. Clusters also facilitate innovation by the rapid exchange of technological information ensuring that innovations in individual firms upgrade the overall cluster through reducing the risk of failure of the entrepreneur (small firm), since other specialized suppliers in the cluster assume part of the risk of innovation and rapid exchange of technological information through proximity, trust together with rivalry, and extensive outsourcing arrangements.

REFERENCES

1. Anderson, Alistair, John Park, and Sarah Jack, (2007), "Entrepreneurial Social Capital: Conceptualizing Social Capital in New High-Tech Firms", International Small Business Journal, 25, pp. 245-272

2. Beugelsdijk, Sjoerd and Sjak Smulders, (2004) "Social Capital and Economic Growth", March. Retrieved on 4/2/08 from http://www.dur.ac.uk/economics.guestspeakers/2003_04/Smulders.pdf

3. Calvin Wang, Elizabeth A. Walker and Janice Redmond, "Explaining The Lack Of Strategic Planning In SMEs: The Importance Of Owner Motivation", International Journal of Organisational Behaviour, Volume 12 (1), 1-16.

4. Casson, Mark and Marina Della Giusta (2007), "Entrepreneurship and Social Capital", International Small Business Journal, 25:3, pp. 220-244

5. Christina Boari & Manuela Presutti, (2004) "Social Capital and Entrepreneurship inside an Italian Cluster - Empirical Investigation, occasional paper 2004/2. Retrieved on 12 October from www.diva-portal.org/diva/getDocument?urn_nbn_se_uu_diva-4287-1__fulltext.pdf

6. Das, Keshab (2005) "Indian Industrial Clusters", Ashgate Publishing Limite, England

7. Das, Keshabanbad, (1996) "Flexible Together: Surviving and Growing In A Garment Cluster, Ahmedabad, India", The Journal Of Entrepreneurship, 5:2, pp. 153-177

8. Datanet India Pvt. Ltd. Delhi, India, retrieved on 12 December from www.indiastat.com

9. Debt restructuring mechanism for Small and Medium Enterprises (SMEs) – Announcement made by the Union Finance Minister, retrieved on 12 December, 2007 from http://www.rbi.org.in/scripts/NotificationUser.aspx?Id=2502&Mode=0

10. Drucker, Peter (1985), "Innovation and Entrepreneurship: Practices and Principles", Heinemann, London

11. Durlauf, Steven N. and Marcel Fafchamps, (2004), "Social Capital", May, National Bureau of Economic Research (NBER) Working Paper 10485. Retrieved from http://www.nber.org/papers/w10485 on 12/12/ 2007

12. Greve, Arent and Janet W. Salaff, (2003), "Social Networks and Entrepreneurship, Entrepreneurship Theory & Practice, 28:1, pp 1-22

13. Iyer, Sriya , Michael Kitson and Bernard Toh, (2005) "Social Capital, Economic Growth and Regional Development" Regional Studies, November, Vol. 39.8, pp. 1015–1040

14. Joshi, Gopal (2001), "Entrepreneurship Development for SMEs in the 21st Centaury", Productivity, July- September, 42:2, pp 186-190

15. Kansititorn, Poopparadai and Phumisak Smutkput (2005), "e-commerce issues in SMEs of Thailand", Asia Pacific Tech Monitor, 22:6, pp. 33-40.

16. Khan, Jamshed H and Jawaid A Ghani, (2004), "Cluster and Entrepreneurship: Implications for Innovation in a Developing Economy", Journal of development entrepreneurship, December, 9:3, pp. 221-238.

17. Maèerinskas, Jogaila and Akvilë Pakalnienë, (2004) "The Impact of Embeddedness on the Economic Performance of Firms", Ekonomika, 67, pp. 1–14

18. OECD Economic Surveys: India, (2007), Organization for Economic Co-Operation Development, Academic Foundation, New Delhi.

19. Porter, Michael E (1980), "Competitive Strategy", The Free Press, New York

20. Porter, Michael E., (1998), "Cluster and the New Economics of Competition", Harvard Business Review, November-December, pp.77-90. Retrieved on 12 October from www.oregoneconomy.org/Porter%20Clusters%20New%20Economics%20of%

21. Porter, Michael E., (2000), "Location, Competition, and Economic Development: Local Clusters in a Global Economy" Economic Development Quarterly, 14: 15 http://edq.sagepub.com/cgi/content/abstract/14/1/15 electronic version retrieved on November 2, 2007

22. Prasad, C S, Vibha Mathur and Anup Chatterjee, (2007), "Sixty Years of The Indian Economy 1947-2007" Volume II. New Century Publications New Delhi

23. Purrushotham, P and V M Rao, (1993) "Employment Potential of Rural Industries", National Institute of Rural Development, Hyderabad, India.

24. Raghunath, S, (2001), "Managing Inter-Organizational Alliances: The Challenge For SMEs", Productivity, July- September, 42:2, pp 181-185

25. Rao, M. Koteswara, (2000) "Rural Employment: The Non-Farm Sector", published by Deep &Deep Publications Private Ltd, New Delhi

26. Saith, Ashwani (2001) "From Village Artisans to Industrial Clusters: Agendas and Policy Gaps in Indian Rural Industrialization, Journal of Agrarian Change, January, 1:1, pp 81–123.

27. Satish, D, (2007), "Indian SMEs: clustering growth", ICFAI Reader, September, 10:9

28. Sjoerd Beugelsdijk and Ton van Schaik, (2003) "Social Capital and Regional Economic Growth", Paper submitted to ERSA, Jyvaskila (Finland). Retrieved on 4/2/08 from www.jyu.fi/ersa2003/cdrom/papers/518.pdf

29. Sampath, Divya (2006) "How Can Indian SMEs Become Export Competitive"?, Dissertation, CRISIL, Young Thought Leader Series, Symbiosis Institute Of Business Management, Pune.

30. Schmitz, Hubert and Bernard, Musyck, (1994) "Industrial Districts In Europe: Policy Lessons For Developing Countries?, World Development, 22:6, pp. 889-910

31. Subrahmanya, M. H. Bala, (2006), "Why Should Indian SMEs Innovate?" Pravartak, October- December, 2:1, pp. 22-28

32. Sury, M.M., Vibha Mathur and Niti Bhasin (2006) "Economic Planning in India: 1951-52 to 2006-07", Indian Tax Foundation, New Century Publication, New Delhi

33. Swedberg, Richard (2000) "Entrepreneurship: The Social Science View",(eds) Oxford University Press, New Delhi

34. Smyth, Ines, (1992) "Collective Efficiency and Selective Benefits: The Growth of the Rattan Industries of Tegalewangi (Indonesia)", IDS Bulletin, 23:3, pp. 53-63

35. Torsvik, Gaute (2000), "Social Capital and Economic Development: A Plea for the Mechanisms", Rationality and Society, 12:4, pp. 451-476

36. Varma, Shri Ravindra, (2002) "Report on the National Commission on Labour" 2nd Labour Commission Report, October, Volume I (part 1and 2), Akalank Publications, New Delhi

37. Walker, Gordon, Bruce Kogut and Weijian Shan "Social Capital, Structural Holes and the Formation of an Industry Network" edited in Lesser, Eric, L, (2001)

38. Weijland, Hermine (1999) "Microenterprise Clusters In Rural Indonesia: Industrial Seedbed and Policy Target" World Development, 27: 9

39. Wolfe, David A, "Social Capital and Cluster Development in Learning Regions" Retrieved on 12 December from www.utoronto.ca/progris/pdf_files/Wolfe_SocialCapital.pdf

40. Wu, Steven Hung-Chi (2001), "IT Application in SMEs-Impacts of e-Commerce & Corresponding Solution", Productivity, July- September, 42:2, pp 256-264

IS SMALL BEAUTIFUL (I)? [1]

Krishna Kumar

Indian Institute of Management Lucknow

The Board of Directors of Institute of Information Technology East (IITE) was wondering what course of action be taken to get over the precarious situation it was facing on account of non-availability of land, which was holding it from moving further on academic activities.

BACKGROUND OF THE INSTITUTE

The Institute was promoted in the year 2000 in the eastern coast by the State Government as a non-profit making joint stock company with the purpose of grooming software professionals and spreading the use of IT in the government. This was in line with the general sentiments prevailing at that time, with several State Governments as well as Government of India promoting institutes of Information Technology. It had an eminent Board with Shri. Komal as the Chairman, two leading luminaries from IT Sector, Secretary (IT), Secretary (Finance) and Secretary (Higher Education) of the State Government.. Dr. Suresh Kanchan was appointed as Managing Director. He was an experienced academician from one of the leading technological institutes of the country. He had great dreams to make the Institute an Institution of higher learning with focus on research and advanced application of IT in various sectors and services, especially the neglected ones like agriculture, education, health etc. The Institute also had educational focus, starting with an 18-month Postgraduate diploma in IT in the year 2003.

THE CRITICALITY OF LAND ISSUE

The Institute started functioning from part of a rented building in Technopark, a major IT hub created by the state government. The Technopark was a very successful venture of the state government. The area of 10000 sq feet, for which

---

[1]Case prepared by Prof. Krishna Kumar. Data has been disguised as necessary. This case material is prepared as a basis for class discussion and not for commenting on proper or improper handling of administrative problems.

the Technopark charged over Rs.50,000/- a month, however, was too small to accommodate training / teaching activity or even for taking up IT projects on a large scale. At the time of establishment, the Technopark had indicated that it will allot about 10 acres of land. However, later the land was given to a software company, as the economic consideration weighed against the IITE. The Institute then proposed acquisition of a 30,000 sq. ft. building in the Technopark which was earlier taken by a software company. The company went broke. The State Bank of India, which had given loan to the company, was willing to give it to the Institute, but the minimum auction price set was twice the valuation of the building done by different departments of the government over a period of two years. Government, therefore, refused to give permission to acquire the same. The Institute thus had to look for an alternate piece of land.

The land issue had become a critical one in view of the fact that the All India Council of Technical Education had declined to approve the Institute's 18-month long MS (IT) programme, which the Instituted had started in 2003.

In view of the non-availability of AICTE recognition to the MS (IT) Programme, it was decided that the programme may be offered as PGDIT with same content and duration for the coming year. The applicants, who had responded to the advertisement for MS (IT) Programme, were informed that the Institute was offering the programme named PGDIT and that they could give their interest to take the PGDIT Programme. It was also decided to refund the admission fee collected to those who were not interested in doing the PGDIT Programme.

However, out of 67 students who had applied only 28 of them indicated that they were willing to join PGDIT programme. It has been decided to dispense with the entrance test and have only interview.   However, only 18 confirmed that they would be appearing in the interview.

The Institute was worried at the development and its likely impact on the programme. The first batch of MS (IT) had done well. 37 of the 39 students had been placed through the Institute in about 15 companies with an average salary of Rs. 3.0 lakhs per year.

THE FINANCIAL CRUNCH

The decline in number of students also had financial ramifications for the Institute. Despite reasonably high fees of Rs. 1.50 lakhs per year for the MS programme, the fee collected during 2006-07 was only Rs. 1.20 crores. One reason was the fact that Institute could not fill all the sixty seats (which could fetch Rs. 1.80 crores), as many students left after joining the programme, thanks to the booming software industry. With the problem of non-approval of MS (IT) by AICTE and change in the name to PGDIT, the fee collection could take a nose dive.

The financial problem worrying the Institute was not only caused by the decline expected in the number of student registration in the PGDIT. The other major source of income namely the research projects taken up by the Institute, which started with a big bang of Rs. 455 lakh Education-Grid grant, were also declining (see exhibit 2), both in terms of numbers as also the amount. The sustenance of the projects was also becoming a cash drain, as government funds were not coming in time for the purpose. The Institute was not yet ready with the economic model to announce it to the public, although the physical infrastructure was ready for use. The projects like Education-Grid although ready for use were not being subscribed by the beneficiary (students or teachers). The Security portal (for Police) and Farmer's Friend portals were ready and being used extensively, but the running expenses were expected to be met by government grants, which was not forthcoming as expected. No subscription from public/farmers was envisaged. The financing of the portal itself was not yet received from any funding agency. Therefore, Institute's funds were used for the purpose.

REMEDIAL ACTION PLANS

Perturbed over the impending financial crunch (see Exhibit-1A & 1B), the Institute proposed a major change in its growth plan to face the challenge. There was a gap of about Rs 1.50 crore between receipts and expenditure and this gap had to be bridged. It was proposed that new initiatives (as shown in the Table-1 below) should be taken to generate internal resources to bridge the gap.

Table 1
New Initiatives

Sl No	Particulars of Items for Generating Income	Estimated Income
1.	20% of project expenditure as Institute Overheads. Project staff 40 and value addition @ Rs 10.0 lacs per engineer. Expd. estimated at Rs. 4 lacs	Rs 100 lacs
2.	Income from Offer of Finishing School /short term courses. Assumptions: 4 class rooms would be available, courses for 200 man days would be offered, Each batch to have min 20 students i.e. 80 students x 200 days. Realization Rs 1000/- per student per day, 50% of which to account for institute overheads	Rs 80 lacs
3.	Institute share of Consultancy undertaken by faculty. Assumption Max. 58 , days by 8 faculty. Consultancy charges 10000/- per consultancy day + travel + local hospitality. Institute share 40% + expenses borne by Institute. Estimated max. 100 consultancy days	Rs 4 lacs
4.	Income from project students. Assumption – charging min 4000 per student and take max. 50 students in a year. 80% of income to Institute	Rs 2 lacs

INCENTIVE SCHEME FOR FACULTY, STAFF & EMPLOYEES

It was thought that the above would be possible if the Institute offers incentives for higher performance level. The following schemes were proposed for approval in principle, for which details were to be worked out later.

1. Professional Compensation Scheme – 30% Savings on a research project after providing for intellectual fee and institute overheads will be shared 20% with project team and 10% with all staff. 70% of surplus would be go to the Institute's Corpus Fund.

2. Rs 2000/- per session was proposed to be realised for taking classes. 50% of 'the fee realised would be shared with faculty/ staff, after the faculty completes 90 class contact hours of teaching the flagship programme PGDIT. Out of 50% earmarked for distribution, 75% of the amount so allocated would be distributed among faculty/ staff directly engaged and remaining 25% distributed among all employees.

3. 40% of Consultancy charges realized on any consultancy assignment shall be shared with the faculty concerned provided consultancy charges agreed is not less than Rs 10,000/- per day per person and no expenditure is charged to the Institute.

STAFF POSITION

The Institute had three broad categories of regular staff namely, faculty, project staff and administrative staff. There were 8 faculty members, three project engineers and twelve administrative staff (see Exhibit-3). Rest of the staff members were contract staff, who were recruited for different projects. The project staff could ordinarily be recruited for one year or project duration (envisaged in the project proposal). In no case it could be extended beyond three years. The Institute was finding it difficult to get and retain the faculty and project staff, in view of the booming software industry that was sucking away anyone who had even the minimum qualification and any experience in the IT field.

Completing the project itself was becoming difficult as the project duration ranged from 1 to 3 years and after engaging in project, the engineers left midway seeking greener pastures. Director himself had to come to the forefront for many research projects (see Exhibit-3). Even some faculty members were vulnerable to attraction in technical and management schools elsewhere

LAND OPTIONS AVAILABLE

As on date the Institute perceived three options open to it, and accordingly put up the same for consideration of the Board.

1. Wait for the final decision of the State government to allot 10 acres of land as required under AICTE regulations for starting a Master's Degree level Programme. The Secretary (IT) had informed that the department was in the process of acquiring around 100 acres of land in the vicinity of technopark. Technopark may allot the 10 acres of land to the Institute on lease for 25 years.

2. Apply to the government for allotment of 150 acres of land. The Government was acquiring about 700 acres of land, some 45 km away, a little in the interior. (Technopark was on National highway close to the main city centre). The Government of India was planning 20 Institutes of Information Technology and five of them were being proposed to commence from the year 2008 itself. The minimum land to be provided by the state government for the purpose was 165 acres. Director felt that the State government could swiftly move to capitalize this opportunity.

3. Approach State Agricultural University (SAU) at Merad, which had over 700 acres of land and was willing to provide 10 acres. The Institute had a major

project Farmer's Friends and e-agri, which fitted in the charter of SAU to allow it give land to the Institute. It was, however, about 300 km away from the existing location. Merad was a midsize industrial city with rich cultural heritage, but was not known for IT, unlike the existing location, which had become an IT hub, and the Institute frequently drew the support of IT experts available in over 110 software companies in close vicinity, in Technopark. The Institute also could get project works done by the students in these companies.

CONCERNS OF BOARD MEMBERS

All the three options proposed by the Director for consideration of the Board seemed to have some of advantage and some disadvantages from the short and the long term view and had varying opportunities and demands/management challenges that different activities of the Institute posed.

Another major factor that was occupying the minds of Board Members was requirement of various resources (other than the land) that future activities proposed by the Institute will need, especially the financial resources. The Government had neither given nor promised any funds for capital and revenue expenditure and the proposal of the Director did not seem to be very clear on these aspects.

QUESTIONS

1. Which of the three alternative proposals for acquisition of land should the Board approve?
2. Discuss the strategy followed by the Institute for academic growth of the Institute.
3. Critically evaluate the activity plan proposed by Director to overcome the financial crisis.
4. What additional managerial tasks and challenges are involved, beyond acquisition of land to fructify the activity targets proposed?

Exhibit 1(A)
Institute of Information Technology East
Grant Received (in 000's) from State Government

Year	Grant	Others	Total Receipts	Capital Expense	Revenue Expense	TOTAL Expense	Net Balance	Closing Balance
2000-01	350	16	366	238	37	275	91	
01-02	110	33	143	45	102	147	- 4	87
02-03	475	31	506	11	123	134	372	459
03-04	50	49	99	14	137	151	-52	407
04-05	0	63	63	13	153	166	-103	304
05-06	300	79	379	8	143	151	228	532
06-07	80	61	141	22	213	235	-94	438
TOTAL	**1365**	**332**	**1697**	**350**	**908**	**1258**	**439**	

Exhibit 1(B)

Revised Estimates for 2007-08 and Budget Estimates for 2008-09 (Rs. In '000)

EXPENDITURE

	Particulars	Actual Expend. Apr-Sep 2007	Estd. Expend. Nov-Mar 2008	Total Revenue 2007-08	Budget Estimate 2008-09
1	Salaries and Allowances	6890	5938	12828	15600
2	Building Related Charge		2938	6062	6825
3	Academic Expenses	1019	750	1769	1700
4	Travelling Expenses	533	400	933	950
5	Postage & Telephone	559	485	1044	1050
6	Printing & Stationery	9	100	109	325
7	Library	687	108	795	850
8	Repairs and Maintenance	125	200	325	1000
9	Other Expenses	206	622	828	1050
	Total Revenue Expenses	**13151**	**11541**	**24692**	**29350**
1	Capital Expenditure	2861	900	3761	650
2	Capital WIP at new premises	7300	1500	8800	1000
	Total Capital Expenditure	**10161**	**2400**	**12561**	**1650**
	Grand Total	**23313**	**13941**	**37253**	**31000**

INCOME

	Particulars	Actual Expend. Apr-Sep 2007	Estd. Expend. Nov-Mar 2008	Total Revenue 2007-08	Budget Estimate 2008-09
1	PGDIT	440	1688	2128	2050
2	Short Term Courses	343	834	1177	1500
3	Training Fees	126	50	176	125
4	Others	89	414	503	325
	Total Receipts	**998**	**2985**	**3984**	**4000**
	Grant from the State Govt.	5100		5100	
	Total Income	**6098**	**2985**	**9084**	**4000**
	Excess of Expenditure over Income	**-17214**	**-10955**	**-28169**	**-27000**

Exhibit 2

Details of Research Projects (Rs. In '000s)

Sl	Project		2002-03	2003-04	2004-05	2005-06	2006-07	Total	Coordi-nator
1.	Project 1	Receipt	30000	15000	0	450	0	45450	Director
		C/F	0	27370	7608	3242	532		
		Expenses	2630	34762	4366	2715	1138	45610	
		Balance	27370	7608	3242	978	-606	-160	
2.	Project 2	Receipt	10	3029	6162	1720	5551	16471	Director
		C/F	0	-552	-1911	-949	-3216		
		Expenses	562	4388	5200	3987	2069	16205	
		Balance	-552	-1911	-949	-3216	266	266	
3.	Project 3	Receipt	0	1500	2770	0	0	4270	Director
		C/F	0	0	167	1637	-163		
		Expenses	0	1333	1300	1799	409	4841	
		Balance	0	167	1637	-163	-571	-571	
4.	Project 4	Receipt	5	1500	16	0	0	1521	Director
		C/F	0	-55	1355	1222	1191		
		Expenses	60	90	149	31	0	329	
		Balance	-55	1355	1222	1191	1191	1191	
5.	Project 5	Receipt	419	640	460	108	0	1627	Dr. Vijaya
		C/F		-10	162	193	240		
		Expenses	429	468	429	61	15	1402	
		Balance	-10	162	193	240	225	225	
6.	Project 6	Receipt	300	0	100	0	0	400	Director
		C/F	0	192	122	222	222		
		Expenses	108	71	0	0	0	178	
		Balance	192	122	222	222	222	222	
7.	Project 7	Receipt				1000	0	1000	Director
		C/F				0	455		
		Expenses				545	232	776	
		Balance				455	224	224	
8.	Project 8	Receipt				322	14	336	Dr. Ganesh
		C/F				0	294		
		Expenses				28	109	137	
		Balance				294	199	199	

SUPPLY CHAIN (SC) DEPARTMENTS
OF DEFENDERS, PROSPECTORS AND
ANALYZERS:
A LITERATURE REVIEW AND FEW
PROPOSITIONS

R.R.K. Sharma
Rahul Sharma
H. Hazarika

Indian Institute of Technology, Kanpur - 208016, India

INTRODUCTION

Strategic orientation is useful because it defines the organization's dominant competitive posture and provides a synthesis of the cognitive mental models of its key strategists. Strategic orientation characterizes how a firm sees the competitive process, and subsequently prescribes how the firm will approach the competitive arena (Engelland and Summey, 1999). According to Hayes & Wheelwright (1984), a consistency is required between corporate strategy and functional strategies such as new product development (NPD), manufacturing and marketing strategy or, in other words, a strategic consistency.

Strategic fit means that both the competitive and supply chain strategies have the same goal. It refers to consistency between the customer priorities that the competitive strategy is designed to satisfy and the supply chain capabilities that the supply chain strategy aims to build. A company's success or failure is closely linked to the following keys:

1. The competitive strategy and all functional strategies must fit together to form a coordinated overall strategy. Strategies of all the functions must be complementary to each other to help a firm reach its competitive strategic goal.
2. The different functions in a company must appropriately structure their process and resources to be able to execute strategies successfully (Chopra & Meindl, 2001).

A company may fail either because of a lack of strategic fit or because its process and resources do not provide the capabilities to support the desired strategic fit (Chopra and Meindl, 2001).

Strategy implementation is the process by which objectives and practices (i.e. processes, technologies, organizational arrangements and/or managerial systems and approaches) are put into action. One of the key principles associated with successful strategy implementation is that at any time, strategy and practices need to be consistent with, and supportive of, each other (Chandler, 1962; Owen, 1982).

Many generic corporate (e.g. Miles and Snow, 1978; Porter, 1980; Kotler et al., 2001) and manufacturing (e.g. Hayes and Wheelwright, 1984; Richardson et al., 1985) strategies have been proposed. These literatures suggest that different strategies require different organizational and managerial practices.

Many authors on strategic management (e.g. Andrews, 1971; Porter, 1980) suggest that strategy should be about aligning the business with its environment. This means that strategy is an adaptive mechanism. Miles and Snow (1978) see strategy as a constraint for the organization to respond to its environment.

The firms need to adopt new systems that cannot be observed in the traditional organization structure where independent functional areas such as production and marketing prevail (Bowersox et al., 1995).

There are different types of organization having there own set of objectives with respect to supplier, production, distribution and customer satisfaction. As it is not possible to present a single type of organization structure that will best suit the strategy of different type of organizations (defenders, prospectors and analyzers), each of these adopts an organization structure which aligns with most of their objectives.

Defenders search profitability by maintaining existing products in established markets through 'technological efficiency' (Miles and Snow, 1978). Prospectors continuously develop new products and markets and, consequently, tend to have difficulties achieving operational efficiency. Analyzers combine efficiency in their operations with effectiveness pursued by adding new products and markets.

Supply chain organizations first started in the early 1990s. Before we can answer the questions of what makes a good supply chain organization we need to understand the goals of such an organization. The objective of supply chain groups differ based on their organizational maturity. As the supply chain organization matures, the focus shifts from manufacturing to the support of cross-functional process like sales and operation planning(S&OP) and new product launch. As part of this maturation process ,the organization moves from a forecasting orientation to the demand sensing one and from functional measures to the business metrics that are shared across the organization(Lora Cecere,2006).

LITERATURE REVIEW

Types of Organizations

There are essentially three strategy types : Defenders, Analyzers, and Prospectors. Each type has its own unique strategy for relating to its chosen market, and each has a particular configuration of technology, structure, and process that is consistent with its market strategy (Miles and Snow, 1978). Defenders primarily stay in their existing domains and stable market niches. Product development for these companies is limited to the improvement of existing products. Efficiency and control are important factors for these companies. Defenders tend to ignore developments outside of domain. Defenders search profitability by maintaining existing products in established markets through 'technological efficiency' (Miles and Snow, 1978). Defender type organizations favor mass production. It involves a detailed functional division of labor and limited authority to lower level management i.e. most of the objectives are decided by top level management without considering the lower level management. Also, the customers have limited options, so delivery performance level suffers for defender type organizations.

Prospectors are the most innovative type and emphasize the development of new products and technologies and the exploration of new markets. They try to be first in the market with new products, and continuously experiment with responses to emerging trends and changes in the market place. They are characterized by a low degree of formalization, and have greater decentralized decision making and higher flexibility.

In prospector type organization higher authority is given to lower level management and they are involved in decision making along with top level management. Also the customers have variety of options and hence, delivery performance is of greater importance for the prospector type organization.

While defenders tend to establish only a single core technology, the Prospectors develop multiple technologies. Prospectors systematically add new products and new markets to their portfolio and put a lot of effort into monitoring 'a wide range of environmental conditions, trends and events' (Miles and Snow, 1978). Prospectors are inclined toward product innovation, so their organizational structure needs to be flexible and prepared for quick adaptation to market changes. Many studies have indicated that such companies are best managed with a low level of formalization, i.e. not based on rules and procedures (Burns and Stalker, 1961, Hage and Aiken, 1970, Miles and Snow, 1978).

Analyzers try to combine the exploration capability and innovativeness of the prospectors with the defenders ability to serve existing markets effectively. These companies pursue efficiency in the stable markets they serve, and try to be adaptive to and prepared for change in the turbulent markets in which they are also active at the same time. However, analyzers are not first movers. Rather their focus is on quick adoption of new concepts launched by successful prospector companies. Analyzers combine cost-leadership and a mechanistic system orthogonally with differentiation and an organic system. That is, they either spatially or temporally separate innovation and operation, but do not do both in the same part of the company or at the same time (Volberda, 1998).

Miles and Snow et al. (1978) described the fourth type of organization (Reactors), but considered it to be an organization that lacks a viable strategy or is in transition from one of the three ideal strategies to another. Doty et al. (1993) compared the effectiveness of the typology with and without reactors, and found empirical support for these (excluding reactors).

Dimensions of SC Structure

Moreno-Luzon and Peris (1998) addressed level of decision-making centralization and level of formalization-standardization as the basic organizational design variables of the contingency model relating to quality management. Formalization can be defined as the degree to which roles and tasks performed in the organization are governed by formal rules, and standard policies and procedures. If higher level of flexibility is required by the organization, then level of formalization should be low whereas if the organization requires a rigid structure then higher level of formalization will be suitable. Degree of formalization can be explained by the existence of independent department responsible for supply chain management and the strategic positioning of the department and the degree of centralization which reflects the scope of responsibilities and the power of SC department within the organization (Kim, 2007). The concept of formalization refers to "the extent that the rules governing behavior are precisely and explicitly formulated and the extent that roles and role relations are prescribed independently of the personal attributes of individuals occupying positions in the structure". In other words, formalization describes the degree to which work and tasks performed in the organization are standardized (Dewsnap and Jobber, 2000; Mollenkopf et al., 2000; Manolis et al., 2004).

Bowersox and Daugherty (1995) and Daugherty et al. (1992) suggest that the concept of formalization in SCM perspective can be consistent with it in organizational perspective. They define formalization as the degree to which decisions and working relationships for SC activities are governed by formal rules and standard policies and procedures. Centralization can be defined as the pattern of authority distribution for various departments within the organization. The management decides the authority distribution pattern on the basis of objectives to be achieved and type of strategy to be followed by the organization. For example, defender's strategy is cost oriented, so centralization should be high whereas prospector's strategy is product innovation oriented, so lower level of centralization will be suitable. Centralization is defined as the extent to which the power to make SCM decisions is concentrated in an organization (Mollenkopf et al., 2000; Manolis et al., 2004). Higher degrees of centralization correspond with concentration of decision making authority at more senior levels (Dewsnap and Jobber, 2000). The degree of centralization is determined partly by hierarchical relationship between SCM department and other functional areas over the control and responsibilities for SCM activities (Leenders et al., 2002). According to Bowersox and Daugherty (1995) and Tsai (2002), three structural components-formalization, centralization and specialization have considerable influence on organization performance. Factors favoring centralization include standardization of products and business processes, cost reductions created through opportunities to allocate resources efficiently and economies of scale and improved levels of knowledge and expertise through the dedication of staff and resources (Droge and Germain, 1989). Decentralization offers business units autonomy and control over key functional activities, supporting the principle that business units must carry responsibility for major decisions if they are to be held accountable for performance (Johnson and Leenders, 2006). Potential advantages of centralization include greater buying specialization, coordination of policies and systems and consolidation of requirements. Meanwhile, decentralization improves service and lowers costs by pushing decision-making responsibility closer to the end user, promotes closer working relationships between suppliers and end users and provides increased opportunities for end users to manage total cost of ownership factors (Leenders and Johnson, 2000). There can be other objectives like cost, flexibility, quality, and innovation, on the basis of which organization structure can be decided. The competitive dimensions can include cost, quality, flexibility, and delivery performance among others (Corbett and Van Wessenhove, 1993; Minor et al., 1994; Vickery, 1991).

The manufacturing strategies of firms today are increasingly reflecting attempts to excel on a number of competitive dimensions. Competitive advantage can be gained from excelling at both cost and quality; flexibility and delivery; or possibly any combination of the four (Stock, Greis and Kasarda, 1999). Cost as a competitive priority can be interpreted as the firm's intention to be the lowest cost producer in its industry. Different type of organizations have different cost objectives like defenders main focus is to achieve cost efficiency whereas prospectors do not care for the cost prospective. Flexibility refers to the ability of the organization to deal with the uncertainties associated with the market and the environmental conditions. Higher flexibility implies quick adoption to the changes in the market. If any organization is more inclined towards the product innovation, then its structure should be more flexible. Flexibility can be considered to be two different categories: design flexibility and volume flexibility. Design flexibility is the "capability to make rapid design changes and/or introduce new products quickly." Volume flexibility refers to the "capability to respond to swings in demand" (Miller and Roth, 1994).

Supply chain can achieve organizational flexibility, the ability to change generic operations, in two ways: through organic change or through modularity. In organic change scenarios, organizations shift to new activities. They have the advantages of retaining established relationships, communication links and higher level management positions (Chandrashekar and Schary, 1999). In a competitive marketplace where organizations compete for customers, delivery performance is also an important dimension for deciding the organizational structure. Delivery performance can be defined as the level upto which products and services supplied by an organization meet the customer expectation. Delivery performance provides an indication of how successful the organization is at providing products and services to the customer. If an organization has higher delivery performance, then its relationship with its customers will be stronger. A company's customer relations practices can affect its success in managing the supply base as well as its performance (Scott and Westbrook, 1991; Ellram, 1991; Turner, 1993). Innovation in either product or process development is often considered to be an element of flexibility, as well (Parthasarthy and Sethi, 1992). Hage and Aiken (1970) argue that centralization might have a negative influence on innovation.

On the basis of above discussion this paper has considered five dimensions on the basis of which SCM objectives can be described: Cost orientation, Flexibility (product and volume), Delivery performance, quality and risk. Similarly there are five dimensions of on which supply chain activities can be structured: Formalization, Centralization, Standardization, Specialization and Complexity of work flow.

Types of SC Structures

SC structure can be defined on the bases of organization's strategy. As defenders, prospectors and analyzers have different strategies, there should be a strategic fit between their supply chain and competitive strategies.

To achieve strategic fit, supply chain activities of an organization must support their objectives. Three steps have been defined for achieving strategic fit–

1. Understanding the customer.
2. Understanding the supply chain.
3. Achieving the strategic fit (Chopra and Meindl, 2001).

SC structure has been defined and classified in a number of ways in the literature. A very simple way of describing SC structure differentiates between organizations on the dimension of centralization or decentralization (Ghoshal, 1994). One of the major problem of decentralized organization is that the goals of the agents are not aligned with the overall goal of organization (Dirickx and Jennergren1979, Milgrom and Roberts, 1992).Different business subunits have their own objectives .To pursue their private interests, these units may choose to send false, or biased, information to headquarters and other departments (Jennergren and Muller, 1973). Modularity replaces permanent organizations in order to perform different specialized tasks. It mirrors the virtual chain, in that a pool of specialized organizations is linked in a complementary task-oriented network. They are recruited as latent members, brought in as needed and then released as the task ends (Chandrashekar and Schary, 1999). Companies must adjust their organizational structure and management processes to adapt to changes in the external competitive environment or its strategy in order to maximize performance (Galunic and Eisenhardt, 1994). The two extremes (prospector and defender) are consistent with findings put forward by the other authors, e.g. Burns and Stalker (1961) and Porter (1980). They labeled these extremes the mechanistic and organic management system, respectively. Burns and Stalker (1961) explicitly mention that mechanistic firms have a functional organization structure with high level of formalization i.e. extent to which rules and roles are precisely and explicitly formulated Organic firms, on the other hand, have low level of formalization.

Mechanistic firms have a hierarchical structure and the way of coordination between the members of the organization is limited to vertical, that is, between superior and subordinate. Mechanistic systems are appropriate in stable conditions and have a functional organization structure, a high degree of formalization, and many rules and procedures. Organic systems are most appropriate in changing conditions and are characterized by loose structures and few rules. Miles and Snow's (1978) prospector corresponds with Burns and Stalker's organic system and Porter's differentiation strategy, while the defender strategy corresponds with Burns and Stalker's mechanistic system and Porter's cost leadership strategy. Analyzers combine cost-leadership and a mechanistic system orthogonally with differentiation and an organic system. That is, they either spatially or temporally separate innovation and operation, but do not do both in the same part of the company or at the same time (Volberda, 1998).

According to Chopra and Meindl (2001), a product-focused organization performs many different functions in producing a single product whereas a functional-focused organization performs few functions on many types of products. A product focus tends to result in more expertise about a particular type of product at the expense of functional expertise that comes from a functional manufacturing methodology. Hybrid organizational structure approach is defined as the structure having features of both centralized and decentralized structures (Leenders and Johnson, 2000). While previous research has found that the hybrid organizational model is the most commonly used within large supply organizations (Johnson et. al., 2006), there is still considerable variation with respect to how the hybrid model is implemented. In 1960s, matrix structures became a popular organizational framework for managing new product and service development. A hybrid approach between the two extremes (functional and programme approaches). Matrix organization approach manages coordination of activities across unit lines within the organization. The matrix combines the benefits of project and functional organizations by integrating the work of various specialists. The matrix structure operates through a two-dimensional system of control: a project/product-line chain of command and a functional chain of command (Lawrence, Kolodny and Davis, 1982). Project managers retain responsibility for developing products, while functional managers concentrate on the organization's capability to make use of up-to-date technical knowledge (Katz and Allen, 1985).

On the basis of above arguments we have main SC departments' structures as mechanistic, organic and matrix structure.

New Propositions

It can be said that most appropriate basic SC structure for defender, prospector and analyzer type of organization is mechanistic, organic and matrix respectively. SC activities may have positive effect on the organization if there is no conflict between them. We can reduce these conflicts by assigning the responsibility to each of these SC activities as clear as possible.

There are two questions related to the problem on the status of exclusive SC department. The first question is on how the existence and status of an exclusive department in charge of strategic SC activities within the organization affects the improvement of SCM performance. This is related to the discussion on the necessity of exclusive SCM department in terms of SC performance. The second question is on whether or not the SC department must take all responsibilities for the implementation of SC activities, and what relationship it has with the existing functional departments. (Kim, 2007). Further, the hierarchical level of each of the departments including SC department should be clear within the SC organization structure. Each of the department has varying importance which is directly associated with the type of organization. SC organization structure for defender requires higher level of formalization, centralization, cost efficiency, standardization and lower level of innovation, risk, flexibility and delivery performance. Their planning is always toward the production and cost control. These objectives can be achieved by having a mechanistic type of SCM organization structure. Also most of the logistics activities are controlled by production department.

Thus, we can suggest the following hypotheses.

H1. SC in Defender type organization will have higher efficiency if it uses mechanistic type of organizational structure.

H2. In Defender type organizations finance and production departments are enjoying higher importance compared to other departments.

H3. In Defender type organization logistics activities will be under the control of production department.

SC structure for prospector requires higher level of innovation, risk, flexibility and delivery performance and lower level of formalization, centralization, cost efficiency and standardization. Prospector's problem is how to facilitate and coordinate numerous and diverse operations. Prospector's administration must be able to deploy and coordinate resource among numerous decentralized units and projects rather than to plan and control the operations of the entire organization centrally (Miles and Snow et al. (1978). As they are more inclined toward the new product innovation, so their planning is mainly towards marketing and research and development. These objectives can be achieved by having an SC structure as organic. All SCM related activities are performed under the supervision and control of other functional department (Kim, 2007). As prospectors are market oriented so marketing department is likely to have higher importance compared to other departments within the organization. Also delivery performance level is relatively higher as compared to defender and analyzer type organizations. So, marketing department controls most of the logistics activities. We suggest the following hypothesis on the basis of above arguments.

H4. SC in Prospector type organization will have higher performance if they adopt organic type of structure.
H5. In Prospector type organizations marketing department enjoys higher importance compared to other departments
H6. In Prospector type organizations logistics activities are under the control of marketing department.

SC structure for analyzer requires higher level of cost efficiency and delivery performance, medium level of formalization, centralization, innovation, flexibility, standardization. These types of characteristics can be achieved by having a matrix type of SC structure with each of the department having its relevant SC activities. For firms employing this type of organization, SC department focuses on coordination and connection with other departments for efficient utilization of SC activities rather than the direct control of SC activities (Kim, 2007). According to Miles and Snow (1978), Analyzers main problem is how to differentiate the organization's structure and processes to accommodate both stable and dynamic areas of operations. As they try to be cost efficient as well as updated with the new product –market relationship, so marketing and production department plays a major role. We suggest the following hypotheses on the basis of above arguments.

H7. SC in Analyzer type organization will have higher efficiency and effectiveness if it uses a matrix type of structure.
H8. In Analyzer type organizations marketing and production departments enjoy higher importance compared to other departments.
H9. Analyzer type organizations will have the logistics activities under the marketing and production department.

Pilot Study and Results

<u>**The Sample:**</u> The sample selected comprised of companies with varied backgrounds, locations and into different businesses. The questionnaire was filled up the various

functional departments of these companies viz. their Purchase, Marketing, Production, and Supply Chain Management departments. The companies selected for the study are:

> Ghadi Industries Pvt. Ltd, Kanpur
> Prachi Leathers Pvt. Ltd, Kanpur
> ITW India Limited (Chemin division), Hyderabad
> Bharat Petroleum Corpn Ltd (Industrial lube division), Kolkata

These companies are into different businesses like for example, Ghadi Industries are into the manufacturing of detergents and soaps; Prachi Leathers are into leather shoes and bags, ITW India Limited (their Chemin division) are into coolants, rust preventives and MRO chemicals and Bharat Petroleum Corporation Limited (their Industrial lubricants division) are in the business of industrial lubricant products.

A visit was made to Ghadi Industries's production plant at Kanpur and the questionnaire was filled by their Sales department. According to them they don not maintain inventory of their finished products and dispatch them to their retailers and distributors on a daily basis. Since they do not have a warehouse located in Kanpur, an in depth study on their Supply Chain Department could not be made.

Two visits were made to Prachi Leathers in Kanpur which is a prominent leather production and processing center of India. They are also well known in the international market as a supplier of leather and leather products with highest quality standards at reasonable prices. Here the questionnaires were filled by their Marketing and Purchase Departments. Their Marketing department takes care of their dispatch and other logistics operations and therefore they answered the questions related to their Supply Chain.

The questionnaire for ITW India Limited and Bharat Petroleum Corporation Limited (BPCL) were emailed to their Purchase, Marketing, Production, and Supply Chain Management (SCM) departments. In ITW India Ltd the questionnaires were filled by their Sales, Purchase, and Production departments. Here the Supply chain decisions are mostly taken by the Purchase department and hence the questions pertaining to their Supply Chain were answered by this department.

In BPCL, the questionnaire was filled only by their Sales department as the other departments were reluctant to participate in the online survey. A telephonic conversation was also made with one of the Sales Executives of BPCL for a more in depth analysis.

Hence, a total of seven responses could be gathered from these four different organizations for the study. We will take up these organizations one by one and analyze them based on their responses and the hypothesis as stated above.

ANALYSIS AND RESULTS

Based on the questionnaires filled by the various departments of these four companies and comparing them with the salient features each of the three types of organizations viz. Defender, Prospector, and Analyzer and their hypothesis as stated earlier we carry out an analysis as under :

1. Ghadi Industries Pvt. Ltd, Kanpur:

Here the response made by their Sales department is analyzed. The responses to the questions related to the Flexibility of the organization were low on rating on a scale of 1 to 6 and hence the organization can be safely accepted to be low on flexibility. From the responses to the questions pertaining to the level of Standardization, the ratings are on a higher side of the scale (the ratings were 1- for custom made products and 5- for standardized products, etc) and hence the organization has a high level of Standardization. In response to the questions on Specialization, the company has rated high on the scale and hence it has a high degree of Specialization. For level of Centralization in the organization, their responses to the questions indicate that most of the decisions are being taken by their higher management of the company (e.g. their Managing Director of their Board of group). Hence, their decision making process is highly Centralized. The level of Formalization is also on a higher side as can be inferred from their responses to the questions on the level of Formalization. The Complexity of workflow is found to be low as they mostly manufacture standardized products. Their frequency of Market research is also being rated low and they do not stress much on product innovations. Their Production department enjoys higher importance in their organization as compared to other departments of their organization. Both their Production and Marketing departments control the logistics activities of the company. The company competes solely on costs and has economies of scale. The analysis on Ghadi Industries shows that its organization structure has higher levels of formalization, centralization, cost efficiency, standardization and lower level of innovation, flexibility, and complexity of work flow which are the salient features of a Defender type of organization. Hence based on this analysis and the hypothesis considered above it is therefore found that Ghadi Industries Pvt. Ltd. is a Defender type of organization and is supported by a Mechanistic type of SC structure.

2. Prachi Leathers Pvt. Ltd, Kanpur:

Here the responses made by their Marketing and Purchase departments are analyzed. On a scale of 1 to 6, the responses to the questions related to the Flexibility of the organization were high on rating and hence the organization can be safely accepted to be high on flexibility. For level of Standardization, the ratings are on the lower side of the scale (the ratings were 1-for custom made products and 5- for standardized products, etc) and hence the organization has a low level of Standardization (hence high level of customization). In response to the questions on Specialization, the company has rated low on the scale and hence it has a low level of Specialization. This is because they keep on changing their product designs and varieties as per the market demands. For level of Centralization in the organization, their responses to the questions indicate some of the decisions are also being taken by the middle management of the company (e.g. their Production and Marketing manager). Hence, their decision making process is not very Centralized. The level of Formalization is also on a lower side as can be inferred from their responses to the questions on the level of Formalization. The Complexity of workflow is found to be high as they mostly manufacture customized products which keep changing very frequently. Their frequency of Market research is also being rated very high and they stress a lot on product innovations. Their Marketing team carries out frequent market research and, in turn, gives feedback to their Design team to come up with new designs in shoes and bags. Their Marketing department enjoys higher importance in their organization as compared to other departments of their organization. It is mostly their Marketing department that controls the logistics activities of the company. The company does not compete on costs but in quality and new designs (product innovation). Moreover it does not have Economies of scale. The analysis on Prachi Leathers therefore shows that its organization structure has lower levels of formalization, centralization, cost efficiency, standardization, specialization and higher level of innovation, flexibility, and complexity of work flow which are the salient features of a Prospector type of organization. Hence based on this analysis and the hypothesis considered above it can therefore be concluded that Prachi Leathers Pvt. Ltd. is a Prospector type of organization and is supported by an Organic type of SC structure.

3.   ITW India Limited (Chemin division), Hyderabad:
Here the responses made by their Sales, Purchase, and Production departments are analyzed. For the questions on the level of Flexibility, the responses to the questions on a scale of 1 to 6 were high on rating and hence the organization can be safely accepted to be high on flexibility. For level of Standardization, the ratings are on much lower side of the scale and hence the organization has a low level of Standardization. For level of Centralization in the organization, their responses to the questions indicate some of the decisions are also being taken by the middle management of the company (e.g. their Production manager). Hence, their decision making process is not very Centralized. The level of Formalization is also on a lower side as can be inferred from their responses to the questions on the level of Formalization. The Complexity of workflow is found to be high as they mostly manufacture customized products. Their frequency of Market research is also being rated very high and they stress a lot on product innovations. Their Sales team carries out frequent market research through customer visits and in turn gives feedback to their R&D department to come up with new products. Their Marketing department enjoys higher importance in their organization as compared to other departments of their organization. It is mostly their Sales and Marketing department who control the logistics activities of the company. The company does not compete on costs but in quality and new products (product innovation). The analysis on ITW India Limited (Chemin division) therefore shows that its organization structure has lower levels of centralization, standardization, formalization, specialization and higher level of innovation, flexibility, and complexity of work flow which are the salient features of a Prospector type of organization. Hence based on this analysis and the hypothesis considered above it can therefore be concluded that ITW India Limited (Chemin division) is a Prospector type of organization and is supported by an Organic type of SC structure.

4.   Bharat Petroleum Corporation Limited (Industrial lube division), Kolkata:
Here the response made by their Sales department is analyzed. The telephonic interview conducted with one of their Sales Executives has also been

considered. The response to the questions related to the Flexibility of the organization was medium on rating on a scale of 1 to 6 and hence the organization can be safely accepted to be medium on flexibility. From the responses to the questions pertaining to the level of Standardization, the ratings are on a medium to high on the scale (the ratings given were 1-for custom made products and 5-for standardized products, etc) and hence the organization has a medium to high level of Standardization. In response to the questions on Specialization, the company has rated high on the scale and hence it has a high degree of Specialization. For level of Centralization in the organization, their responses to the questions indicate that most of the decisions are being taken by their higher management of the company (e.g. their Managing Director of their Board of group) and few by the middle management (e.g. the Production manager). Hence, their degree of Centralization can be treated to between medium and high. The level of Formalization is medium (ratings given on a scale from 1 to 7 were 5, 6, 5, and 7) as can be inferred from their responses to the questions on the degree of Formalization. The Complexity of workflow is also found to be low to medium as they mostly manufacture standardized products and sometimes customized products depending on the market demands (as per the telephonic interview with their Sales Executive). The company also has high Economies of scale. Their frequency of Market research is also being rated low and they do not stress too much on product innovations (which can be treated to be low to medium as they innovate products occasionally). Both their Production department (production department takes care of cost efficiency and economies of scale) and Marketing department (marketing department is also responsible for product innovations) enjoy higher importance in their organization as compared to other departments of their organization. Both their Production and Marketing departments jointly control the logistics activities. The company competes mainly on costs and has economies of scale. The analysis on Bharat Petroleum Corporation Limited (Industrial lubricants division) shows that its organization structure has medium to high level of Standardization, medium level of Flexibility, between medium and high level of Centralization, low to medium Complexity of workflow, low to medium level of innovation, which matches closely with the characteristics of an Analyzer type of organization. Hence based on this analysis and the hypothesis considered above it can therefore be concluded that Bharat Petroleum Corporation Limited (Industrial lubricants division) fits into an Analyzer type of organization and is supported by a Matrix type of SC structure.

Based on the analysis of the four companies considered in the sample survey as discussed above, the following conclusions can be drawn:

1. **Ghadi Industries Pvt. Ltd.** is a Defender type of organization and is supported by a Mechanistic type of SC structure.
2. **Prachi Leathers Pvt. Ltd.** is a Prospector type of organization and is supported by an Organic type of SC structure.
3. **ITW India Limited (Chemin division)** is a Prospector type of organization and is supported by an Organic type of SC structure.
4. **Bharat Petroleum Corporation Limited (Industrial lubricants division)** fits into an Analyzer type of organization and is supported by a Matrix type of SC structure.

LIMITATIONS OF THE STUDY:
1. In most of these organizations, not all their departments viz. Purchase, Marketing, Production, and Supply Chain Management departments participated in the survey.
2. For the companies ITW India Ltd and BPCL, where the questionnaires were filled online and no personal interaction was possible, a more in depth study of their Supply Chain departments could not be made.
3. For Ghadi Industries Pvt. Ltd. an in depth study of their Supply Chain department could not take place as they do not have a warehouse located in Kanpur and only their Sales Manager showed interest in filling the questionnaire.

CONCLUSIONS

The purpose of this study is to relate the SC structure to its objectives which we do by using the classification of Miles and Snow et al. (1978), i.e., defenders, prospectors and analyzers. Interesting hypotheses are presented (and these are supported by limited pilot study) which need to be verified by a future study undertaken on a larger scale.

REFERENCES

1. Andrew, D.R., 1971. The concept of corporate strategy. Dow Jones Irwin, Homewood.
2. Bowersox, D.J., Daugherty, P.J., 1995. Logistics paradigm: the impact of information technology. Journal of Business Logistics 16(1), 65-80.
3. Burns, T., Stalker, G.M., 1961. The management of innovation. Tavistock, London.
4. Cecere, L., 2006. Supply Chain Organization Enter Second Decade. Supply Chain Management Review, 17-18.
5. Chandler, A.D., 1962. Strategy and structure. MIT Press, Boston.
6. Chandrashekar, A., Schary P.B., 1999. Toward the Virtual Supply Chain: The Convergence of IT and Organization. International Journal of Logistics Management 10(20), 27-39.
7. Chopra, S., Meindl, P., 2001. Supply chain management: Strategy, planning and operation. Pearson Education Asia.
8. Corbett, C., Van Wassenhove, L., 1993. Trade-offs? What trade-offs? Competence and competitiveness in manufacturing strategy. California Management Review 35(4), 107-122.
9. Daugherty, P.J., Stank, T.P., Rogers, D.S., 1992. The impact of formalization on warehousing firms. International Journal of Logistics Management 3(2), 49-61.
10. Dewsnap, B., Jobber, D., 2000. The sales-marketing interface in consumer packaged-goods companies: a conceptual framework. Journal of Personal Selling & Sales Management 20(2), 109-119.
11. Dirickx, Y.M., Jennergren, L.P., 1979. Systems Analysis by Multilevel Methods. John Wiley, Chichester, New York.
12. Doty, D.H., Glick, W.H., 1993. Fit, equifinality and organizational effectiveness, A test of two configurational theories. Acad Management Journal 36(6), 1196-1250.
13. Droge, C., Germain, R., Daugherty, P.J., 1989. Servicing the exchange relationship: organizational configuration and its effects on intra-firm and buyer-seller communications. In: Annual Conference of Council of Logistics Management, St. Louis, MO.

14. Ellram, L.M., 1991. Supply chain management: the industrial organization perspective. International Journal of Physical Distribution and logistics management 21(1), 13-22.

15. Engelland, B.T., Summey, J.H., 1999. An extended typology of strategic orientation and its linkages to product innovativeness. The Journal of Marketing Management 9(2), 19-31.

16. Galunic, C.D., Eisenhardt, K.M., 1994. Renewing the strategy-structure-performance paradigm. In: Staw, B.M., Cummings, L.L. (Eds.), Research in Organizational Behaviour 16, 215-255.

17. Gerwin, D., 1987. An agenda for research on the flexibility of manufacturing processes. International Journal of Operations & Production Management 7(1), 38-49.

18. Ghoshal, S., Korine, H., Szulansi, G., 1994. Interunit communication in multinational corporations. Management Science 40(1), 96-110.

19. Hage, J., Aiken, M., 1970. Social change in complex organizations. Random House, New York.

20. Hayes, R.H., Wheelwright, S.C., 1984. Restoring our competitive edge: competing through manufacturing. John Wiley & Sons, New York.

21. Jennergren, L.P., Muller, W., 1973. Simulation experiments of resource-allocation decisions in two-level organizations. Soc. Sci. Res. 333-352.

22. Johnson, P.F., Leenders, M.R., 2006. A longitudinal study of supply organizational change. Journal of Purchasing & Supply Management 12, 332-342.

23. Katz, R., Allen, T.J., 1985. Project performance and the locus of influence in the R&D matrix. Acad. Management Journal 28(1), 67-87.

24. Kim, S.W., 2007. Organizational structures and the performance of supply chain management. International Journal of Production Economics, 323-345.

25. Kotler, P., Armstrong, G., Saunders, J., Wong, V., 2001. Principles of marketing. Prentice Hall, London.

26. Lawrence, P.R., Kolodny, H.F., Davis, S.M., 1982. The human side of matrix. Readings in the Management of Innovation, 504-519.

27. Leenders, M.R., Fearson, H.E., Flynn, A.E., Johnson, P.F., 2002. Purchasing and Supply Management. McGraw-Hill Companies Inc, New York.

28. Leenders, M.R., Johnson, P.F., 2000. Major structural changes in supply organizations. Center for Advanced Purchasing Studies, Tempe, AZ.

29. Manolis, C., Gassenheimer, B., Winsor, R.D., 2004. The moderating effect of solidarity as conduct: a theoretical and empirical perspective. Journal of Marketing & Practice 12(3), 48-60.

30. Miles, R.E., Snow, C.C., 1978. Organizational strategy, structure and process. McGraw Hill, New York.

31. Miles, R.E., Snow, C.C., 2003. Organizational strategy, structure and process. Stanford University Press, Stanford, California.

32. Miles, R.E., Snow, C.C., Meyer, A.D., Coleman, H.J., 1978. Organizational strategy, structure and process. Academy of Management Review July, 546-562.

33. Milgrom, Roberts, P.J., 1992. Economics, Organization and Management. Prentice Hall, Upper Saddle River, NJ.

34. Miller, J.G., Roth, A.V., 1994. A taxonomy of manufacturing strategies 40(3), 285-304.

35. Minor, E.D., Hensley, R.L., Wood, D.R.., 1994. A review of empirical manufacturing strategy studies. International Journal of Operations & Production Management 14(1), 5-25.

36. Mollenkopf, D., Gibson, A., Ozanne, L., 2000. The integration of marketing and logistics: an empirical examination of New Zealand firms. Journal of Business Logistics 21(2), 89-112.

37. Monczka, R.M., Trent, R.J., Handfield, R., 2002. Purchasing and supply chain management, second ed. South-Western Thompson.
38. Moreno-Luzon, M.D., Peris, F.J., 1998. Strategic approaches, organizational design and quality management-integration in a fit and contingency model. International Journal of Quality Science 3(4), 328-347.
39. Owen, A.A., 1982. How to implement strategy. Management Today, 50-53.
40. Parthasarthy, R., Sethi, S.P., 1992. The impact of flexible automation on business strategy and organizational structure. Academy of Management Review 17(1), 86-111.
41. Porter, M.E., 1980. Competitive strategy: Techniques for analyzing industries and competitors. The Free Press, New York.
42. Richardson, P.R., Taylor, A.J., Gordon, J.R., 1985. A strategic approach to evaluating manufacturing performance. Interfaces 15(6), 15-27.
43. Scott, C. and Westbrook, R., 1991. New strategic tools for supply chain management. International Journal of Physical Distribution and Logistics 11, 23-33.
44. Stock, G.N., Greis, N.P., Kasarda, J.D., 1999. Logistics, strategy and structure: A conceptual framework. International Journal of Physical Distribution & logistics management 29(4), 224-239.
45. Tsai, W., 2002. Social structure of "cooperation" within a multiunit organization: coordination, competition, and intraorganizational knowledge sharing. Organization Science 13(2), 179-191.
46. Turner, J.R., 1993. "Integrated supply chain management: what's wrong with this picture?". Industrial Engineering 25(12), 52-5.
47. Vickery, S. K., 1991. A theory of production competence revisited. Decision Sciences 22, 635-643.
48. Volberda, H.W., 1998. Building the flexible firm, how to remain competitive. Oxford University Press, Oxford.
49. Zahra, S.A., Pearce, J.A., 1990. Research evidence on Miles –Snew typology. Journal of Management 16(4), 751-768.

SMUGGLING PROBLEM .... BROUGHT ON TRACK!

H.S. Gupta

Professor, Indian Institute of Forest Management, Bhopal

"…….. and the trail of destruction left in its wake brought home forcefully the fact that India's forest were not inexhaustible. Railway requirement (is) 'the first and by far the most formidable' of the forces thinning Indian forests. (Cleghorn 1860)."

One of the most vivid descriptions of the transformation in the ecological landscape brought by the railways is found in Cleghorn's work, The Forests and Gardens of South India. The Melghat and North Arcot hills, formerly crowned with timber, were 'now to a considerable degree laid bare' by the insatiable demand of the railways. All around the tracks, where once there was forest, there now lay wide swathes of cleared land stripped bare of cover, and consequently of protection to wild animals. (Gadgil,M.and R.Guha 1992)

This observation would have fitted well if the past history of conservation effort in Saranda forest were followed but for a very bold legal measure. This case would go down the tunnel of legal history, as one of the rare cases where the Indian Railway has been penalized and train bogey confiscated, for the fault of railway and their operating staff for smuggling the illegal forest produce.

Development and ecology can never exist, simultaneously as is best exemplified in the southwest corner of Jharkhand. This remote corner of Jharkhand adjoins the remote north west corner of Orissa and here lies the best Sal forest of Singhbhum district of Jharkhand. Far from the civilization, with hardly any human pressure, this tract had the pristine forest cover, till 50 years ago. But alas, with the advent of industrialization, particularly coming of Tata steel plant in the eastern part of the district and after the independence, the coming up of steel plant at Rourkela in the west, doomed this forest tract. Incidentally these forests also harboured the largest concentration of elephants of the Jharkhand state, besides other wildlife. These two big industrial nuclei of development at both ends brought ever-increasing hunger for wood. With rail and road links improving, the inaccessible forests started opening up, more for illegal pilferage than for the legal harvesting.

The network of roads in inaccessible forest tract has torn down their sanctity. The skeletal forest protection machinery with its limited resources and knee jerk reaction policies could hardly contain this systematic devastation process. This tract of forest in Singhbhum, namely Saranda, Kolhan and Porahat paid the price of "development", and ever-increasing cases of human-wild animal conflict are just an indicator to it.

If the paths or roads could be used for illegal transport of forest products, how can railways remain untouched by this malady? In fact in India,(particularly after independence) it is presumed to be a birth right of an Indian to travel ticketless and misuse the railway property. The problem of transporting illegal wood in passenger trains is a national phenomenon for the last many decades. But in recent years, under the patronage of some misguided political leaders, who encouraged indiscriminate felling of forest in the name of "Jharkhand agitation " (but basically for encouraging encroachment/cultivation to their constituencies), the problem of illegal transportation of wood by passenger and goods train increased alarmingly.

Initially overlooked by forest staff, as the problem was confined to fuel wood but later it took worse shape with poles, timbers, sleepers started smuggling out not only in passenger trains but even in goods trains. The ingenious ways of hiding timber in the toilets, sides, undersides of railway carriage, even concealing inside the loaded wagon were devised by the smugglers, for its shipment to Industrial township of Rourkela and Tatanagar. But the worst "actors" of the story were unscrupulous railway staff and lower functionary of Railway Protection Force (RPF), Govt. Railway Police (GRP), who colluded in this nefarious game plan and abetted this destruction of forests for "Development"!

This unholy alliance of these "saviors" of national property for their "ulterior motives' and helplessness of forest staff (sometime, they also colluded) played havoc with the pristine forests; the prime habitat for elephants, tigers and other creatures. The decimating fringes of forests became obvious to everybody and the forest department could not afford to ignore this systematic devastation and loot.

When this author took over the charge of Saranda Forest division in 2001, a casual flip of satellite imageries of forest pertaining to previous years, showed the gnawing of edges of forests as if eaten by termites. These damages were more pronounced on the forests falling along the railway line connecting Tatanagar to Rourkela.

The protection staff, when questioned replied that the earlier efforts to contain this menace came to naught due to non cooperation of other agencies. In fact, this was the classic example of "Bureaucracy" -where so many agencies of Govt. had the common objective of protecting Government property, but all of them working independently (without any coordination) and most of the time against the interest of the Government. No amount of request to make coordinated effort of patrolling, raiding Railway station, trains (both goods and passenger) could yield any favorable result. In fact, these agencies had invisible but more specific border lines drawn for their territory and any intrusion was not tolerated kindly. Railway station and platform by GRP, moving trains by RPF, approach to Railway stations by state police, entry to platform, bogey's/wagons by rail ticket checking staffs were the different domain. It seems that this concept of territoriality was created more to facilitate the vested interest of allowing, storing, loading and unloading of illegal forest produce by the different agencies and they were, in turn, obliged in monetary form by the organized gang of smugglers. Further enquiry also revealed that in the past some enthusiastic efforts of a range officer to conduct raid on Manoharpur railway station led to altercation with GRP and landed him in jail on charges of trespassing and obstructing the railway police to perform their official duties. This particular incident became the biggest stumbling block to starting any effective operation to control the smuggling activities by railways.

Whenever senior officers of railways were approached about this matter, it evoked their non cooperation or indifference. On many occasions, the railway official would suggest to Forest Department (in friendly manner) or rather dictate (when not friendly...) to keep forest produce off the platform by checking the problem of cutting of trees etc. in jungle itself. It was very difficult to make them understand that with very meager staff, how difficult it is to control the felling activities in jungle itself and that's why there is a provision of control and checking the forest produce in transit. This provision was there in all the earlier version of Indian Forest Act also. But by no amount of imagination could the senior railway official believe that the foresters can not stop all the felling in the forest itself and hence there is a necessity to check the points of exit, loading, unloading of forest produce.

But with constant motivation, request and persuasion - sometimes foresters could conduct occasional raids on railway platform with the permission of stationmaster. This had some check on illegal transport, but main activities went on as greedy Guards/Drivers of the train could stop the train and allow the loading/unloading of forest produce at inaccessible, remote points in jungle. Similarly GRP and RPF would allow free passage to these smugglers by charging "protection money" from them. The unfortunate part of the story was that the general public and media remained mute spectators, who thought it was the general practice and rarely commented on this state of affairs.

When repeated requests to railway officials and Railway police officials to stop this smuggling by trains failed, it was planned by Forest Department, one day, to conduct a surprise raid on Manoharpur railway station and this time not only to seize forest produce or nab the offender but to seize the railways also. The raiding party boarded the train at Chakradharpur and as planned the train was raided at Manoharpur railway station with prior request to the station master, forest produce was seized but at the same time three offenders were nabbed. When seizure-report was being prepared at the railway station, the bogey number of Tatanagar -Nagpur passenger train was also mentioned. The forest staff was perplexed and not prepared to mention it in seizure list as it was beyond their imagination to seize the train. Yet sheer persuasion or command of the DFO, prevailed and the seizure list included "the Bogey of Tatanagar- Nagpur Passenger", with driver and guard of the train as co-accused, based on the statements of other arrested accused. The arrested accused also stated that they were in continuous habit of smuggling forest produce in connivance with drivers and guards of the railway. Since the seriousness of this organized crime was not taken cognizance by railways, which played no proactive role in stopping this nefarious activity. Since the railways who were the owner of the all the rolling stock and were requested, warned umpteen times earlier to not allow their passenger trains/good trains to facilitate the smuggling of forest produce. Hence, this was sufficient to presume that railways had not taken enough precaution to prevent their property in omission and commission of smuggling activities. This point was well thought of for all its possible legal repercussions and ultimately it was decided that the railways as owner were not very cautious or rather were negligent in controlling their staff who despite several prior warnings allowed the rolling stock in smuggling activities.

In fact this was the most crucial logic while fixing such responsibility of negligence to railways; which eventually made the railways liable for confiscation.

When the decision for confiscation of railway bogey was initiated; it was scoffed even within the foresters' community. The foresters of all hue with varying seniority, even retired ones, were at their wit's end to digest the concept of "confiscation of railways". The real crisis precipitated when the notice by the "authorized officers" were served to railway authorities, right from "Railway Board" to "station-master" to explain why the seized bogey of train should not be confiscated. This notice must have created some furore in railway officialdom, which started contracting the senior forest officials for the misdemeanor shown by the local foresters. Soon this issue became hot topic for discussion in senior bureaucracy, and legal fraternity, as for them it was the case of height of impudence by Forest department. But the legal process had started and railways moved to the High Court, Jharkhand, by filling writ petitions No. 4162/2001 to 4166/2001 for quashing the whole confiscation case started by the Forest department.

As is the usual practice, forest and environment are such 'useless' issues for Government pleaders, they did not even bother to inform Forest department about the filing of above case in High court and the lawyers of railways got the order for stay of this confiscation case, *ex parte*. Not only that; they could also get the order of release of trains immediately. It is most unfortunate that the picture painted by lawyers of the railway before the court was that the train seized by the high handed foresters was causing great difficulty to general public. This happened because forest department was not given any opportunity to explain their stand. The order of the High court was served by district collector to be implemented immediately, and it asked for personal appearance of the D.F.O. and other senior functionaries of Government for explaining the so called high handed, 'mischievous' action of Forest department or 'vexatious /totally unwarranted' seizure.

It would be interesting to clarify that the bogey in question had been seized, but was immediately handed over to railway station master for further interim possession and with freedom to operate it, and hence suffering of traveling public did not arise at all. This step was carefully taken to avoid any public hue and cry of "high handedness" and also with the simple reason that Forest Dept. had no stockyard to store such trains in their custody. But all these points were suppressed by railways before High Court, to get its sympathetic order.

The "quarterfinal" match going in favour of railways, the "seized" railway bogeys were again released in order to comply with the court's order.

Now the real heat was on foresters, due to this order of court; as even senior foresters and bureaucrats believed that it was a case of "high handedness" of field foresters who were making mockery of "legal provisions". The forest department had to file a show cause; and the senior most functionary of department, including the departmental secretary and Chief Secretary of the state had also to file show cause. Hence all the points raised by railways were carefully replied with strictest legal scrutiny. The provisions of seizure of railways, whether the railway property could be confiscated etc. were carefully dealt with in the light of involvement of Central Government agency.

All the legal points were elaborated in the context of general negligence of railways and failure to take effective action to control the menace. Even then the senior bureaucrats of the state, who were impleaded by Railways, were not convinced with the logic of the show-cause and were apprehending the wrath of High Court; when they would appear in person. But then the Advocate General was the only person who was some how convinced of the logic of forest department stated in the show-cause.

The dooms day arrived and the court was packed to capacity. Every lawyer in the court was interested to hear the arguments, whether railways "could be confiscated" or not. The first "fire" started from the "battery of top lawyers of railways", who argued for the railways that being Central Government organization, the "railways" can never be confiscated or attached and it was sheer case of high handedness of Forest department to conceal their failure to protect forest in the first place. The vociferous and emphatic logic seemed impressive and was supported by continuous nod of the judge (who made occasional remarks about forest department's failure to protect the general greenery and wildlife of the country). Simultaneously, the internal discussion going in whispers by state govt. officials present (including the Chief Secretary) was to blame the impetuous DFO for initiating this intemperate act, which had landed them in such a poor position. This cursing by senior bureaucrats, who had started apprehending severe stricture from the court as the argument moved, made the heart of DFO sink.

Then suddenly came the loud voice of the presiding judge with word "But...". He elaborated that on that very day he happened to visit the Railway station of Ranchi , the capital town of Jharkhand. He himself narrated, how filthy it was, with firewood and small wood bundle littered all over the platform. It was beyond his comprehension, how this could happen in station premises despite the presence of RPF and GRP. After this observation, the shaky lawyer of the forest department was asked by the court to explain his point. Alas, he could hardly speak, and the forester present himself was made to explain the case. When the whole episode unfolded with its genesis, the court also started appreciating it. Finally the court observed that the forest department had law on their side. The railways represented by all their very senior official present were shocked to hear this comment and the court ordered the Chief Secretary present there to call a meeting of Railway and forest officials on that very day to see how railways can cooperate with forest department in controlling the smuggling activities by trains. The earlier shaky Chief Secretary and senior foresters were now feeling confident enough to instruct senior railway officers (of course by the backing of High court). The poor DFO heaved a sigh of relief; had the Court taken an adverse view of his actions, the case would have spelt doom for him. Also the case was adjourned for further hearing with exemption from personal appearance to forest officials.

After prolonged hearing and with written and verbal arguments; it was very well appreciated by the court that law permitted the seizure of Railway and its subsequent confiscation but in general public interest directed to close the confiscation proceeding in question, in its order dated 2/12/2002.

In another case where another bogey was seized, this earlier case provided the precedent to allow confiscation. Finally in July 2004, after detailed hearing of both sides; the rail bogey in question was confiscated under the provisions of Indian Forest Act. It may be a unique case when "train" was confiscated in legal history and it had a still more satisfying end for "forest and its wildlife", as now the "Railways" were duty-bound to act and to *suo-moto* cooperate with the forest department in controlling the smuggling of forest produce both in trains and on platforms.

REFERENCES

1. Cleghorn, H., 1860. Forests and Gardens of South India, W.H. Allen, London. pp. 60
2. Gadgil, M and R. Guha (1992) This fissured Land, Oxford University Press. New Delhi.pp.120-121

Section 4

EMERGENT RESOURCES

'Emergent Resources' here implies the increased emphasis that is now being given to some types of resources. Two *resources* have progressively acquired a larger space in strategy discourse. One of these is 'innovation'. In the paper on innovation, authors discuss the contribution of 'innovation' in various industries. They examine various kinds of innovation, and what drives the innovation in the auto-component manufacturing firms, as well as in other manufacturing sectors in India.

The other paper in this section is a theoretical contribution to understanding the "social capital" resource of organizations. It develops a dependency based index of power to measure structural social capital, looks into aspects of 'reputation capital', and shows the long term effect of 'reputation capital' on organizations.

THE DRIVERS OF CHANGE IN INDIAN AUTOCOMPONENT INDUSTRY: A STUDY OF INNOVATION ATTRIBUTES

Manoj Mishra
GenNext Business Consultants & Management Dev Instt., Gurgaon
A. Sahay
Management Development Institute Gurgaon

INTRODUCTION

The famous adage "The only thing that is constant is change" in no less relevant in today's times with world facing economic crises, the economic balance of the world shifting towards east and BRIC economies becoming more powerful and drivers of the global economic growth. This change has also forced organizations evolve newer methods of managing the change while beating competition, for remaining on the top. Organizations have used various innovations in strategy in the arenas of Product and Process to create an edge over competitors.

The global auto industry, which has proven to be a driver to many successful economies globally, has also been no less affected with this global change and crisis. The western economies have witnessed a drop of 35 to 46 % in their automotive sales and the same has put pressures on the auto component manufacturers which directly depend on the OEM industry. The global projections of the vehicles by top auto manufacturers of passenger vehicles, which was projected to grow to 72 million by 2012, is now projected to taper down from 66 Million to 59 Million.(Source: CSM Worldwide).India and China have been the fastest two countries which have shown double digit growth for last 10 years and even in this times of recession have maintained the same growth. In addition to demand, another major change which the global auto industry is experiencing; is the shift towards higher fuel economies resulting into increase in use of small cars, government offering cash discounts for purchase of small cars and fuel efficient utility vehicles and also a big drive by all companies towards greener, hybrid, fuel cell based, electric vehicles. The developed world is also looking at Low cost countries (LCC) and high potential demand countries, like China, India, Brazil, Thailand, Malaysia, Indonesia etc to drive their growth as well as make their manufacturing cost effective.

Indian Auto Industry forms over 5% of GDP of the country. With automobile penetration of passenger vehicles (which accounts for 70% of auto industry sales) of 7/1000 people as compared to over 400/1000 in developed nations, industry is slated for growing at over 20% CAGR till year 2015 (ACMA-Mc-Kinsey report, 2005.*Vision 2015*). Government of India has worked out an Auto Mission Plan (AMP) with a vision to take the industry contribution to 10% of GDP ,generate additional 25 Million employment and have a sales revenue of 145-180 Billion US$. The contribution of Auto Component Manufacturing sector is also likely to go from current 18 Billion US$(2006) to a whopping 40 Billion US$ by 2016. The exports are also likely to grow from 4 Billion US$ to over 15 Billion US$ including aftermarket sales. There are almost 10000 Indian Auto Component Manufacturers (ACM) out of which only 10% are organized players and only 860 are members of ACMA (Auto Component Manufacturer's Association).

The graphs and tables in Annexure-A (1 to 6), represent growth of Indian OEM and Component auto Industry which comprises of Cars, Multi Utility and Utility Vehicles, 2 Wheelers (Motor Cycle and Scooters), Commercial Vehicles (which included Heavy, Medium and Light Commercial vehicles— HCV, MCV and LCV), 3 Wheelers and Tractors. As per statistics of Society of Indian Automotive Manufacturers (SIAM), the industry has a Compounded Annual Growth rate (CAGR) of 12 % for domestic sales while of 30% for Exports, over last 5 years. In the same way as per ACMA, the CAGR of ACM have been 20%. In ACM sector, 65% of the share of sales comes from Domestic OEMs, 20% from After Market sales and balance 15 % comes from exports. Tables in Annexure-A give the growth trends, capacity, vehicle category wise sales growth etc for OEMs and ACM sectors.(ACMA-McKinsey Report, 2005).

Post economic liberalization in 1991, India has witnessed a boom, in Auto vehicle as well as component industry which has further been accelerated and intensified in last 5 years (2002 onwards) .Today many auto manufacturers globally have decided to set up their manufacturing and sourcing operations in India to realize cost advantages. This has also brought intense competition from local players, which are expanding and setting up their units outside India while global players are setting up shops in India. This has made competitiveness an extremely important parameter for survival and growth. Indian companies are now exposed to manufacturing excellence techniques .They need to scale up on innovations to remain competitive.

In the present context of severe competition, where even survival is not an easy task, growth and more so faster growth is imperative and is the biggest challenge for all top management executives.

RESEARCH GAPS, INNOVATION TYPES, IMPORTANCE, DRIVERS, PROFITABILITY& CREATIVITY

In a global survey of top management executives, innovation is rated as one of the top 3 agendas of the Global CEOs (Business Standard, Jan 28, 2008; Carrier Executive, Jan 2008). Long term growth will be an outcome of sustainable competitive advantage which can only be achieved through **innovation in products, processes and strategy**. All types of innovation, namely Incremental (Continuous), Modular, Architectural, as well as Breakthrough and Disruptive will be required in organizations. Its selection will depend on severity of competition, urgency and scale of growth required and the gap with respect to benchmarks in various organizational efficiency parameters. (Tushman, 1997)

Though Indian Auto component manufacturers (ACM) have started focusing on innovation as strategy for last 5 years, practically no research has been done on Indian innovation climate and that too, in the emerging auto component industry in India. The development of technological and innovation capabilities thus are the defining strategies to survive the severe competition and also to accelerate growth. Although many countries world over have demonstrated good success by taking route of Imitation as first step to innovation, absorb the product and process technology and then have ramped up the levels further. Drivers of imitation (not innovation) have been mapped by Eric Bonabeau (2005) but the same cannot be applicable for the innovation climate and InQ mapping. Most of the other work on Innovation Index has been at country level mapping and hence does not find relevance to this work (George K. Beard, 2007).

Works of Porter (2006) and World economic Forum have been more focused on competitive advantages of nations and help in assessing innovation climate of countries.

Though innovation can take place in any segment of the value chain of the firm, innovations in the field of technology make business more competitive. Technology-based economic development focuses on enhancing the technology life cycle so that technology enters the economy where it can have a positive effect on such things as per capita income (the average income per person) or gross state product (the total value of goods and services produced in the state). Economists have studied the technology life cycle for many years, concluding that these activities are important for economic development. The Innovation Index goals of Mississippi Technology Alliance are given in Table-1.

Table 1: Mississipi Innovation Outcomes and 10-Year Goals

W e a l t h   C r e a t i o n
Increase high Tech employment to 7.9% of total manpower
S t a t e w i d e   R e s e a r c h   C a p a c i t y
Increase total R&D Expenditures to $ 17 for every $ 1000 of Gross State Product (GSP)
U n i v e r s i t y   R e s e a r c h   C a p a c i t y
Increase University royalties from Patents and Licences to $ 2.50 for every $ 1000 University R&D Expenditure
B u s i n e s s   R e s e a r c h   &   D e v e l o p m e n t
Increase Small Business Innovation Research (SBIR) Awards to $.10 for every $ 1000 GSP
T e c h n o l o g y   B u s i n e s s   D e v e l o p m e n t
Increase Net Growth in the Number of Technology Intensive Firms to 33%
I n d u s t r i a l   P r o d u c t i v i t y
Increase Value-added in Manufacturing to $ 84000 per Manufacturing Employee
T e c h n o l o g y   W o r k f o r c e   D e v e l o p m e n t
Increase the %age of Scientists & Engineers in Workforce to .30%
I n v e s t m e n t   C a p i t a l
Increase Venture Capital Invested in Mississipi companies to $ 1.00 for every $ 1000 GSP

Auto component Industry profitability has been very low traditionally and more so in last 5 years due to severe domestic competition, entry of global players forcing local manufacturers to cut prices in spite of increasing costs and pressure from OEM on price reduction to ensure their own competitiveness. The Profit after Tax (PAT) and Earnings before Interest, Depreciation and Taxes (EBIDTA) margins of ACM with respect to other industry players were collected by ACMA and are very low (SeeTable-2 below). This further emphasizes the need for Innovation required in the ACM in areas of product, process and Strategy so as to improve these margins.

Table-2

Industry wise Profit After Tax (PAT) & Earnings Before Depreciation, Interest and Taxes (EBIDTA) of Top three companies in ACM in various technology category and other industry sectors		
S no Industry	Average PAT	Average EBIDTA
1 SME Auto component-Sheet metal-Below Rs 1 Billion sales/yr	0.4%	6%
2 Sheet Metal Assembly (Large companies-Rs 3 Billion sales/yr)	6%	14%
3 Forging/ Casting	8%	16%
4 High-tech Assembly	10%	18%
5 Precision Machining	12%	22%
6 IT- Software	20%	26%
7 Real Estate-construction	30%	40%
8 Food -catering	25%	30%
9 Food - Restaurant	35%	42%

Realizing the importance of an employee working like an entrepreneur; today's organizations speak of creating an entrepreneurial culture and mind set for their employees .Entrepreneurship build on the bedrock of innovation which has creativity as its main ingredient. The Innovation, Entrepreneurship and creativity are inter-twined in an organisation and result in a sustainable profitable organisation.

Various studies have been done on relationship between Innovation, Entrepreneurship (Considered here as Entrepreneurial Manager/Employee) and Creativity. These studies throw light on how we nurture and increase the innovation climate in the organisation and improve profitability. Findings from some of these studies are given below to derive attributes of Innovation, Creativity, relationship of them, their impact on profitability etc.

Innovation can be defined as the successful implementation of creative ideas (Brazeal and Herbert, 1999). Innovation is the phase in which new ideas are developed and it includes the ability to change an idea into a money-generating activity. Innovation is seldom a systematic, structured process in the case of the small business venture. Creativity is the starting point of innovation (Pretorius et. al., 2006).

Innovation has also been defined by Ireland, Hitt, Camp and Sexton (2001) as the sum of invention and the commercialization of that invention. Innovation thus involves having the idea and turning that idea into an opportunity through commercialization. Opportunity exploitation for an entrepreneur therefore involves innovation. Ireland et al. (2001) further postulate that, to be effective, an innovation has to be simple, and it has to be focused. Effective innovators usually start small, often trying to do one specific thing. Innovation is work (implementation) rather than genius, requiring knowledge, ingenuity and focus; if an innovation does not aim at industry leadership from the outset, it might not be innovative enough. Innovation should be pursued systematically and not left to chance (Pretorius et. al., 2006).

According to Jun and Deschoolmeester (2003), entrepreneurs' innovativeness is demonstrated by their willingness and capability to create a paradigm shift in science and technology and/or market structure in an industry from a macro perspective. From a micro perspective, innovativeness is the willingness and the capability of entrepreneurs to influence the firm's existing marketing resources, technological resources, skills, knowledge, capabilities, or strategy.

Schumpeter defined the entrepreneur as the founder of a new firm and as an innovator, who breaks up established routines and opposes the old way of doing things. Schumpeter's entrepreneur only undertakes those ventures which turn out to be successful (Brouwer, 2000). The entrepreneur's special leadership qualities enable him to see the right way to act. Others will follow in his wake. In order to introduce his innovations, the entrepreneur needs to withstand the opposition of the environment, which is usually hostile to deviating behavior and novelty. The Schumpeterian definition (Shumpeter, 1934) of innovation states that the commercialization of all new combinations is based upon the application of any of the following: new materials and components, the introduction of new processes, the opening of new markets, and the introduction of new organisational forms. Only when a change in technology is involved is it termed an "invention", but as soon as the business world becomes involved, it becomes an "innovation" (Janszen, 2000). According to this definition, innovations are the composite of two worlds, namely the technical world and the business world. Innovation in this sense can be seen as an event: the introduction of something new to the business world as well as a process. In other words, innovation leads to change being introduced in the business environment by the entrepreneur.

In Drucker's view innovation is what entrepreneurs do. It involves changing the value and satisfaction obtained from resources by the customer. Innovation represents the specific tool of entrepreneurs, the means by which they exploit change as an opportunity for a different business or different service (1985).

Drucker argues that there is a need for constant innovation because of the challenge of ever-changing customer needs, technology, and competition. The two primary functions of business are to innovate and to market. Marketing creates a customer, whereas innovation involves doing something better to enhance organizational performance. Entrepreneurship does both and involves doing something different in order to better utilize resources and to expand markets. At its core, entrepreneurship is market-focused and market-driven.

In sum, the phenomenon of entrepreneurship is a complex interplay of opportunity (Shane and Venkataraman, 2000), human action (Kirzner, 1973), learning (Minniti and Bygrave, 2001), and creativity and innovation (Ward, 2004). Each of these elements cannot be examined in isolation.

Drucker (1985) challenges the notion that entrepreneurship and innovation are innate or represent personality-based characteristics or represent the domain of select individuals or scientists. Instead he describes innovation and entrepreneurship as behaviors that most people are capable of learning.

Drucker (1985) argues that innovation rarely arises from "flashes of genius" but rather innovation is purposeful and involves an organized, systematic process of monitoring these sources of innovation for innovative opportunities. He identifies and describes seven sources of innovative opportunity: The Unexpected, Incongruities, Process Need, Industry and Market Structures, Demographics, Changes in Perception, and New Knowledge. Overall, the seven sources represent symptoms of change or "highly reliable indicators of changes that have already happened or can be made to happen with little effort" (p. 35). The role of the entrepreneur is to identify these changes and opportunities and respond through action. The first four of the sources are related to the enterprise or industry; the second three are outside the enterprise or industry.

Drucker also provides a set of principles of innovation representing what he calls "the hardcore of the discipline" (p. 134). He identifies things that should be done (do's), things that should not be done (don'ts), and conditions. The first do is that innovation is purposeful and systematic and begins with the analysis of the sources of opportunity. Next comes testing the analysis against reality. This involves going into the marketplace and ascertaining customers' expectations, needs, and values. Third, for an innovation to be effective, it must be simple and focused on a specific need that it satisfies and a specific end result that it produces. Related, it should also start small. Finally, it should aim at achieving leadership in a given environment, market, or industry. The don'ts include: not trying to be clever, not trying to do too many things at once, and innovating not for the future but rather for the present.

Drucker argues that entrepreneurial management is needed to create an entrepreneurial business. An entrepreneurial business is an organization that fosters and exploits innovation. This type of business and management approach involves building a culture that encourages and provides the resources to its members to be innovative. This must be embedded into the company's philosophy and practice; acquiring another company in hopes of transforming the parent company into becoming innovative usually does not succeed. Examples of companies that are entrepreneurial and practice entrepreneurial management that identifies include Procter and Gamble, Johnson and Johnson, and 3M.

McLean (2007) defines creativity as the process of generating new ideas. He advocates that innovation is quite distinct from creativity and is the implementation of ideas generated via the creative process. Creativity and innovation therefore together are the process of generating and implementing new knowledge. Such knowledge can be used to not only create new products and services but also to enable the organization to learn better and faster than the competitors and to gain and sustain competitive advantage. Innovation results from pattern thinking in the areas of: customer, value chains, organizational forms, products, and channels.

Mol and Berkinshaw (2006) have defined Management Innovation as the implementation of new management practices, processes and structures that represent a significant departure from the current state-of-art practices and are intended to further organizational goals. This aspect of innovation however is most neglected in organizations. While technological and product innovation has been used by organizations to gain sustainable competitive advantage, management innovation is rarely thought of even though it is the driver of technological, service and product innovation.

Innovations improve the productivity of the existing work processes by increasing specialization, redesigning processes, investing in new equipment, which enriches society as a whole. Through innovation firms take risks to commercialize new products and services that meet previously unfulfilled needs. This also enhances society (Govindarajan & Trimble, 2005). Innovation is the core of economic vitality. It drives growth, creates jobs, builds wealth, gives employees new purpose, and revitalizes organizations.

Creativity, by itself, does not define entrepreneurship. Creativity without innovation does not produce results, and innovation without effective management does not produce marketable products, processes or services. Furthermore, not all innovations are creative, as some innovations are incremental changes or were developed by others and adapted for use locally. Creativity therefore cannot directly generate innovation, nor does innovation automatically establish creativity, but the unity and degree of mutuality incorporates the possibilities for further development and a higher level of quality (Pretorius et. al., 2006).

Innovation is considered to be critical for firms to compete. Innovation is the most important component of a firms' strategy (Hamel, 2000). It allows a firm to set the direction of the evolution of an industry. Because the competitive space is non-linear it requires non-linear thinking. Hamel (2007) reports the results of a survey of 500 CEOs who largely agreed that their industry had been changed in the last 10 years by new-comers and incumbents. These new-comers have done this by changing the rules of the business. The reason for success of Silicon Valley is not e-commerce but innovation.

Research has pointed out a high correlation between high innovation and superior profitability (Roberts, 1999). No support has been found for the argument that firms can earn high profits without being competitive and not being innovative. Research has also found that early and fast movers who are first to introduce new goods and services, achieve the highest returns (Lee *et. al.*, 2000) through monopoly profits, until a competitor introduces new products or substitutes. It has also been found that capability to develop and introduce new products to the market is the main driver to a successful global strategy (Subramanium & Venkataraman, 1999), and is to be used systematically and not left to chance (Pretorius et. al., 2006).

According to Jun and Deschoolmeester (2003), entrepreneurs' innovativeness is demonstrated by their willingness and capability to create a paradigm shift in science and technology and/or market structure in an industry from a macro perspective. From a micro perspective, innovativeness is the willingness and the capability of entrepreneurs to influence the firm's existing marketing resources, technological resources, skills, knowledge, capabilities, or strategy.

Schumpeter defined the entrepreneur as the founder of a new firm and as an innovator, who breaks up established routines and opposes the old way of doing things. Schumpeter's entrepreneur only undertakes those ventures which turn out to be successful (Brouwer, 2000). The entrepreneur's special leadership qualities enable him to see the right way to act. Others will follow in his wake.

RESEARCH QUESTION & METHODOLOGY

Based on the literature review and the research gaps identified, it is clear that no work has been done to define the Innovation attributes extensively across various Industry sectors. Further, although drivers to innovation has been attempted in some researches, , no work has been done for Auto Component Industry and more so for Indian Industry, Thus this work will fill this gap. The research questions identified are:

1) What are the drivers to Innovation in India across various chosen industry sectors
2) Do these drivers have equal weightages in innovation culture
3) Do some drivers matter more in specific industry with respect to other industries

The methods of case study and surveying of companies were used. For understanding the issues, specific cases have been taken as they were considered to be best suited for theory building. (Eisenhardt, 1989; Mintzberg 1987, 1978; Mintzberg & Walters, 1985; Yin, 1994; Wieck, 1989). The process for the study is described below: .

1. Identification of the attributes and enablers for innovation through a cross sector, cross organization level survey. The sectors identified were IT, Auto component, Pharma, Food, Engineering and Reality. These sectors were chosen as they represented key sectors in economy as well as the sectors where innovation is taking place at a higher level. Innovation is urgently needed for survival and growth in these sectors as also in emerging sectors.
2. Categorization of the attributes to identify factors.
3. Rating of these attributes, through a survey questionnaire, on a 5 point scale, to define their relevance to innovation in selected sectors.
4. Finalizing the drivers(attributes) of Innovation for Auto Component Industry.
5. Basis of sample selection: The ACM organizations selected represent various regions of country, size(in terms of sales, investment and people employed) as well as type namely Ancillary units of OEM, Joint ventures with OEM, JV with foreign collaboration, as well as type of product tier (assembly—Engine, Drive line, axle and Turbocharger; Sheet metal, Machining and Forgings). The study has also been done of at least one unit each of few other key sectors so as to compare and neutralize the sector impact.

EXPLORING INNOVATION DRIVERS, THEIR IMPORTANCE & WEIGHTAGES

A pilot study was done to explore the attributes with various senior and middle level executives across different sectors in auto component, IT, Pharma, Real estate and Construction etc. The attributes were sought from 41 executives and experts through a questionnaire; asking Six attributes/respondent (total 300 entries). The 27 respondents, who replied, included executives and entrepreneurs from auto component manufacture (in majority since this is the sector of interest - 70%) as well as from IT (19%), Pharma (7%); services and other sectors (Engineering and Reality) accounted for the rest.

Although Factor analysis would have been the idea tool to derive at Categories from these factors (attributes) of innovation, if the sample size was over 100 organisations; as the sample size was less, these attributes were processed logically for duplication, ambiguity, similarity and affinity. The categories emerged were:

a. culture related (13 attributes)
b. employee related (8 attributes)
c. environment related (5 attributes)
d. management related (11 attributes) and
e. network of technology partner, suppliers, customers, competitors etc. (3 attributes)

These were finalized under 5 categories and 40 attributes and are listed in Table-3 below:

Table-3: Attribute Consolidation and Categorization

S.No.	Category	Attributes which drive / enable / facilitate Innovation
1	Culture	Global orientation
2	Culture	Attitude towards Cost competitiveness
3	Culture	Peaceful working culture of the Organization
4	Culture	Culture of respecting others' ideas
5	Culture	Flexibility
6	Culture	Quick decision making
7	Culture	Learning Environment /continuous education
8	Culture	Promoting creativity at work
9	Culture	Encourage risk-taking
10	Culture	Innovation sustaining Organizational culture
11	Culture	Continuous improvement/Kaizen culture
12	Culture	TQM practices
13	Culture	TPM practices
14	Employee	Employee Involvement
15	Employee	Employee Empowerment
16	Employee	Employee Development/nurturing
17	Employee	Technical Competence
18	Employee	Motivated employees

Table Contd…

19	Employee	Intrapreneurship- entrepreneurial mind set of employees
20	Employee	Dedicated talent pool for ideation
21	Employee	Live by values of the organization
22	Environment	Competition from the foreign companies
23	Environment	Global exposure
24	Environment	Market leader
25	Environment	Deep understanding of the Key Factors of Success in the Industry
26	Environment	Deep understanding of the trends in global auto business
27	Management	Management Commitment to Change
28	Management	Willingness to Change
29	Management	Accept the need of change
30	Management	Financial backup /support
31	Management	Appropriate Incentive policy to reward/share innovation benefits
32	Management	Visionary/strong leadership
33	Management	Clear business goals
34	Management	Strong-big -challenging Vision
35	Management	Encourage organizational Transparency
36	Management	Good R&D set up
37	Management	Strong KMS (Knowledge management system)
38	Network	Strong communication network with customers
39	Network	Collaboration and Partnership with their buyers
40	Network	Access to newer technology trends-alliance/partner/networks

The attributes finalized were sent as questionnaire (refer Annexure-B) to the same pool of cross sectoral respondents to arrive at the importance of these drivers to the promotion of innovation. This was done by seeking their rating on a 5 point Likert scale. The scale for rating was chosen to be on 0 to 5 for ease and familiarity of the respondents and to provide a step of 20% rating differential for each step of the scale. Due to the phenomenon under study, **it may not be possible for the respondents to differentiate the attributes on lesser scale justifiably and would**

have other wise created scale bias in case respondents do not actually perceive to differentiate but they chose their response differently while rating. The zero on the scale represented no relation of that attribute on the innovation while a rating of 5 meant a very high impact of this attribute on driving the innovation.

Based on the above attribute study, category wise maximum score of each category works out as under:

1. Culture: 13 Attributes *5 Maximum rating =65 (32.5% of total score)
2. Employee: 8*5=40 (20% of total score)
3. Environment: 5*5=25 (12.5% of total score)
4. Management: 11*5=55 (27.5% of total score)
5. Network: 3*5=15 (7.5% of total score)
6. Total score: 40*5=200

(Refer attached Annexure- B for Weights and Importance rating of Organizations)

The above category score, shown as a Percent of total score for each category, can be considered as its weightages in driving innovation in an organization with each factor (attribute) contributing a maximum score of 5. The rating of these attributes was between 4 and 5 for most of the attributes by many of the respondents, proving that all these attributes contribute a great degree in driving innovation in any organization. After discussion with experts, it was also felt that these factors at a score of 5, will contribute, for sure, their maximum to Innovation and hence the rating given by a respondent for individual attribute was considered to be the executive and organization specific (respondent biased).Thus, this was not taken to moderate the weightages of categories as found earlier through category % score in total score. The order of importance or weightages for all the attributes thus was taken to be equal.

DISCUSSION AND CONCLUSION

The categories and Drivers (Attributes) to Innovation are although arrived with a larger weightages of ACM in the sample studied (as this was the prime objective of the study), but they can be generalized to other sectors as well. Other sectors studied are also helping remove the bias and neutralize the effect of skewness of drivers even for ACM . These sectors like IT and Pharma are the ones where the level of Innovation is good are not found to have some attributes which are just not there in ACM. Thus the attribute may contribute differently in different sectors, the exhaustive list presented in the annexure 1 above if prevalent in all sectors and organizations. As discussed above, Innovation would be the defining parameters for creating winning organizations. The organizations which would not only assess their level of Innovation but would also demonstrate good ability to manage transition from current to global benchmark levels of innovation, would surely be the winner in long run. The need although is urgent in auto industry, in light of intense competition with global players.

LIMITATIONS

Following are the limitations and directions for future research.

a. Further exploratory study can be done through interviewing the sample respondents to understand the causality of innovation drivers.

b. Study of key successful companies in various technology segments can also be done to study the effect of innovation climate across technology and tiers e.g. machining, forging, casting, sheet metal etc as well as engine assy., axle assy., gear box assy., steering assy. etc.

c. The study has not been statistically tested and verified for validity due to small sample size and being case study based work.

d. The various attributes and categories are taken using rating and clubbed for simplicity to arrive at Innovation drivers using relative weightages of each category and attribute. These can be further studied to arrive at actual weightages in a broad based exploratory study and further through benchmarking study of successful global companies on innovations.

e. Since many attributes may also be related and may have a stronger co-relation among them, a large scale study with 100 companies minimum may be taken up to reduce the attributes and come out with factors through Factor analysis and co-relation method.

f. No foreign company or subsidiary of a foreign company was taken. If taken, it will further improve the case for generalization

DIRECTION FOR FUTURE RESEARCH

A further study can be done to define the measurement of Innovation through an Innovation Quotient and also then assessing the same organization wide sector wide so as to understand the status of Innovation in various organizations. Authors plans to do further study of the same in their future works

A further analysis through questionnaire and exploratory interview is suggested for all units. This can further be studied by the author himself to analyze the improvement aspects in detail though a collaborative study with the industry, especially the units involved, it will be more valuable as the units in the study will then commit to act on the innovation front to improve their InQ

Authors plan to extend this study further to enhance the current study, validate statistically the findings and arrive at stronger road map to accelerate innovations in auto component sector of India.

BENEFITS AND CONTRIBUTIONS

This study will help organizations understand drivers of innovation in their own industry and organization. Further it will also facilitate bench marking innovation drivers on various categories and attributes with respect to global and domestic best. When extended further, this will form basis to help them identify gaps overall and in various categories and attributes to devise strategies for improving specific attributes of innovation. When extended, the benchmarks can be taken beyond specific sectors for best in class for various categories and attributes so as to create best practices irrespective of which sector one operates.

Even Industrial associations and Government bodies may use the study for devising surveys, assessing innovation climate and areas needing improvement so as to develop local industries to global levels.

REFERENCES

1. ACMA-McKinsey Report (2005), *Vision 2015 for the Indian Automotive Components Industry*
2. Brazeal, D.V. and Herbert, T.T. (1999). The genesis of entrepreneurship. *Entrepreneurship: Theory and Practice, 23* (3): 29-45.
3. Brouwer, M. (2000). Entrepreneurship and uncertainty: Innovation and competition among the many. *Small Business Economics, 15*(2), 149-160.
4. Business Standard (2007, Oct.2). Interview of Tucker, R. *If you donot innovate, some one else will*
5. Business Standard (2007, Dec.18). A McKinsey global survey-*How companies approach innovation*
6. Business Standard (2008,Jan 28); Carrier Executive (2008,Jan).Top 10 priorities of the Global CEOs
7. Drucker, Peter F. (1985). *Innovation and entrepreneurship: Practice and principle.* New York : Harper Business
8. Eisenhardt, K.M. (1989). Building *theories from case study research.* Academy of management Review, 14, 532-550.
9. Eric Bonabeau (2004). *The perils of imitation age.* Harvard business review,June,2004
10. George k.Beard (2007) 'What's your Innovation quotient' downloaded from web site of Government technology's www.prbliccio.com on Mar.17,2008
11. Government of India,2005.*Auto Vision 2015,2005*
12. Govindarajan, V. & Trimble, C. (2005). *10 rules for strategic innovators: From idea to execution.* Boston, MA : Harvard Business School Publishing
13. Govindrajan. V (2008). Ten Myths of Innovation. Business Today, April 2008
14. Hamel, G. (2007). The future of management. *Management Today*, Sept., pp. 48-51.
15. Hamel, G. (2000).Leading the revolution. Boston, MA: Harvard Business School Press.
16. Higgins, J. (1996). Achieving Innovation,the core competencies, R&D Innovator.Volume 5,Number 6
17. Hitt, Michael A. , Ireland, Duane R, Camp, Michael S, & Sexton, Donald L. (2001).Guest editors' introduction to the special issue: Strategic entrepreneurship: Entrepreneurial strategies for wealth creation. *Strategic Management Journal, 22*(6/7), 479-491.
18. Ireland, R. D., Hitt, M. A., Camp, S.M. & Sexton, D.L. (2001). Integrating entrepreneurship and strategic management actions to create firm wealth. *The Academy of Management Executive. 15*(1): 49-64.
19. Janszen, F. (2000). *The Age of Innovation.* London: Prentice Hall.
20. Kirzner, I.M. (1973). *Competition and Entrepreneurship.* Chicago, IL: The University of Chicago Press.
21. Lee, H., Smith, K. G., Grimm, C. M., Schomburg, A. (2000). Timing, order and durability of new product advantages with imitation. *Strategic Management Journal 21*(1), 23-30.
22. McLean, J. (2007). The art of thinking outside the box. *The British Journal of Entrepreneurship*

23. Minniti, M. and Bygrave, W. (2001). A dynamic model of entrepreneurial learning. *Entrepreneurship Theory and Practice, 25*(3), pp. 5-16.

24. Mintzberg, H. (1987). The strategy concepts: I. Five Ps for strategy. In G.R. Caroll, & D. Vogel (Eds.), *Organizational approaches to Strategy* (pp. 123-145). Cambridge, MA: Ballinger.

25. Mol, Michael J. and Birkinshaw, Julian. (2006). Against the Flow: Reaping the Rewards of Management Innovation, *European Business Forum,* Winter 2006, 27, pp. 24-29.

26. Pretorius, M., Millard, S. M., & Kruger, M. E. (2006). The relationship between implementation, creativity and innovation in small business, South African Journal of Business Management, 2005,36(4)

27. Roberts, P. W. (1999). Product innovation, product-market competition and persistent profitability in the U.S pharmaceutical industry. *Strategic Management Journal, 20*(7), 655-670.

28. Schumpeter, J.A. (1934). *Change and the Entrepreneur.* Cambridge, MA: Harvard

29. Shane, S. and Venkataraman, S. (2000). Promise of entrepreneurship as a field of research. *Academy of Management Review, 25*(1), pp. 217-26.

30. Shiba S.(2006).Breakthrough Management, Tata McGraw Hill-CII publication

31. Subramanium, M. & Venkataraman, N. (1999). The influence of leveraging tacit overseas knowledge for global new product development capability: An empirical examination

32. Tushman, M. L., & O'Reilly, C.A. (1997) *Winning trough innovation.* Cambridge, NA: Harvard Business School Press.

33. Yin, R. K. (1994). *Case study research: Design and Methods* (2nd ed.) London: Sage.

Trends of Indian Auto OEM and Component Industry
Trend of Vehicle sales in India (Source SIAM,India)

	2001-02	2003-04	2005-06	2007-08
CARS	5,64,052	8,43,235	11,12,542	14,16,480
MULTI UTILITY VEHICLES	1,05,667	1,46,325	1,96,371	2,44,648
LCVs	65,756	1,08,917	1,71,781	2,54,062
BUSES & TRUCKS	96,752	1,66,123	2,19,297	2,91,114
SCOOTERS	9,37,506	9,35,279	10,20,013	10,74,933
MOTOR CYCLES	29,06,323	43,55,168	62,01,214	65,03,532
MOPEDS	4,27,498	3,32,294	3,79,574	4,30,827
3-WHEELERS	2,12,748	3,56,223	4,34,424	5,00,592
TRACTORS	2,07,324	1,91,633	2,96,080	
Total 2 and 3 Wheelers	44,84,075	59,78,964	80,35,225	85,26,641
LCVs	65,756			
BUSES & TRUCKS	96,752			
ALL CVs (H,M&LCVs)	1,62,508	2,75,040		

Two Wheelers: Capacity of Two wheelers is 10 Million including scooters which is likely to be raised to 18 Million by 2014. The share of capacity is 60%, 25% and 20% by Hero Honda, Bajaj Auto and TVS Motors. Balance 5 % is shared by Honda Motor Cycle and Scooters Limited, Suzuki Auto, Yamaha Motors, Kinetic Honda etc. Some more manufacturers (Local and Global) are also exploring entering Indian market.

Annexure A(2): Existing capacity and plans of Auto OEMS- Non Two Wheelers

Srl	Name	Product	Locations	Capacity		
				Existing	New by 2010	Total
1	Tata	Car/SUV	Pune	250000	100000	350000
			Singrur	250000	250000	500000
		LCV	Pune	300000	200000	500000
			Utrakhand	0	200000	200000
		MCV/HCV	Lucknow	100000	50000	150000
			Pune	100000	100000	200000
			Jamshedpur	150000	100000	250000
2	Leyland	MCV/HCV	Chennai	80000	50000	130000
			Hosur	20000	20000	40000
			Alwar	10000	10000	20000
		LCV	Chennai	0	50000	50000
3	Eicher	MCV/HCV	Pithampur	5000	15000	20000
		LCV	Pithampur	25000	40000	65000
4	Bajaj	3 Wheeler	Pune	400000	200000	600000
		Car/SUV	Pune		250000	250000
5	Maruti	Car/SUV	Gurgaon	900000	600000	1500000
6	Mahindra	Car/SUV	Nasik	150000	50000	200000
		Tractor	Mumbai	20000	0	20000
			Utrakhand	50000	25000	75000
			Nagpur	20000	10000	30000
		3 Wheeler	Utrakhand	100000	50000	150000
			Zahirabad	25000	25000	50000
		LCV	Zahirabad	10000	20000	30000
		MCV/HCV	Pune		20000	20000
7	Hyundai	Car/SUV	Chennai	300000	600000	900000
8	Toyota	Car/SUV	Bangalore	60000	140000	200000
9	GM	Car/SUV	Halol	80000	20000	100000
			Pune	50000	50000	100000
10	Ford	Car/SUV	Chennai	50000	50000	100000
11	Mercedes	Car/SUV	Pune	5000	5000	10000
12	Nissan	Car/SUV	Chennai		400000	400000

Annexure A(2) Contd...

13	Hero-Daimler	MCV/HCV	To decide		100000	100000
14	Sonalika	Tractor	Hoshiarpur	50000	50000	100000
		Car/SUV	Baddi	20000	30000	50000
15	Punjab tractor	Tractor	Chandigarh	50000	0	50000
16	New Holland	Tractor	Noida	30000	20000	50000
17	Mitsubishi	Car/SUV	Chennai	10000	10000	20000
18	BMW	Car/SUV	to decide	5000	5000	10000
19	Volkswagen	Car/SUV	Pune	5000	5000	10000
20	Audi	Car/SUV	Aurangabad	5000	5000	10000
21	Skoda	Car/SUV	Aurangabad	20000	10000	30000
22	Fiat-Tata	Car	Ranjangaon	0	300000	300000
23	Off highway	Bull dozer,etc	N & W india	10000	10000	20000
	Total			**3715000**	**4245000**	**7960000**

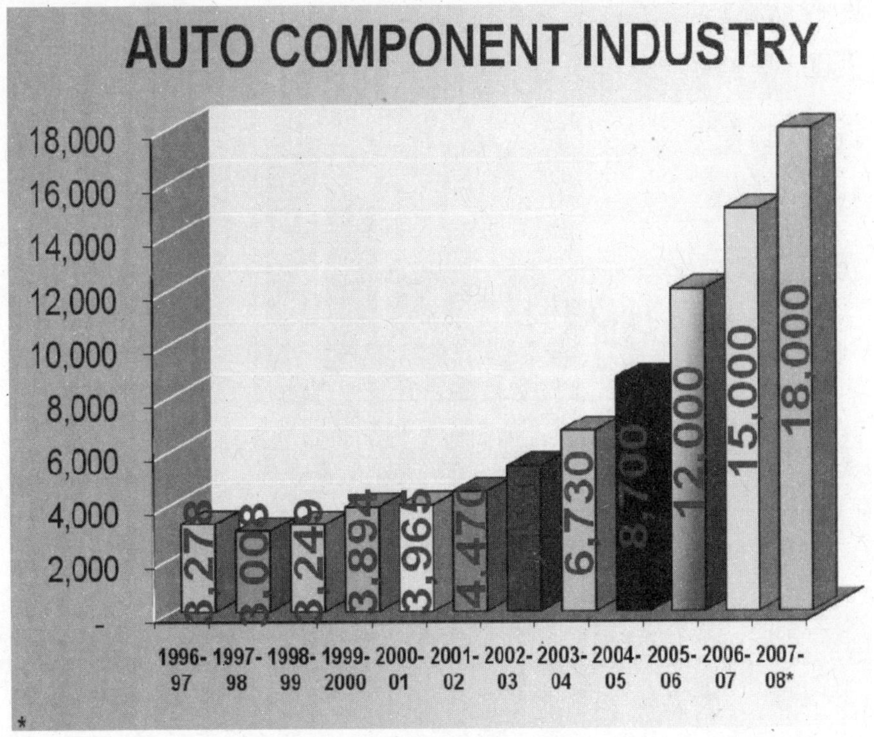

Annexure A(3): Sales in Million US$ of Auto Component Industry

AUTO COMPONENT INDUSTRY

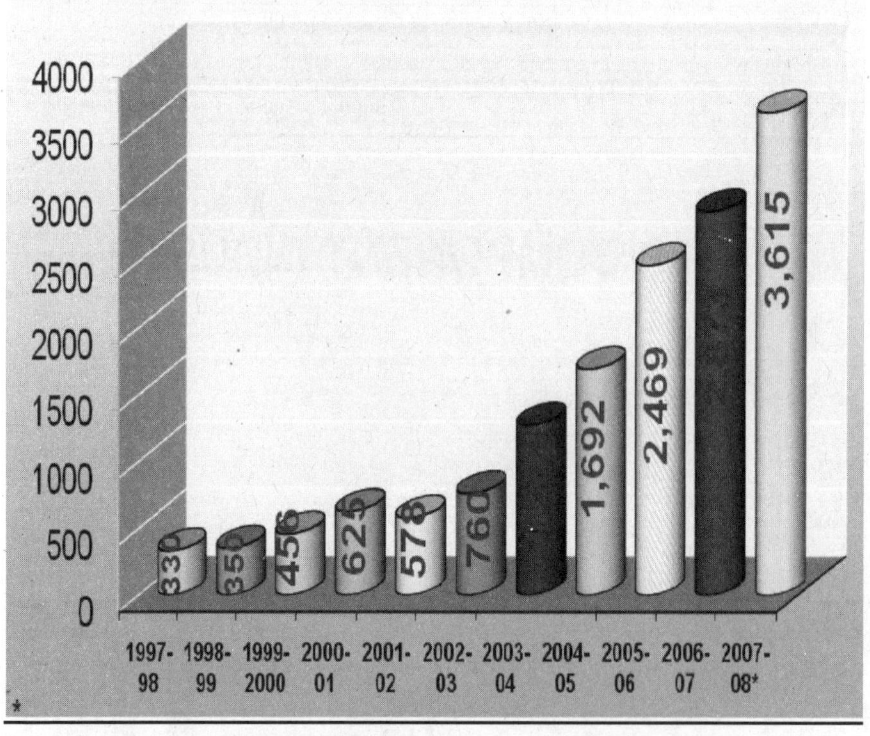

Annexure A(4): Export Sales in Million US$ of Auto Component Industry

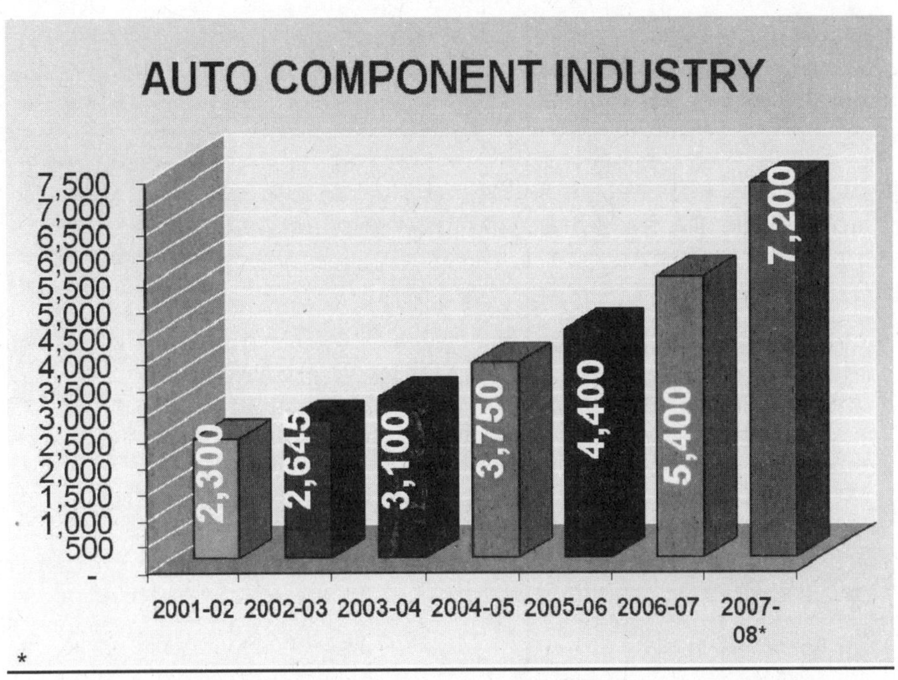

Annexure A(5): Domestic OEM Sales, mn US$, of Auto Component Industry

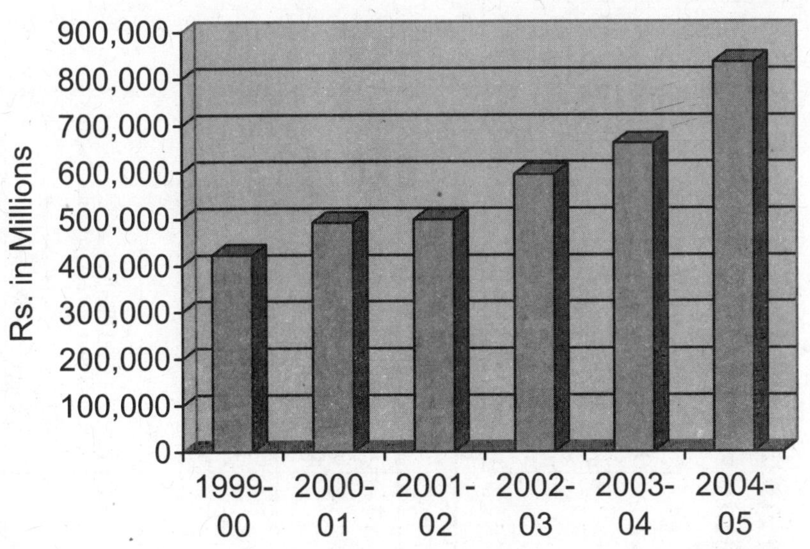

Annexure A(6): Turnover of Automobile Industry 1999-00 to 2004-05

Annexure B:
Attribute rating summary

Organisation profiles--->	Turbo assy	Engine assy	Drive line assy	Axle assy	Sheet metal	Tool mfg.	Forging machining	Machining-ancillary	Sheet metal-ancillary	Forging	Sheet metal ancilary	Pharma	EnggConstn eqpmt	IT s/w	Food -Spices
	1	2	3	4	5	6	7	8	9	10	11	12	13	14	15
Sales,Rs Crores	400	800	450	800	560	20	140	1.5	6	160	6	400	20	75	12
Employees	200	900	900	450	1050	70	550	70	150	650	120	180	400	150	60
Tech tie up	JV	TA	no	JV	MUL	no	no	no-	no-	JV	no-	no	no	no	TA

S.No.	Category	Attribute which drives/enables/facilitates Innovn	Scale Ratings														
1	Culture	Global orientation	4	5	2	3	4	4	3	4	4	5	4	5	4	4	4
2	Culture	Attitude towards Cost competitiveness	4	5	3	2	4	4	2	4	4	5	4	5	2	4	4
3	Culture	Peaceful working culture of the Organization	1	2	2	4	4	1	4	4	1	2	1	2	4	4	4
4	Culture	Culture of respecting others' ideas	4	4	4	4	4	4	4	4	4	4	4	4	5	4	4
5	Culture	Flexibility	2	5	4	4	3	2	4	3	2	5	2	5	5	3	3
6	Culture	Quick decision making	2	3	4	3	5	2	3	5	2	3	2	3	3	5	5
7	Culture	Learning Environment /continuous education	3	5	4	5	4	3	5	4	3	5	3	5	5	4	4
8	Culture	Promoting creativity at work	4	5	4	5	5	4	5	5	4	5	4	5	5	5	5
9	Culture	Encourage risk-taking	4	5	4	5	4	4	5	4	4	5	4	5	5	4	4

#	Category																	
10	Culture	Innovation sustaining Organizational culture	4	4	4	5	4	4	5	4	4	4	4	4	5	4	4
11	Culture	Continuous improvement/Kaizen culture	4	2	4	5	3	4	5	3	4	2	4	2	5	3	3
12	Culture	TQM practices	2	4	3	4	4	2	4	4	2	4	2	4	4	4	4
13	Culture	TPM practices	2	4	3	4	3	2	4	3	2	4	2	4	4	3	3
14	Employee	Employee Involvement	4	5	4	5	5	4	5	5	4	5	4	5	5	5	5
15	Employee	Employee Empowerment	4	5	4	4	5	4	4	5	4	5	4	5	4	5	5
16	Employee	Employee Development/nurturing	3	4	4	5	5	3	5	5	3	4	3	4	5	5	5
17	Employee	Technical Competence	2	5	3	5	4	2	5	4	2	5	2	5	5	4	4
18	Employee	Motivated employees	4	5	4	5	5	4	5	5	4	5	4	5	5	5	5
19	Employee	Intra/Entre-preneurial mind set of employees	2	5	4	5	4	2	5	4	2	5	2	5	5	4	4
20	Employee	Dedicated talent pool for ideation	1	4	4	5	4	1	5	4	1	4	1	4	5	4	4
21	Employee	Live by values of the organization	3	5	3	4	4	3	4	4	3	5	3	5	4	4	4
22	Environmt	Competition from the foreign companies	3	5	3	4	3	3	4	3	3	5	3	5	4	3	3
23	Environmt	Global exposure	3	5	3	5	4	3	5	4	3	5	3	5	5	4	4
24	Environmt	Market leader	2	2	2	4	4	2	4	4	2	2	2	2	4	4	4
25	Environmt	Deep understanding of key success factors of Industry	2	5	3	5	4	2	5	4	2	5	2	5	5	4	4
26	Environmt	Deep understanding of trends in global auto business	2	5	3	5	5	2	5	5	2	5	2	5	5	5	5
27	Mgmt	Management Commitment to Change	4	5	4	5	5	4	5	5	4	5	4	5	5	5	5

Annexure B Contd…

No.	Category	Item															
28	Mgmt	Willingness to Change	5	4	4	5	5	5	5	5	5	4	5	4	5	5	5
29	Mgmt	Accept the need of change	5	4	4	5	5	5	5	5	5	4	5	4	5	5	5
30	Mgmt	Financial backup /support	1	5	4	3	4	1	3	4	1	5	1	5	3	4	4
31	Mgmt	Appropriate Incentive policy to reward/share innovation benefits	3	5	4	4	4	3	4	4	3	5	3	5	4	4	4
32	Mgmt	Visionary/strong leadership	2	5	4	4	5	2	4	5	2	5	2	5	4	5	5
33	Mgmt	Clear business goals	3	5	2	3	4	3	3	4	3	5	3	5	3	4	4
34	Mgmt	Strong-big -challenging Vision	2	5	2	4	5	2	4	5	2	5	2	5	5	5	5
35	Mgmt	Encourage organizational Transparency	4	4	2	3	4	4	3	4	4	4	4	4	5	4	4
36	Mgmt	Good R&D set up	2	5	3	5	5	2	5	5	2	5	2	5	5	5	5
37	Mgmt	Strong KMS (Knowledge mgmt system)	2	5	4	5	4	2	5	4	2	5	2	5	5	4	4
38	Network	Strong communication network with customers	1	5	4	2	4	1	2	4	1	5	1	5	2	4	4
39	Network	Collaboration and Partnership with Suppliers	1	5	4	4	4	1	4	4	1	5	1	5	4	4	4
40	Network	Access to tech trends- alliance/partner/networks	2	5	4	5	5	2	5	5	2	5	2	5	5	5	5

A DEPENDENCY BASED VIEW OF ORGANIZATIONAL SOCIAL CAPITAL (OSC)

: Understanding the Structural and Reputational aspects of OSC, and its effect on Performance

Saroj Kumar Pani

Doctoral Student, Indian Institute of Management Bangalore

Social capital literature has contributed immensely to organization and management science. From strategy perspective, it has enhanced our understanding on how an organization and its economic activities are dependent on the context of social structure in which it operates. There are mainly two perspectives on social capital - structural view and individualist view. Structural view emphasizes that social capital available to a firm is dependant on its external links and its structural position in a larger network such as industry (c.f. Adler and Kwon, 2002; Coleman, 1990). The individualist view (also termed as bonding view, collective view) opines that social capital is sourced from the internal ties, structure and capabilities of a collective such as firm (c.f. Adler and Kwon, 2002; Kilduff and Tsai, 2003). Nevertheless, most of the studies have treated social capital from structural perspective in inter-organizational and organizational context. This is despite the fact that social capital has long been accepted as a resultant asset sourced from internal attributes and capabilities of the organization, as highlighted by the individualist view. In this background this paper presents a fused theorization of social capital in a socio-economic network (SEN) while considering both the perspectives. The paper argues that social capital available for an organization termed as Organizational Social Capital (OSC), is the net of the social capital derived from external sources (termed as structural social capital -SSC) as well as from internal sources (termed as reputational capital -RC). Thereafter the paper presents a formal index to measure SSC and discusses the dynamics of RC.

The structural view of social capital, having its epistemological underpinning on social network analysis, assumes that social capital primarily has three benefits such as (a) information (b) influence, control and power (3) solidarity, abidance to norms and beliefs (Adler and Kwon, 2002). However, most of the studies on social capital focus on information flow and the benefit that accrues to the subject. In organizational and inter-organizational context very few studies have considered social capital as a function of power. Contemporary constructs of power in social capital study are either proxies for control over information or are measures of tie distance and tie numbers. This impediment has severely restrained the measurement of social capital as a real function of power, especially in a socio-economic network (SEN). In this context it is proposed here that in a SEN, power is a function of mutual dependency and that structural social capital can be quantitatively captured by mapping the structural position and magnitude of dependency. As a result, this write-up contributes to the structural perspective by introducing a dependency based power index called Nodal Power. The second part this piece contributes to the individualist perspective by studying the dynamics of social capital sourced internally. Considering organization as a collective, net social capital from internal sources is conceptualized as the resultant of the capability of each internal source and their relations within. This discussion assumes that the net social capital from internal sources has a reputational value for organization and theoretically shows the dynamics and effect of this reputational capital on organization over time.

Subsequent sections of this write-up are organized as follows. First it takes a quick look-back on the genesis of social capital and on defining organizational social capital. This definition will synthesize both structural and individualist perspectives. The next section delves into structural i.e. network perspective of social capital and introduces the concept of nodal power. This section uses elementary mathematical logic and graph theory to do so. The following section focuses on the dynamics of reputational capital. Finally propositions are developed followed by a brief discussion and conclusion.

SOCIAL CAPITAL AND ORGANIZATION: A BRIEF LOOK BACK

The concept of social capital is not new [i] and dates back to several centuries. However, the modern literature on social capital originated with the work of Hobbes (1651). In his book *Leviathan,* Hobbes argued that the individual's standard of living depends on his/her social and political resources. Weber (1922) furthered this argument and opined that individual's standard of living can improve with three types of resources: economic, political, and symbolic; where the latter two resources are subject to the quantity and quality of social interaction. The whole perspective of social capital is built on the idea that an actor and its activities including economic activities can't be proscribed of the context and social structure in which it operates. The action and its consequences affect and are affected by this social structure which creates an intangible asset at the disposal of the actor and can be mobilized to facilitate socio-economic gain. This intangible asset is termed as social capital in management, sociology, and economics literature. Conceptualization of social capital as an value enhancing system resource and a tradable asset stock (Black and Boal, 1994) has given rise to study it's affect on performance and success at individual, organizational and inter-organizational level in the field of organization and management science.

In the context of business firms, the positive effect of social capital on resource allocation, innovation & learning, it's effect on availability of human resource and attrition, as a facilitating function to strengthen relation with members of value chain (for an overview of the social capital literature in the context of business organizations, see the review paper by Adler and Kwon, 2002), to explain longevity and economic performance of firms including prospect of start-ups (Ingram and Baum,1997; Maurer and Ebers 2006), relation between investment in social capital and economic growth of firm (Westlund and Nilsson,2005; Wu and Leung, 2005); effect on pre-investment behavior (Sorheim, 2003) has been investigated, to name a few. Most of the researchers mentioned above, has explored the effect of social capital on variables those have direct impact on firm's existence, firm performance and profitability. Though describing details of the results is out of scope for this paper, the literature in social capital fairly establishes that a positive relationship exists between organizational social capital and organizational performance (Adler and Kwon, 2002).

In organizational context, conception of social capital is viewed from two perspectives. The structural perspective views social capital 'as the resource located in the external linkage of a focal factor' (ibid). Hence this view of social capital attributes more importance to the structure in which the organization operates and takes into account the number of ties, structure, and content of relation as base of empirical analysis. It considers organization as one single unit like an individual. It treats impact of social norms, rules, obligations, individual actions and their consequences from a holistic view (Kilduff & Tsai, 2003). The other view called individualist view (also named as collective view and bonding view) focus 'on collective actor's internal characteristics' (Adler and Kwon, 2002). According to this view social capital of a collectivity such as organization is not so much derived from its external ties but originates from its internal structure and cohesiveness (ibid).

From both the perspectives the epistemologically dominant feature of social capital analysis is analyzing the tie between two single units - individual or a collective- and the reciprocal relation between them. From this standpoint social capital involves expectation and reciprocal obligation between two units (Degenne and Forse, 1999: 116). This implies that it is not sufficient to know how many members one is attached to but it is also important to judge whether the individual is capable enough to meet the expectation of its network members and whether it will be able to continuously manage reciprocal action up to their satisfaction. So in case of an individual, its traits such as individual capability, efficiency, and personality definitely affect the quantity and quality of relations the individual establishes within its network. In case of organization, if we consider it as a single unit, meeting the reciprocal obligations requires the resources of organization, their efficient and effective utilization, supportive human resource, their enabling interaction, overall cohesiveness, and a supporting internal structure. In organization context the collection of these mentioned attributes can be conceived as the capability of organization. This statement is in agreement with Nahapiet and Ghoshal's (1998) assertion that organization as a collective is a cohesive entity and its capability is the net resultant of the internal resources available and the interaction among them. This internal capability of organization when successfully meets expectations increases organizational social capital. The discussion leads us to the following questions: where does an organization sources its social capital from – from the structure or from the relational content? If the nature of social capital changes according source then what exactly organizational social capital is?

DEFINING ORGANIZATIONAL SOCIAL CAPITAL (OSC)

Social capital is defined differently by different authors. The definition varies according to the importance given to structural aspect, relational aspect or content aspect of the actor's network. Defining organizational social capital in a socio-economic network such as an industry also has its own peculiarity because of two reasons. (1) As structural view suggests, organizations considered as a single unit can generate social capital by the virtue of their structural position in the network and (2) As individualist view suggests, an organization is a network by itself consisting individuals and groups, and hence the organization as a separate entity also enjoys social capital from its internal networks. Therefore, prior to defining organizational social capital we need to have a look back into the existing definitions and the context they were defined. While synthesizing social capital theory, Adler and Kwon (2002) list eighteen definitions of social capital, both from structural as well as individualist perspective. However, they favor the definition those are neutral to both the perspectives and opine that the two views are not mutually exclusive. This suggestion seems very appropriate in the context of organization as it can be observed that behavior of actors and their relationship inside organization affects social capital of the organization as a whole which in turn affects the network structure in which it operates (Maurer and Ebers, 2006). Thus, in organization context definition of social capital should acknowledge both the structural contribution and individual contribution to the resultant social capital of the organization.

Adhering to this principle and considering the fact that an is a separate entity having its own existence, this paper defines organizational social capital as, "The aggregate of intangible assets and resources available at the disposal of firm for facilitating socio-economic gain in its interaction with internal and external constituents of network. It is the aggregate of structural social capital (SSC) and reputational capital (RC). Structural social capital is sourced from the organization's position, relations and dependency structure in the embedded network where as Reputational social capital (or simply Reputational Capital) results from the relation, action and shared belief of the collectiveness that is internal to the organization." $\Rightarrow$ OSC = f (SSC, RC)

This definition synthesizes both structural and individualist perspective and acknowledges the mutual reciprocity principle. The definition also adheres to the structural, relational and cognitive dimensions of social capital (Nahpiet and Ghoshal, 1998) and simultaneously considers social capital as a tradable asset stock (Black and Boal, 1994).The definition of structural social capital is synonymous with Uphoof's (2000) definition where it is defined as 'a relative objective and externally observable social structure such as networks, associations and institutions they embody'. Reputational capital is subjective and is based on Nahpiet and Ghoshal's (1998) cognitive and relational aspects. It is the net result of interaction between organization capabilities, norms, behavior, shared values which build organization's reputation over time. Because organization is itself a network this definition assumes that the net contribution of the mentioned internal capital results in reputational capital.

MEASURING STRUCTURAL SOCIAL CAPITAL (SSC) WITH NODAL POWER

SSC caters to the structural perspective of social capital which depends on social network analysis as an epistemological tool. The fundamental logic of this perspective is that an organization, its action and resultant consequence is embedded in the structure and the context in which it operates. Context encompasses the whole networked economic system which includes the organization's competitors, suppliers, consumers and all those who affect and are affected by it. In a networked economic system each individual participant seeks an exchange with others. Hence a network is based on mutual dependence and division of work. Such type of network is stable but not static because relationships often go through renovation, change, and disruption. These relationships are complementary in nature and are specific to inter-firm dependence (Johanson and Mattsson, 1987). Power of a participant in such an economic system is naturally derived from the variation in mutual dependence. Though mutual dependence is the main source of relational power, contemporary network analysis lacks to inculcate dependency based power perspective while analyzing the effect of network structure. Primarily contemporary network analysis subscribe to centrality based indexes, which conceive power as a function of importance of a node in the network and measures the same as the number of connections to a node, the distance of the node from alters[ii] or their path of connection. Hence, power in these indexes is based on absence or presence of links but based neither on the quality of links nor on mutual dependence. Moreover, the strength of relation between a node and alter is calculated by its direct or indirect connectedness i.e. either an alter is directly attached to the node or has an indirect path with other alters in between. In some cases, strength is calculated by frequency of contact which is by any means a qualitative judgment (Degenne and Forse, 1999). This indicates that in contemporary network analysis, primary importance is given to distance and accessibility of a node to alters. Though such treatment is very effective in few contexts, the missing consideration of need based mutual dependency and direct economic reciprocity limits our understanding of economic networks such as industrial networks and value nets. Such networks, whose primary action entails economic transactions, are termed as socio-economic network (SEN) in this paper.

The next section constructs Nodal Power as a function of mutual dependency. It argues that the network effect on organization which is same as structural social capital (SSC) can be quantitatively captured based on the structural position, relations and dependency an organization establishes with other members in the network. In the context of SEN, this paper quantifies the power index based on economic dependency, which can be objectively measured in value terms. However the power index can also be used in pure social networks if social dependency can be quantified.

Defining Nodal Power in a Socio-economic Network (SEN)

The concept of nodal power is based on the idea of mutual dependency of actors in an economic network. A socio-economic network is defined as a relationship between a node and more than one alters where at least one alter enjoys a one-to-one relationship with the node.

Definition 1 (Socio-Economic Network, SEN) : Let $X = \{x_1, x_2, \ldots x_n\}$ represent a finite node set of cardinality n, and $R = \{r_1, r_2, \ldots r_k\}$ represent a finite set of relationships of cardinality k, such that $X, R \neq \phi$ and $\forall x_n \in X, \exists r_k \in R$

Then, a socio economic network N: = (X, R) such that

    (i) X = $\{x_1, x_2, \ldots x_n\}$

    (ii) R = $\{r_1, r_2, \ldots r_k\}$ elements of the Cartesian product $X \times X = \{(x,y)/x \in X, y \in X\}$ and

    (iii) $k \leq n(n-1)/2$.

Note: r_k is a bidirectional relationship and for each one-to-one bidirectional relationship there exists two unidirectional relationships. The maximum number of unidirectional relationships possible in SEN is $K_{max} = n(n-1)$.

By definition a SEN is a set of nodes and their relationships. These nodes are quasi-independent units such as individual or organization those either as individuals or as collective[iii] constitute a socio-economic system such as SEN.

Each one-to-one relationship in SEN is an arrangement for mutual need satisfaction, thus SEN can be considered as a system of mutual need satisfaction. The need may be economic, social, or personal. Higher the need, higher the dependency, stronger is the desire to build relationship with someone. In a need based relation the strength of relationship depends on the magnitude of need that one satisfies or seeks to satisfy from the other. It includes present need(s) and/or anticipated need(s). The needs may not be mutually exclusive but can be valued independently. So in a one-to-one relationship node's strength is negatively related to the need it satisfies from alter and positively related to the alters' need that it satisfies. The resultant magnitude determines the power; the node has in its disposal. This adheres to Emerson's (1962) view that "Dependency in a socio-economic relation is the reverse of power" and subsequently provided the main urge in finding out the factors that cause variance in dependency and power in organizational context. This treatment of power is inherently different than the earlier 'number of relation' or 'connectedness' based measures as it consider the relative strength of each node.

Definition 2 (Nodal Power) In a SEN, the 'Nodal Power' P_i for any node 'i' is defined as the net power derived by the node from the variance of dependency in a given relationship. For N= (X, D), the net nodal power P_i for any node i is defined as

$$P_i = \sum_{j=1}^{k} (d_{ji} - d_{ij}) \;\; ; \text{ such that } -1 \leq (d_{ji} - d_{ij}) \leq 1 \text{ and } k \leq |R|$$

As mentioned, d_{ij} is dependence of node i on alter j and d_{ji} is dependence of alter j on node i. Both d_{ij} and d_{ji} are termed as *dependency factors. (d_{ij}-d_{ji})* is called the *Marginal Power Contribution* for P_i from the one-to-one relation between i and j.

In this definition each unidirectional relationship with the node represents one unit of dependency having minimum value 0 and maximum value 1. That means, if i is fully dependant on j and no one else for a specific unique need, then dependency of i on j, $d_{ij} = 1$ and if j is not at all dependant on i then $d_{ji} = 0$. However in a SEN, for all practical purpose, it is assumed that each unidirectional dependency is non-zero. Note that when both d_{ji} and d_{ij} are positive and equal it represents symmetric relation and when $d_{ji} \neq d_{ij}$ the relation becomes asymmetric. Hence this formula is applicable to both symmetric and asymmetric networks.

Case 1: Imperfect substitutes having equal value: In N (X,R), iff $\exists$ $S_i \subset X$, $C_j \subset X$ such that

    i) $S_i = \{s_1, s_2, \ldots s_i\}$ and $C_j = \{c_1, c_2, \ldots c_j\}$

    ii)   One-to-one relationship set $R_{ij} = \{r_1, r_2, \ldots r_k\}$ elements of the Cartesian product $S_i \times C_j = \{(x,y)/x \in S_i, y \in C_j\}$ and $r_1 = r_2 = \ldots = r_k$

    iii) $\forall r_k \in R_k \, \exists! \, d_m \in D$

Then for $s_i \in S_i$ and $c_j \in C_j$; the relationships $r_k \in R_{ij}$ are imperfectly substitute, as each relationship fulfills/ has potential to fulfill the same need. Hence, $d_{ji} = 1/|S_i|$; $d_{ij} = 1/|C_j|$

Case 2: Imperfect substitutes having unequal value: In N (X,R), iff $\exists$ $S_i \subset X$, $C_j \subset X$ such that

    (i) $S_i = \{s_1, s_2, \ldots s_i\}$ and $C_j = \{c_1, c_2, \ldots c_j\}$

    (ii) One-to-one relationship set $R_{ij} = \{r_1, r_2, \ldots r_k\}$ elements of the Cartesian product $S_i \times C_j = \{(x,y)/x \in S_i, y \in C_j\}$ and $r_1 = r_2 = \ldots = r_n$

    (iii) $\forall r_k \in R_k \, \exists! \, d_m \in D$

And there exists a Value set $V_{ij} = \{v_1, v_2, \ldots v_z\}$ such that $\forall \, r_n \in R_{ij}$, $d_m \in D$ $\exists! \, V_z \in V_{ij}$ then, $d_{ji} = V_{ij}/V_i$; $d_{ij} = V_{ij}/V_j$

d_{ji} = the value of utility provided by j / total value of the unique utility for i
   = value of i's dependence on j / i's total value of dependence
d_{ij} = value of *i*'s dependence on j / *j*'s total value of dependence

$$\text{then } P_i = \sum_{j=1}^{k} \sum_{1}^{m} (d_{ji} - d_{ij})$$

; such that $-1 \leq (d_{ji} - d_{ij}) \leq 1$ for each dependency of 1 to m derived from each relation of 1 to k

Case 4: Critical Complements: In N(X, R), $r_k \in R$ is called a critical relation, iff $\exists \, d_m \in D$ such that for the $d_m \in D \, \exists! \, r_k \in R$

Iff a need is divisible and is a function of multiple dependencies then a critical complement is defined as the colligating dependency of a node on an alter such that all other relations do not satisfy the need if the colligating dependency is not satisfied. Thus critical complement has a dependency factor of one irrespective of the monetary value of the dependency and remains critical if and only if a single one-to-one relation satisfies that dependency i.e. no imperfect substitutes available.

Measures of Nodal Efficiency:

Definition 3: (Average Nodal Power). The average nodal power is defined as the nodal power per relation per dependency and is denoted as P_{avg}

$$P_{avg\,i} = \left[\sum_{j=1}^{k} \left\{ \sum_{1}^{m} (d_{ji} - d_{ij}) \right\} / m \right] / k$$

such that $-1 \leq (P_{avg\,i}) \leq 1$;

where *m* is the number of utility per relation and *k* is the number of one-to-one relation.

Average nodal power signifies the efficiency of relationship i.e. The power derived from each relationship and power derived from each utility. In a dynamic situation it reflects power derived from each transaction that in turn affects the future of the relationship. This index has critical implications as there is a natural limitation for a node to have relationships. The number of direct relationships a node can maintain simultaneously is a function of its capability. In this scenario the index proves to be beneficial as it helps in establishing the optimal number of relations for a node and the trade-off between number of relations and *marginal power contribution*.

Definition 4: (Space of operation). In N (X,R), iff $\exists$ $S_i \subset X$, $C_j \subset X$ such that

(i) $S_i = \{s_1, s_2, \ldots s_i\}$ and $C_j = \{c_1, c_2, \ldots c_j\}$

(ii) $s_{1\,to\,i} \in S_i$ and $c_{1\,to\,j} \in C_J$ are homogenous but $S_i \cap C_j = 0$

(iii) E_i is the set of "established" one-to-one relationship set and $e_i \in E_i$ elements of the Cartesian product $S_i \times C_j = \{(x,y)/x \in S_i, y \in C_j\}$

(iv) $E_i \subset R_{ij}$ and $|E_i| \leq j(j+1)/2$

Then the 'Space of Operation' SO: $= 1 - \left[2E_i / j(j+1)\right]$ such that $0 < SO < 1$

Property of Nodal Power (P_i)

Here are briefly described the operational properties of nodal power as an index. Each property described hereafter corresponds to at least one characteristic of various indexes[iv] used in the contemporary network analysis.

(1) P_i is directly proportional to the number of relations if and only if for each one-to-one relation the marginal power contribution is positive. (This takes care of the earlier shortcoming of network analysis where power was a function of number of relations but not the nature of relation. P_i adheres to the principle of Network centrality)

(2) P_i is inversely proportional to the number of imperfect substitutes available for alter *j*.(This considers the structural accessibility of alters while determining nodal power)

(3) P_i is directly proportional to the alter's dependency on a second alter if and only if the second alter have high dependency on the node. (It adheres to the principle of complementary relationship and the principle of transitivity)

(4)   If there exists more than one utility for a relationship between a node and an alter then P_i is directly proportional to the number of utilities it provides. (It includes the possibility of multiple value addition and adheres to the principle of multiplexity)

The definition of Nodal Power considers only direct relationships. Researchers have argued that it is essential to consider effect of both direct and indirect relations of a node because the action of a node and consequences there of is considered to be embedded in the whole network, which goes beyond direct relations. Careful observation of the concept of nodal power will reveal that the 'net nodal power' captures the trickle down effect of entire network on node such as effect of indirect relations. The reason as follows *One* It can be observed that total utility[v] of an alter is divisible[vi] . Hence each relationship it establishes with others caters to a part(s) of that utility. Thus the part of utility an alter derives from node is also dependant on the utility it derives from all other alters except the node. Thus the power of node not only depends on its relationship with the alter but also on the alter's relationship with all other's in the network. *Two* According to the principle of substitutability the alter can substitute the node provided substitutes available, thus can reduce its power. If many nodes are available for the alter offering the same utility and if the alter can establish relationship with all of them, then the power derived by a single node decreases proportional to the established relationship with other nodes offering same utility. Thus the direct relationships of a node is affected by alter's direct relationships with all other alters. Hence the node's indirect relationships are taken care of in the dependency-based power structure. In other words an alter's nodal power is affected by it's direct relationships, hence the nodal power a node derived from its relationship with that alter is also affected by alter's other relationships and this takes care of nodes indirect relationships[vii]. For a more detailed explanation with an example refer *Appendix II*. For a brief comparison of nodal power with other transformations (i.e. how treatment of social capital with nodal power is similar or different from Coleman's and Burt's treatment of social capital) refer *Appendix III*.

DYNAMICS OF REPUTATIONAL CAPITAL: THE INDIVIDUALIST PERSPECTIVE

The individualist perspective considers an organization as a single collective. Being a network by itself, an organization has its own capability which is derived from its internal resources and the people involved. So an organization in this sense is similar to an individual, who is not only known by his/her external relations but also by his/her personality, reputation and other personal traits, which more often than not is internal (which affect his/her capability of establishing and sustaining relationships). In the context of organization, this paper argues that the intangible capital sourced from the internal sources of organization has a reputational value which complements the structural social capital. As described earlier, this reputational capital is a function of firm capability and is path dependant. Researchers have shown that reputation not only affects network formation but also triggers structural change (c.f. Sherwood, 2006; Stuart, 1998).

Social capital derived from internal sources (in this case the reputational capital) has been treated by researchers as simple aggregation of individual capitals. For example, Pennings, Lee & Witteloostuijn (1998); Tsai and Ghosal (1998) have measured entrepreneurial firm's social capital as the aggregate of social capital of individual firm members. Maurer and Ebers (2006) have opted for the same when studying dynamics of social capital for start-up biotechnology firms in Germany. It is indeed perfect to identify an organization with entrepreneurs in the very conception stage of firm but as firm grows its takes its own identity and creates its own reputation which is different from the individuals involved[viii] (even though not mutually exclusive). It shows that the treatment by researchers fails to appreciate the separate identity of a firm in subsequent periods when the organization grows beyond individual identities. Hence with time the reputational capital of an organization, though depends on individuals, is not an additive function of each individual's reputational capital. With passing of time the organization creates its own value, its own identity and own structural position in the network. Therefore in this paper organization is considered as an ongoing concern which is separate from individuals or sum of them. Resultantly internal sourced social capital (reputational capital) is considered to have its own existence, dynamics, and effect. It is already established that internal sourced social capital not only has positive impact but also negative impact on firm performance depending upon changing environment, internal structure, capability, and in-firm, out-firm relations (Edelman, Bresnen, Newell, Scarbrough & Swan, 2004; Maurer and Ebers, 2006; Gargiulo and Benassi,2000). As internal sourced social capital affects performance which in turn affects reputation, we can reason that decrease in internal sourced social capital decreases reputation and vice-versa. Because reputational capital is path dependant and is based on capability, it changes with time and varies with firm's internal capability.

Capability is derived from resources at the disposal of an organization. Organization's reputational capital directly depends on its capability. In inception stage organization capability depends on the number of persons involved with the organization and their capabilities. It also depends on the numbers of relations the individuals have in and out of the organization. This is in agreement with the view that for a start up reputational capital is the addition of entrepreneurs' individual capital hence more individuals more will be reputational capital and from more diverse background they are, more is the reputational capital (Maurer and Ebers, 2006, Burt, 2000). We also know increase or decrease in social capital depends on the action of related persons and nature of relations. Combining these perspectives we can study the rate of change of reputational capital for a firm for given number of relations and nature/type of action. The paper considers three types of action i.e. positive action, negative action and inaction or absence of action. From organization's perspective any inaction is assumed to have no value addition, thus considered as inactive form of negative action. The following section studies the dynamics of reputational capital for negative action/inaction (i.e. rate of change with respect to time). The result is also applicable for positive action and will help in measuring reputational capital at a given time for a given capability. The next section measures the effort taken to replenish the lost reputational capital created by a negative action.

Rate of Change of Reputational Capital

Preceding arguments consider reputational capital as a collective good which is particularly true in case of internal sourced social capital which is nonrivalrous (Adler and Kwon, 2002). As reputational capital is directly proportional to the number of individuals in an organization (in the inception stage) and net value it gains there of, we can assume that the change in reputational capital (i.e. increase or decrease) is proportional to the number of individuals (or resources) internal to the organization. Let $S(t)$ be the total unit of social capital present with the organization at time t. Note that $S(t)$ is not the simple addition of numbers of individuals attached but it is the whole total of intangible asset available at firm's disposal. We also know that if expectation of individuals attached to the organization (internal stakeholders) doesn't match with performance of organization then reputational capital decreases (c.f. Sherwood, 2006). This may happen because of firm's inaction or negative action. Lets denote the unit of social capital decrease per unit time as ds/dt because unit of social capital decay is proportional to $S(t)$. The change in t is always positive and it represents passing of time, changing circumstances, or environmental change.

Clearly $\dfrac{-ds}{dt} \propto s$ {Negative symbol denotes decrease and $S(t)$ is simply denoted by S}

$$\Rightarrow \dfrac{-ds}{dt} = ks \quad \text{where k>0} \tag{1}$$

k is the *decay constant* for a specific action or inaction. It signifies the gravity or value of a specific inaction or action. Here a negative sign signifies inaction or negative action.

The above equation reflects Adler and Kwon (2002) view of social capital, where they explain the nature of social capital and comment, "Social capital needs maintenance. Social bonds have to be periodically renewed and reconfirmed or else they lose efficacy. Like human capital but unlike physical capital, social capital doesn't have a predictable rate of depreciation for two reasons, *First*, it depreciates with non-use and abuse but not with use; *Second,* while social capital some time is rendered obsolete by contextual changes (Refer Sandefur and Laumann,1988 for examples), the rate at which this happens is typically unpredictable"

$$\Rightarrow \dfrac{ds}{s} = \dfrac{-k}{dt}$$ integrating we get log S = -kt + log I   where I is a constant and defined below.

Thus $S = I\,e^{-kt} \Rightarrow$ At t=0, S=I   where I = initial social capital or social capital at time of inception of organization and this is equal to the net aggregate of individual social capitals of entrepreneurs.

By treating an organization a different entity than its founders we can safely assume that an organization at its inception (time t_0) doesn't have any social capital of its own. The social capital it uses is sum of founder's social capital (Pennings et al,1998; Tsai and Ghosal, 1998; Maurer and Ebers, 2006). This situation is reflected in the above equation. Let S_0 be the sum of promoters' social capital at time t_0.

Thus $S_0 = I \Rightarrow S = S_0\,e^{-kt}$ -------- (2a) where $1 \leq k \leq \infty$ for negative action and inaction and $-1 \geq k \geq -\infty$ for positive action[ix].

Hence for positive actions equation (2) becomes, $S = S_0\,e^{+kt}$ $\hspace{2em}$ (2b) which signifies increase in social capital. Thus we get: the change in social capital at any time t_n is the initial social capital at time t_0 exponentially multiplied with elapsed time and *decay constant* k which captures the gravity of the situation/negative action, which is specific to a situation. The more the value of k, more is the seriousness of negative action.

So Reputational Capital at time $t_1 = S_1 = S_0\,e^{\pm kt} \Rightarrow RC = S_t = S_{t-1}\,e^{\pm kt}$ $\hspace{1em}$ (3)

Where negative sign (-k) signifies inaction or negative action and positive sign (+k) signify positive action or expectation match at time t_0.

This equation provides insight to a few important properties of social capital and reputational capital. It says social capital is not only the sum of individual social capitals in an organization but also it is a function of how the firm manages its relations. It is a function of firm's positive or negative actions. Implicitly it points towards firm's capability to satisfy stakeholder's expectations. It is also dependant on time thus path dependant. Since, t will always increases, to maintain the same level of reputational capital an organization has to do positive actions, i.e. to increase capability and matching the expectations in a changing environment. From, equation (1) it can be observed , as t increases with no change in $-k$ value (inaction) the net social capital decreases. Only with positive action, i.e. $+k$ value, the net social capital increases. It subscribes to Maurer and Ebers (2006) finding that, with change in environment one has to change the capability and the nature of relations to have positive impact of social capital on firm performance. The equation also shows that inaction is paid by heavy price as reputational capital decreases exponentially. It also shows if one 'matches the expectation then reputational capital increases exponentially (For example It can explain word-of-mouth phenomena).Relating such results with firm performance we can infer that, firm performance will increase when increased expectation is matched by increased capability, thus having a $+k$ value. If expectation increases without increase in capability then the equation takes $-k$ value, means decreasing performance. However, one of the interesting findings is: if capability increases without increase in expectation, then performance is unaffected. For example a capacity increase with no additional business (means no new relation/ no additional demand from existing relations) doesn't increase the revenue of a firm. The equation also says that each positive and negative action, inaction has its effect on the reputational capital of the firm.

Replenishment of Lost Reputational Capital

Suppose for inaction or a negative action some amount of reputational capital is lost. Let's assume the period of inaction/negative action started at time t_{-1} and reputational capital was lost according up to time t_0. Equation (1) captures the lost reputational capital. In other words we can say that some amount of reputational/social capital was utilized for that specific action. This equation also reflects the properties of social capital where it is considered as 'tradable asset stock' and 'substitutability across time[x]. Let us name the social capital lost or amount of social capital used in the above-described scenario as '*social capital debt* R'. Thus R_0 is the social capital debt at time t_0.

Let R(t) = Unit of existing capital debt at time t . Now onwards it will be denoted as R. Let t is the time taken by an alter to extract information from a node who is affected by inaction or negative action. In other words t is the rate of information dissemination in a social network. For simplicity let's assume that the information dissemination is liner (i.e. It takes same time to transfer from one affected alter to other alters).

Let W(t)= Amount of inaction or negative action (for which social capital was lost) up to time t. Now onwards it will be denoted as W. In an economic system this amount may be valued in monetary terms i.e. loss in value for alter.

Let $S_N(t)$= Social capital needed (Effort/action needed which will result in positive reputational capital) to replenish the lost social capital leading to regain the original position. For example if a firm lost some sales or lost goodwill because of a negative action, that is the value of social capital they lost (i.e. W) and S_N is the value/money/effort they need to come to the initial position. From now on it is denoted by S.

So in a time interval Δt, say from t to t+Δt, an organization's amount of inaction/negative action results in Δw such that an amount of Δs was needed to replenish it. Because amount of social capital debt is directly proportional to amount of inaction (w∝r), the net change in Δr, in time Δt can be written as

$$\Delta r = k\Delta w - \Delta s \tag{4}$$

as loss of social capital is simultaneously replenished by social capital created by positive action in the specified time length. Here k is the *decay constant*.

Dividing by Δt to get the rate of change and obtaining the value as $\Delta t \to 0$ we get

$$\frac{dr}{dt} = k\frac{dw}{dt} - \frac{ds}{dt} \qquad \Rightarrow \frac{dr}{dt} = kP(t) - \frac{ds}{dt} \tag{5}$$

Where $P(t) = \dfrac{dw}{dt}$ = negative work done .

It is the unit loss of reputational capital for change in unit time. This is a function of capability of the firm and the rate at which information disseminates among alters in a given network. The rate at which reputational capital/positive action is needed is proportional to the deficiency/lost social capital. In other words social capital needed is directly proportional to amount of capital debt.

$$\Rightarrow \frac{ds}{dt} = c\,r(t) \quad \text{------(6)}$$

where c is called *capability constant* specific to a firm. It is the capability or power of the firm that affects the rate of replenishment. High capability will result in swift and effective corrective action. Thus c is directly proportional to the rate of replenishment. Note: In a structural analysis, nodal power can be taken as a proxy for c.

Combining equation (5) and (6) we get

$$\frac{dr}{dt} + c\,r = kP \tag{7}$$

Equation (7) is a first order liner differential equation and can be solved to

$$r\,e^{ct} = \int kP\,e^{ct}\,dt + C_1 \tag{8}$$

If r_0 is the amount of reputational capital existing at time t_0 then $C_1 = r_0$

$$\Rightarrow r(t) = r_0 e^{-ct} + k\,e^{-ct} \int P(t)\,e^{ct}\,dt \Rightarrow r(t) = r_0 e^{-ct} + k \int P(t)\,dt \tag{9}$$

The above equation can be used to determine r(t) for different function of p(t) where t is the time period as defined above. The simplest case will be, if P(t)≡0, i.e. no negative work done at time t_0 (remember negative work started at t_{-1} and stopped at t_0)

Then, $r(t) = r_0 e^{-ct}$ $\tag{10}$

This shows the unit of reputational debt at time *t* is the product of previous reputational debt and exponential of the product of capability constant and elapsed time. As *t* will always be positive, the equation means more the time taken to initiate corrective actions more is the reputational debt. More the capability of firm less is the prospect of reputational debt. The equation also shows that reputational debt should be replenished exponentially after the negative action is stopped. For any bad action followed by a time of inaction, the price will be paid exponentially which depends on value of the negative action and the length of time of inaction[xi] i.e. the time period at which no corrective measures were taken following negative action. This equation shows that every negative action is exponentially punished in a network where free flow of information is possible (efficient market) with the condition that negative action is identifiable and containable.

ORGANIZATIONAL SOCIAL CAPITAL (OSC) AND FIRM PERFORMANCE

This section follows the discussion in preceding sections and provides a few propositions to enumerate the effect of structural social capital (measured as nodal power) and reputational capital on firm performance.

Profit, as we know, is a function of both value creation and value appropriation. In a network relationship variance in dependency for a single utility should reflect the valuation of that particular utility by concerned organizations. This valuation of utility is directly proportional to the post-processed value of that utility (firm creates value by processing input into output) and is also proportional to the rareness of fulfilling the utility from other network relations. Thus value creation is a function of variance in dependency. Appropriation of value is a function of creation of value, position & indispensability of the source & user of utility and organization's control over the network. Since Nodal Power as a measure of structural social capital considers these variables it captures the potential of an organization to appropriate value. Based on this link the under mentioned propositions can be made.

P1a: No profitable business organization exists with net negative Nodal Power.

P1b: Nodal Power is directly proportional to the profit potential of a firm.

The existing power of node makes it attractive for alters to establish a relationship with the node (c.f. Stuart, 1998). But in a one-to-one relation a low dependant node will be less vulnerable to alters expectancy and vice-versa. It results in a positive variance of dependency for the node. Combining these to it can reasoned

P2: In any one-to-one alliance/relationship bargaining power will be directly proportional to the Nodal Power.

As discussed, a node in socio-economic network has finite capability to establish and maintain relations. Thus beyond that limit any new relation will have a negative effect to the aggregate gain from relations. This happens because constraint in capability of the node makes it vulnerable to the incremental reciprocal expectation of alters. Hence constraint in capability will result in a negative 'marginal power contribution'. Conversely an optimum selection of number of relations those contribute to positive marginal power will increase the net nodal power with less vulnerability to alter's expectation. Thus

P3a: There exists an inverse 'U' relationship between nodal power and number of direct relations.

P3b: Profitability will be directly proportional to average nodal power

P3c: The node with highest number of connections and highest average nodal power will appropriate most value in a network.

In growth phase of an industry, firms try many business arrangements. However, in this stage a relative stable industry structure is still in the phase of development. This is because of continues technological and market innovations and absence of standards. The established relationships are low in this phase because of unproven capability of individual firms in various segments of value chain. Many firms enter and exit in this phase making it a situation of continues flux. As a result the number of established relations is only a fraction of potential relations. Thus

P4a: In the growth phase of industry high space of operation will be available contributing to increase in nodal power of existing competitors. In that case profit potential will be more a function of industry growth than structural social capital.

P4b: In a mature industry low space of operation will be available and there won't be any significant variation in profit potential among firms after controlling for firm size.

For any node (e.g. organization) fulfillment of alter's dependency depends on its capability. Similarly alter's dependency on a node is a function of alter's expectation. Organizational Social Capital will be positively affected if capability of node matches with expectation of alters. If both capability and expectation increases and have a match then there will be net increase in social capital. This is true for both external as well as internal-stake holders. Thus

P5a: Increase in capability matched with increased expectation increases both structural social capital and reputational capital.

P5b: Low capability with high number of relations decreases structural social capital. Low capability with high expectation from internal stakeholders decreases reputational capital.

P5c: Low expectation/number of relations with high capability doesn't change the level of reputational or structural social capital.

Business environment for an organization changes because of changing expectation of stakeholders such as consumers. Changing expectation might be triggered by circumstances such as technological breakthrough, changing need set, competition. In such a case the firm needs to take action to adapt to that situation. As shown in equation (2a) and (9) social capital decreases if action is not taken. Thus

P6a: Any inaction in a changing environment decreases organizational social capital. Negative action increases the rate of decrease of organizational social capital in the absence of any corrective positive action.

Considering shareholders as internal stakeholders we can infer that if their expectation is not matched by organization then they have higher incentive to detach themselves from the organization and if the reverse is true then many will try to be internal stakeholders. Assuming an efficient share market, the change in reputational capital will also be reflected on performance of firm's shares. Combining this with proposition 5b and 5c we can reason.

P6b: If environment is stable then reputational capital doesn't have an effect on firm's share prices but in unstable environment high reputational capital effects share prices positively and low reputational capital affects share prices negatively.

As discussed above, the nodal power changes with the conduct of network members. In the presence of 'co-density', where two parties indulge in a thick alliance like behavior facilitating free flow of information and willingly help and warn each other in case of contingencies (Baker and Faulkner, 2002), the conduct of individual actors affect other members of the network by either changing the substitutability power or space of operation. In this case

P7a: A co-density in same segment of value chain increases the nodal power of a node in the specific value segment but reduces the nodal power of nodes operating in the colligating value segment. (For example a co-density of suppliers will increase supplier's nodal power but will decrease producer's nodal power).

P7b: A co-density across value segment will increase the nodal power of all those who are involved in co-density but will decrease the nodal power of competitors those are not involved in co-density.

DISCUSSION AND CONCLUSION

The above discussion has explored the possibility of synthesizing both structural and individualist perspective while defining organizational social capital in a socio-economic network (SEN). It is suggested that organizational social capital is a function of social capital sourced from its structural position in the network as well as the net intangible asset an organization gets from the internal resources. Both internal-sourced intangible assets and external-sourced intangible assets and their interaction determine the net social capital of an organization. It is argued that in a socio-economic network (SEN), 'connectedness' based calculations of structural social capital do not explain the power of network members explicitly. To overcome this shortcoming the concept of 'Nodal Power' is introduced, which is based on mutual dependency of relations and it is argued that Nodal Power determines the relative power position and a node's potential for value appropriation in a SEN. It is conceptualized that internal-sourced social capital has reputational value for an organization, and the dynamics of reputational capital for negative actions, inactions, and positive actions are shown. It proves that in an efficient market any negative action or inaction is paid for exponentially.

Potential Research Opportunities

Theoretical research need: Though this discussion introduced the concept of nodal power which reflects dependency based power structure in a network, it is yet to be examined as to what extent nodal power captures the insight provided by 'connectedness' based analysis. This needs studying the effect of nodal power vis-à-vis other contemporary indexes. Such analysis is important to prove that both Burt's view and Coleman's view are special cases of nodal power based formulation. The explanation provided in Appendix II and III which compares Nodal Power with Burt's transformation (i.e. Z transformation) is a first step. However it is highly inadequate as it is based on a single example of closure type network. Hence, the effectiveness of the proposed index is yet to be studied for networks having 'structural holes'. Theoretical exploration is also needed to substantially validate the argument that 'nodal power based on direct relations takes into account all other indirect relations that affects the node'.

Empirical research need: Though the propositions indicates that conduct of nodes in a SEN affect network structure and firm performance, empirical validation is needed to prove them. It is still not clear how nodal power captures the dynamics of competition between rival networks and the winning probability of one network over the other in the same competitive space, even if both networks have net positive nodal power. The dynamics of reputational capital is another area of research to understand how the rate of flow of information affects the "t" value and what the optimal time length is in a specific network to assign a "t" value. The other shortcoming is the lack of objective quantification of organizational capability except that of number of human resources. One of the ways to measure the mentioned capability is using ordinal scale. However it is still subjective and problematic while comparing two organizations. Though Nodal power provides insight about organizational social capital, greater understanding will be achieved by demystifying the 'capability' of a collective i.e. organization, in network context.

To study network dynamics in a longitudinal setting over time, it is important to study the structure and effect of existing relationships. It is so, because these developments facilitate making and changing of future relationships over time. This piece contributes to the first stage of this development by throwing light on power structure in an existing network and the value appropriated by members by virtue of their relative power position and conduct. It also contributes to organizational social capital literature by providing insight into the nature and dynamics of reputational capital of an organization.

REFERENCES:

1. Adler, P. S., & Kwon, S. W. 2002. Social capital: Prospects for a new concept. *The Academy of Management review*, 27(1): 17-40.
2. Baker, W. E., & Faulkner, R. R. 2002. Interorganizational Networks. *The Blackwell companion to organizations. Oxford: Blackwell Publishers Ltd.*
3. Black, J. A., & Boal, K. B. 1994. Strategic Resources: Traits, Configurations and Paths to Sustainable Competitive Advantage. *Strategic Management Journal*, 15: 131-148.
4. Burt, R. S. 2000. The network structure of social capital. *Research in Organizational Behavior*, 22(2): 345-423.
5. Coleman, J. S. 1990. *Foundations of Social Theory*: Harvard University Press.
6. Degenne, A., Forsé, M., & Borges, A. 1999. *Introducing Social Networks*: Sage Publications Inc.
7. Edelman, L. F., Bresnen, M., Newell, S., Scarbrough, H., & Swan, J. 2004. The Benefits and Pitfalls of Social Capital: Empirical Evidence from Two Organizations in the United Kingdom. *British Journal of Management*, 15(s 1): 59-69.
8. Emerson, R. M. 1962. Power-Dependence Relations. *American Sociological Review*, 27(1): 31-41.
9. Gargiulo, M., & Benassi, M. 2000. Trapped in Your Own Net? Network Cohesion, Structural Holes, and the Adaptation of Social Capital. *Organization Science*, 11(2): 183-196.Gibbs, J. P. 1990. Foundations of Social Theory (Book Review), *Social Forces* .69(2):625-633

10. Hobbes, T. 1651. *The Leviathan* (1962 ed.). New York: COLLIER.

11. Ingram, P., & Baum, J. A. C. 1997. Chain Affiliation and the Failure of Manhattan Hotels, 1898-1980. *Administrative Science Quarterly*, 42(1).

12. Johnson, J., & Mattsson, L. G. 1987. Interorganizational Relations in Industrial Systems: A Network Approach Compared with the Transaction-cost Approach. *International Studies of Management & Organization*, 17(1):34-48

13. Kilduff, M., & Tsai, W. 2003. *Social networks and organizations*: SAGE Thousand Oaks, Calif.

14. Maurer, I., & Ebers, M. 2006. Dynamics of Social Capital and Their Performance Implications: Lessons from Biotechnology Start-ups. *Administrative Science Quarterly*, 51:262-292.

15. Nahapiet, J., & Ghoshal, S. 1998. Social Capital, Intellectual Capital, and the Organizational Advantage. *The Academy of Management Review*, 23(2): 242-266.

16. Pennings, J. M., Lee, K., & van Witteloostuijn, A. 1998. Human Capital, Social Capital, and Firm Dissolution. *The Academy of Management Journal*, 41(4): 425-440.

17. Sandefur,R.L.,& Laumann,E.O.1998.A paradigm for social capital. *Rationality and Society,* 10:481-501

18. Sorheim, R. 2003. The pre-investment behaviour of business angels: a social capital approach». *Venture Capital*, 5: 337-364.

19. Sherwood, A. L. 2006. An empirical examination of the relationship between alliance trust,reputation and performance. York University.

20. Stuart, T. E. 1998. Network Positions and Propensities to Collaborate: An Investigation of Strategic Alliance Formation in a High-Technology Industry. *Administrative Science Quarterly*, 43(3): 668-698.

21. Tsai, W., & Ghoshal, S. 1998. Social Capital and Value Creation: The Role of Intrafirm Networks. *The Academy of Management Journal*, 41(4): 464-476.

22. Uphoff, N. 2000. Understanding Social Capital: Learning from the Analysis and Experience of Participation. *Social Capital: A Multifaceted Perspective*: 215-252.

23. Wasserman, S., & Faust, K. 1994. *Social Network Analysis: methods and applications*: Cambridge University Press.

24. Weber, M. 1922.1968. Economy and Society

25. Westlund, H., & Nilsson, E. 2005. Measuring enterprises' investments in social capital: a pilot study. *Regional Studies*, 39(8): 1079-1094.

26. Wu, W., & Leung, A. 2005. Does a Micro-Macro Link Exist Between Managerial Value of Reciprocity, Social Capital and Firm Performance? The Case of SMEs in China. *Asia Pacific Journal of Management*, 22(4): 445-463.

Appendix – I
Legend for some of the Mathematical Notations Used

$N(X, R)$ should be read as	N consists set X and set R
$\exists$ should be read as	There exists
$\exists!$ should be read as	There exists exactly one
$\forall$ should be read as	For all, for each, for any
$\in$ should be read as	is an element of
Iff should be read as	If and only if
$|R|$ should be read as	Cardinality of set R, number of elements in set R
$:=$ should be read as	Defined as
ϕ signifies	A null set

Proof: Direct relationships of a node reflect the effect of all indirect relationships possible for that node. Consider the below figure:

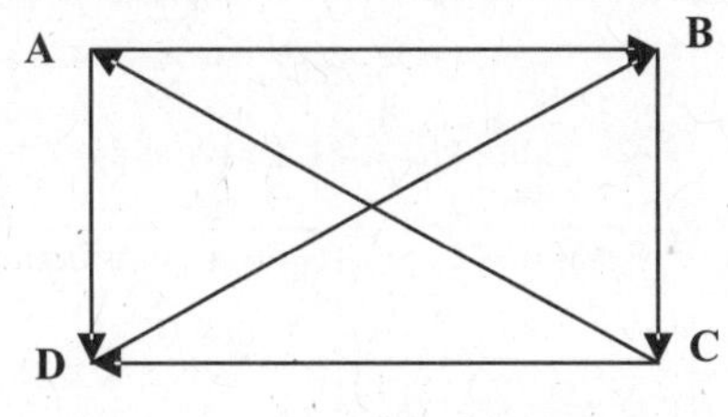

$$\Rightarrow O = \begin{pmatrix} 0 & 1 & 0 & 1 \\ 0 & 0 & 1 & 0 \\ 1 & 0 & 0 & 1 \\ 0 & 1 & 0 & 0 \end{pmatrix}$$

AND

$$Z = \begin{pmatrix} 1 & 0.5 & 0.25 & 0.5 \\ 0.25 & 1 & 0.75 & 0.25 \\ 0.5 & 0.25 & 1 & 0.5 \\ 0.25 & 0.75 & 0.5 & 1 \end{pmatrix}$$

In the above figure "A→B" denotes A depends on B. For simplicity of analysis one part of dependency in the bidirectional relation is taken as zero thus making it an asymmetric network. In the above figure A depends on B but B doesn't depend directly on A. This is synonymous to the traditional analysis. Also it is assumed that each unidirectional relationship reflects equal dependency thus has equal value/contribution to the power. For the notation "A→B"; B gets a single unit of power. Assume no multiplexity i.e. multiple utility .Thus the variables like multiplexity and unequal value of relations are controlled for and the only variable that will affect the power of a node is its position in network i.e. direct relation or indirect relation.

The power analysis Table–1 represents the traditional analysis (according to Burt's transformation) which takes into account both direct and indirect relations. Observe that the power contribution distribution in Table-1 is the exact as the sociometric choice matrix 'O'. From this table we can observe A and C have equal power of 1 unit each where as B and C have equal power of 2 units each. We can observe both B and D establish two relationships each where as A and D have one each. This is reflected in the power table which is similar with the concept of centrality-strength of link that is used in contemporary analysis. But this kind of analysis has an inherent flaw. Because no multiplexity is assumed A's dependence on D and B is for the same utility. As a result though the power derived by B and D will be equal but not as equal to D's relationship with B where D is only dependant on B. Thus B and D's gain of power from A will be half of one unit i.e. number of established relations with substitutes factored by number of parts of utility. Thus even if each utility has same value contribution to power of a node, each dependency's contribution to power varies with the nature of contribution and other relations that the alter established except with that of node.

Table-1

Relation	Power contribution			
	A	B	C	D
A→B & A→D		1		1
B→C			1	
C→A & C→D	1			1
D→B		1		
Total	1	2	1	2

Table-2 (Case1, k=1 and n=4)

Relation	Power contribution			
	A	B	C	D
A→B & A→D		0.5		0.5
B→C			1	
C→A & C→D	0.5			0.5
D→B		1		
Total	0.5	1.5	1	1

Now consider the network relations in the above figure .Clearly A doesn't have any power over B as B doesn't depend on A. Situation is similar for B and C. But C depends on A and B depends on C, thus naturally there exists indirect power of A on B because of its relationship with C. That means effect of AC relationship trickles down to AB relationship which has a positive contribution to the power of A. Except this A depends both on B and D, but B depends only on C. So A's power contribution to B is definitely less than B's power contribution to C. Like wise both of D's dependences are also dependant on others; but D is only dependant on B. So even if B and D have same number of dependants, B's power will be more than D's power simply because of the nature of their respective dependences. Similarly, though A and C both have one dependant each C enjoys exclusive dependence of B but it is not the case for A. So naturally power derived by C will be greater than that of A simply because of the nature of their dependants. The difference of power between C and D not only depends on numbers of dependants but the value that each dependant contributes. The value that each dependant contributes depends on their established relationships and available substitutable alternatives. From the above analysis the power structure that evolves will look like $P_B > P_D \geq P_C > P_A$ .Clearly table-1 misses this analysis but table-2 reflects the analysis. This shows that the concept of nodal power capture the trickle down effect of indirect relationships.

So, we can conclude that by taking into account the direct relationships of a node in a given network, the effect of indirect relationship are also taken care of. Intuitively we can argue that if a node is dependant on an alter then the node is in fact using the power of the alter to the proportion the node is dependant on the alter. So nodes utility from alter includes all the relation the alter has with others in the network. The same is true for other direct relationships. Hence it is redundant to calculate the effect of each and every indirect relationship of the node in this network.

Note: While the above example proved the point large scale simulation and empirical research is needed to generalize it to all kind of network analysis.

Appendix - III

Comparison with 'Z' based Transformation

The nodal power calculates the net intangible asset available for a node emanating from the structural position of the node in a network. It signifies the structural view of social capital. Nodal Power not only considers the number of relations and nature of that relation but also considers other relations the alter has in the network and their effect on nodal power. This is a modification to the indexes based on number of relations and path. For example in the given figure in Appendix–II both B and D has equal number of dependants thus has equal power as shown in table-1 but in calculation of nodal power it is shown that both have unequal power (1.5 >1: table-2). This shows nodal power captures both the quantity and quality of relations. It also captures both positive and negative trickle down effect of alters on node (for B, in table 2 N_P is 1.5 not 2), thus making it redundant to calculate the effect of indirect relationships of node. While doing network analysis of fairly closed and dense networks like intra-organizational networks, calculation of nodal power includes all the structural power available to the node as a result of membership of that network.

In Burt's transformation matrix Z which depends on the path concept i.e. based on geodesic distance, the power derived by each node from their position is as follows. A=1, B=1.5, C=1.5, D=1.25. This follows the hierarchy of $P_B = P_C > P_D > P_A$. The hierarchy according to nodal power is $P_B > P_C = P_D > P_A$. Note that both the formulas don't alter the hierarchical position of nodes. The hierarchical position of nodes only shifts in the same hierarchical space (i.e.> sign don't change into < sign; = signifies the meeting point of two hierarchical space). It is also clear that Burt's transformation gives too much power to the indirect relations and undermines the importance of direct relations. This supports Degenne and Forse's (1999) view that Burt's transformation attributes more importance to infrequent relations even with several intermediaries while minimizing the effect of direct links. In the example this is the reason for B's equal importance to C in case of Burt's transformation. The other reason is it focuses on distance but nodal power is based on dependency. This way nodal power captures the property of Burt's transformation and enhances it by considering the numbers and utility function of alters attached to it.

Coleman approached the structure of interaction in an economic system from competitive equilibrium perspective and indirectly treated dependency while describing linear system of action (Coleman, 1990:681). His treatment is fundamentally a demand model that describes the extent to which first person is interested in what the second person provides/controls. This conceptualization heavily depends on classical (i.e. rationality) and neo-classical (i.e. declining marginal utility) economic theory thus indifferent to empirical applicability in its present form (Gibbs, 1990). It also doesn't explicitly consider the established relation of actors which is fundamental to the network theory; neither has it assumed reciprocal relations based on mutual dependency. It subscribes to institutional and socio-structural assumptions based on hyper rationality where the general idea is that each actor in a system can communicate with others and takes decision (Coleman, 1990:686) where as a network structure given its boundary condition works in a bounded rationality mode. Thus even though the concept of dependency is latent in analysis of Coleman, the assumptions and treatment is different from that of 'Nodal Power'.

---

[i] Fables in *Panchatantra,*(300 BC) describe the virtue of having good friends, good social circle which helps an individual in creating political, economic and reputational resources and also facilitates socio-economic transactions. *Arthashastra* (200 BC*)* prominently discusses the social capital of State and opines that social capital affects and is affected by the conduct and capability of the ruler and its citizens. It also argues that such social capital not only facilitates well being of the state but also enhances performance of institutions in the state.

[ii] In a network, all other nodes except the node on focus are termed as alters. This is a standard network terminology.

[iii] An economic entity such as an organization by itself is a collection of internal ties and can be considered as a network. As organization action and its consequences are the result of its internal ties, resources, cohesiveness and collective goal internal capital can be considered as the outcome of its structural embeddedness of the internal network (Coleman, 1990).Again organization is embedded in a social structure including other organizations and extra-organizational individuals. This forms a greater network such as industry or economy where each single organization is considered as a single 'collective'. However, in a larger network like industry a firm is considered as a single node for all practical purposes.

[iv] For a detailed description of indexes such as centrality, transitivity, multiplexity and other characteristics of socio-economic networks, refer work of Ronald Burt and J.S.Coleman. Books such as 'Introducing Social Networks' by Degenee, Forse translated to English by Borges (1999); 'Social Network Analysis' by Wasserman and Faust (1994) also provide a detailed explanation of structural network analysis.

[v] Utility of a node is the whole of benefit that others get from a particular node. It is the reason of other's dependency on that particular node.

[vi] Recall that network is established for accessing complementary resources, capabilities, and division of work.

[vii] The mathematical proof of the argument is based on matrix algebra and is available with the author.

[viii] For example Infosys' – an Indian IT measure- social capital might be equal to all the entrepreneurs' individual social capital in its inception stage but it is not so now. Infosys as a separate entity has created its own reputational capital based on its own capability and resources that is different than individual reputation. However it may not be mutually exclusive than that of entrepreneurs.

[ix] For example positive action is matching stakeholder's expectation or adhering to principles of corporate social responsibility etc

[x] For example : In a team if a member free rides, other members may not effectively restrain him because either he is a good friend or he has already worked in another assignment of the same group when the other members haven't worked OR the other members expect to have some benefit in future by keeping him in good humor. In all these cases the free rider is substituting his/her already existing social capital or prospect of social capital in future for the capital loss in present. This describes the issue of 'substitutability across time' of social capital.

[xi] For example; suppose a firm cuts cost by compromising product quality that is detrimental to consumers' interest. This was not known to consumers for a significant time period after which they came to know about it. The value of that negative action is the cost advantage gained by the firm. After the incident is known, the firm's reputation decreases and sales decrease. This is a function of the speed of information dissemination from the affected parties/or from the source of information. The price that the firm pays to replenish this loss of reputation and to come to original position will be exponential to the achieved profit which it gained by cutting cost. This price includes value of corrective actions, lost sales and any resulting compensations.

Section 5

GEOGRAPHIC LOCUS AND OTHER ISSUES

Technology has made it possible for firms to reach distant markets more efficiently than ever before. Innovations in media have also ensured that the *village aspires for the globe*. Consumer demand has consequently forced the hand of nationalism. The process of democratization has led further to the demise of isolationist thinking in the national elite. Borders have been softening their barriers, making it more and more feasible for firms to access markets across them.

Another phenomenon adds a vital related trend. Technology has made it feasible, and then competitively necessary, for value-chains to be split. Outsourcing is the biggest contributor to improvements in efficiency. In this process, firms have developed strategies of 'networking' across borders, which build competitiveness for the enterprise. This is what is referred to here as the emergent *geographic locus*.

The first paper in this section tries to find the factors that may chiefly explain the business success of a cross-border alliance between an Indian manufacturing enterprise and a foreign partner. This analysis is based on case studies of alliances of four firms with their overseas partners.

Other papers here deal with a mix of issues. One empirical paper attempts to examine the impact of advertising on profitability of the firm. Another paper, conceptual in nature, applies a selective mixing of two Soft OR methodologies for designing, improving and managing service environment of shopping malls and retail stores. A third paper studies M&A and evaluates the success/failure of some mergers in India.

143

CRITICAL SUCCESS FACTORS TO COLLABORATE IN CROSS BORDER ALLIANCES: EXPERIENCES OF INDIAN MANUFACTURING ENTERPRISES

Mathew Cherian
Department of Management Studies, IIT Madras
Myrna Flores
Collège du Management de la Technologie, EPFL Lausanne
G. Srinivasan
Department of Management Studies, IIT Madras

INTRODUCTION

Manufacturing is the backbone of the economy in most countries, especially in fast-growing markets like India. The Indian manufacturing sector has been averaging 9 % growth in the last four years (2004-08), with a record 12.3 % in 2006-07. For the manufacturing sector to grow from current share of 16% to 30% of GDP requires a) significant increase in the productivity and quality at the plant level, b) pursuit of competitive manufacturing strategies and operations and c) successful integration into global supply chains, meeting stringent quality standards and delivery performance (Ref.1).

Strategic alliances provide flexibility to the partnering firms by committing on fewer resources and activities on which they have competencies and configuring networks of alliance partners to bridge the gap between firm's present resources and the required to compete in highly innovative and global markets. It brings in competitive advantage such as risk reduction and access to new technologies, low cost resources, markets of developing nation, etc. *Cross border alliance* (CBA) is a form of strategic partnership that is formed between two or more firms from different countries for the purpose of pursuing mutual interests through sharing their resources and capabilities. CBAs have resulted in reducing the deficiency gap of manufacturing enterprises in India.

The reasons for success of many Indian Manufacturing Enterprise (IME) alliances and their confidence to thrust into global business have not yet been analyzed by the academic community. We therefore take up here a study of these reasons, the Critical Success Factors (CSFs), of successful cross border alliances (CBAs) of IMEs. This analysis is based on case studies of alliances of four South

Indian firms with their overseas partners. While doing this, a reference has been made to several established theories of inter-organizational relationship. It is aimed that the results of this study will help IMEs to look at potential new alliances as a means of overcoming their deficiency and to give sufficient management attention to critical success factors to manage in a better way cross border alliances.

ALLIANCES RESEARCH: DIVERSE THEORETICAL FRAMEWORKS

The research in "alliances" is characterized by diversity in the theoretical framework and related analysis. These theories can be roughly classified into two streams:

According to the first stream, firms form alliances as an alternative to markets and hierarchies that try to: a) Minimize the transaction costs (transaction-cost theory: Williamson, 1975, 1991) or give access to resources that cannot be acquired from the market at acceptable cost or risk or that could not be developed internally within reasonable time (resource-based theory: Barney, 1991) or create value by pooling or exchanging dispersed knowledge (knowledge-based theory: Grant and Baden-Fuller, 1995) or provide a vehicle for organizational learning of new skills to face the uncertain future (Praise and Henderson, 2001). This structural view of the alliance, therefore, focuses on circumstances under which alliances are formed such as motivations for alliance formation, partner characteristics, etc (Harrigan, 1986).

The other major stream, or the relational view, focuses on the interactive nature of ongoing cooperative and dynamic relationship between firms (e.g. Ring & Van de Ven, 1994) and tries to explain alliance in terms of "soft issues" such as the interpersonal and inter-organizational trust (Dyer and Singh, 1998) or the role of key executives to commit on alliance formation and success (Eisenhardt and Schoonhoven, 1996), etc.

Studies on alliances tend to focus around the determinants of success and failure from a theoretical perspective. The two streams have rarely been combined in order to investigate the underlying factors that promote (or impede) successful outcomes of CBA (Nielson, 2007).

CRITICAL SUCCESS FACTORS

The Critical Success Factor (CSF) approach has the conceptual antecedents from the "success factors" introduced by Daniel (1961). He argued that a company's information system must be discriminative and selective, focusing on 'success factors' (usually three to six activities vital for success for an industry), which in turn, must be tied to goals of the organization and form the basis of management control. Later Anthony *et al.* (1972) sharpened the concept by introducing CSF and uplifted the concept to the managerial level, showing it can vary from company to company. Rockart (1979) defines Critical Success Factors (CSFs) as *those few key areas of activity in which favorable results are absolutely necessary for a particular company to reach its goals.* He introduced the concept of different CSFs based on structural, strategical, environmental, operational requirements of various companies and different levels and positions of the management, and tying to performance indicators. According to Thierauf (1982), if the results in these areas (CSFs) are not adequate, the organization's efforts for the period will be less than desired. The CSFs are those few key areas of activity which must be performed particularly well in order for the organization to outperform its competitors (Vasconcellos e Sá, 1988). For obvious reasons, critical success factors are the key areas of activity where "things must go right" that must receive due attention from management.

RESEARCH QUESTIONS AND METHODOLOGY

Since alliance is an important "strategic tool" for IMEs to develop competences and compete in the era of globalization, it is pertinent to understand the key areas of activity where "things must go right" that must receive due attention from management and "tune" their management control. The basic research question is: *What are the critical success factors for successful cross border alliance among Indian Manufacturing Enterprises (IMEs)?*

This question has further been subdivided so as to form what is known as the *study protocol* (basic framework) for the subsequent interviews or questionnaires.

a) **Rationale for collaborating:** *Why do IMEs go for an alliance?*
b) **Forms of alliance organization:** *What form of alliance organization contributes to success?*
c) **Value creating partners:** *What characteristics of partners bring in alliance success and value creation under a win-win long term perspective?*
d) **Going with Alliance**: *What factors are critical for maintaining alliance?*
e) **Measuring Success:** *What indicators can be taken into consideration to measure and track the success of alliance for an IME and the foreign company?*

CHOICE OF RESEARCH METHODOLOGY

Rockart (1979) recommends for in-depth interview of managers for finding CSFs. Auruškevicienė *et al.* (2001) observe that there is no universal Critical Success Factor (CSF) research method and report that with the growth of the problematic and organizational scope of critical success factors, consultants and researchers used numerous critical success factor methods such as 'onion technique' interviews, analysis of related organizational activities, *a priori* list of critical success factors based on literature sources, mailed questionnaires, interviews in combination with subsequent questionnaires.

Yin (2003) defines case study research method as an empirical inquiry that investigates a contemporary phenomenon within its real-life context; when the boundaries between phenomenon and context are not clearly evident; and in which multiple sources of evidence are used. The boundaries of structural and relational factors involved in success of alliance are not clear (Nielson, 2007), therefore an exploratory case study methodology, based on theoretical framework developed from literature, would bring out what managers consider CSFs of their alliance success.

Case Study Methodology

This framework follows the "replication" logic which states good performance of the factors (*here – CSFs)* under which successful occurrence of phenomenon *(Successful CBA)* is likely to occur in two or more cases (literal replication) (Yin, 2003a, b) and Auruškevicienė *et al.* (2001) "recipe" as described in *Choice of research methodology.* As Miles and Huberman (1984) observed: "…findings are more dependable when they can be buttressed from several independent sources…" Secondary sources were used to check the veracity.

A detailed semi-structured questionnaire was prepared based on several factors. The main sources for questions are from Saxena and Kumar, (2007) for motives, partner selection, performance and termination (employed Likert scales 1-5); Dyer (2004) and Jagersma (2005) for forms of alliance organization and Bamford et al. (2004) for Align strategically – Governance systems - Economic dependencies – Building Alliance Organization.

Face to face interviews were conducted with CEOs and/or managing partners and/or top officials of companies based on the questionnaire prepared. The companies chosen for this study were the ones with good financial performances and successful cross border alliances as per company annual reports, news reports and company websites. It took roughly an hour for each interview. The meetings took place in their head offices. Later on, the three companies returned the filled questionnaires and for the fourth company, it was filled while interviewing. Detailed case studies were prepared. Then major themes were derived out of it. These case studies with their theme summary were sent to each company for their approval. Two companies corrected and approved. The third one approved orally. The fourth company did not respond. Figure-1 displays the methodology.

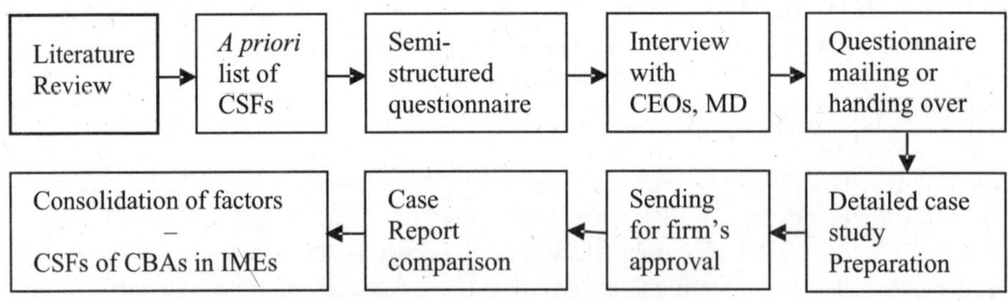

Figure 1: Research Methodology

a. The Rationale for Collaborating

Value creation – The need to collaborate to compete

Value creation is to make "sense" or value to collaborate. Doz and Hamel (1998) further elaborate by identifying three types of "logic of alliance value creation" for firms.

It could be *to co-opt collaborating firms* (networking) in order to develop critical mass by pooling combined customer bases and to build the necessary supporting resources and capabilities of all players of the network taken together, thus exploiting the opportunities opened by globalization, and ultimately, each vying for a "nodal position" in the future in the network of relationship that the firm has built. Yet another imperative could be *to leverage the unique resources and capabilities* of the local and/or technology partners such as to enter into unknown markets across the border of its own nation or into unfamiliar product development, thereby becoming one among the insiders of that market for reaping the opportunities in the future. The third objective could be *to learn and internalize new or deficient skills and technologies* from the partner, thereby building new competencies required for future business to innovate and offer better products to global markets. Besides these, many authors have mentioned that firms are increasingly resorting to CBAs to escape from problems associated *with acquisition and mergers* such as high cost and issues of retaining local skills, particularly for SMEs of developed countries *and with internal development* such as long duration required for building skills internally and indigenously by firms of developing nations (Jagersma, 2005).

Strategic fit occurs when partners value the skills each brings to the alliance (Bierly III and Gallagher, 2007). Eisenhardt and Schoonhoven (1996) found that alliances are more likely to be formed when both firms are in vulnerable strategic positions (i.e., in need of resources) or when they are in strong social positions (i.e., possess valuable resources to share). Strategic fit of alliance of IMEs occurs when both partner firms are in vulnerable strategic positions (i.e., in need of resources), seeking complementary or similar resources for transferring or pooling (Ahuja, 2000). Usually the foreign partner looks for a local firm support to manage the local people, politicians, bureaucrats and market distribution capabilities or to avail low cost resources such as cheap labour, raw materials, etc. In turn, IMEs look for firms that can provide higher technology and process capabilities. Hence ***Cross Border Alliances, provide IMEs and its foreign partners to leverage on unique resources and capabilities of each other, creating value at the time of formation and during its operation.***

Value Capture – Why is it difficult?

The dynamic evolution of learning approach (Doz, 1996) and the viewing alliance as a progression of inter organizational co-ordination (Ring and Van den Van, 1994) from the initial condition at the time of formation considers the success of the alliance in terms of progressive learning and value capturing for themselves (private benefit) and for the alliance (public benefit) in the midst of the cooperation and competition (Khanna *et al.*, 1998) between partners. This inter-organizational learning from the partners' alliance occurs through internalization by information processing leading to change in behaviour (Huber, 1991) or routines embedded in the organization memory (Levitt and March, 1996) of the entity (here the partner firms). Learning in alliances involves significant transfer of tacit, specialized and complex knowledge (Parise and Henderson, 2001). Table-1 gives some of the challenges for the transfer of tacit, specialized and complex knowledge, methods of overcoming the same and some examples of overcoming transfer challenges from the case studies.

The critical challenge for IMEs is to have the alliance learning capability. Levin (1997) looks at technology in a broader perspective as a complex product that entails the tacit knowledge, values, culture and organizational forms. Chaston *et al.* (2001) found that the small firm's growth is critically depending on improving five areas of competence: new product development, human resource management practices, organizational productivity, and management of quality and management of information. Learning requires close collaboration of both firms at various levels of the respective organizations, overcoming the various transfer challenges. Value capture in alliance for IME is the satisfactory acquisition of technology, internalization of the associated tacit knowledge and enhancement of organizational capabilities that reduces its vulnerability due to deficiency of skills and knowledge and equips them to face the challenges of globalization. Hence *successful cross border alliance of IME involves continuous value capture and new value creation based on continuous collaboration.*

b. Forms of alliance organization

In the case of a to-be-formed global joint venture with a stand-alone organization, the classic issues of organization structure and "cultural fit" are the most critical. In the case of a cross-border alliance with little or no organizational integration between the partners, the critical issues often center on how to gain momentum and meet performance targets in the absence of a dedicated organization (Jagersma, 2005). The alliances of firms under study have been classified in accordance with classification by Jagersma (2005) (See table – 2).

c. Value Creating Partner

Capability

Several past studies have shown that the selection of a particular partner has a great impact on the performance of CBA as it determines the extent of skill and resources available to the alliance for achieving its objectives (Geringer, 1991, p. 42). Ahuja (2000) points out that if a partner firm has a high level of technical or commercial capital, its attractiveness as a potential partner increases. Needless to say, any partner that has necessary resources fits the purpose of alliances for IME firms.

Bargaining power

The relative bargaining power of partners can reduce the firm's share of common benefits relative to its share in joint investments (Khanna *et al.*, 1998). Bargaining power depends on two factors of interdependence, i.e. stake of the parties involved in the relationship and the availability of alternatives (Bacharach and Lawler, 1981). Therefore the availability of partner's resources in an alliance is moderated by bargaining power.

Trust-ability

A trustworthy partner builds trust and hence increases effectiveness of alliance as it reduces cost of governance or safeguard mechanisms for deterring opportunistic behaviours of partners and opens possibilities for newer transactions that may not be possible with governance (Barney *et al.*, 1994). *Trust-ability* of a trustworthy firm is increased with social aspects of the relationship, such as Social network in which firms are positioned, Cultural and organizational similarity, reputation, previous ties and propensity to trust (primarily based on past experiences and trusting environment) (Bierly III and Gallagher, 2007).

d. Going with Alliance - *Challenge of maintaining alliance*

The challenge for the implementation of Cross Border Alliance is to build and maintain strategic alignment across the separate corporate entities, each of which has its own goals, market pressures, and shareholders. Bamford *et al.* (2004) advocated four basic factors for successful launch of international joint venture: 1) Align Strategically, 2) Governance system, 3) Economic dependencies and 4) Building Alliance Organization Structure.

1) Align Strategically

The transaction-cost theory stipulates the need to configure at the beginning in order to minimize behavioural uncertainty and the resulting need for control for a successful alliance (Hennart, 1988). Defining a detailed business plan, consisting of scope, future possibilities and financial targets can contain disputes, hindrances for cooperation and overcoming differences later. Some quick and early results will motivate for cementing the alliance. Bamford *et al.* (2004) advise for assigning a senior and respectable person as launch leader who can work in a cross cultural environment for the new CBA and create accountability for the business plan. The use of modern Information and Communication Technology (ICT) will reduce the transaction costs. This initial alignment avoids possible future conflicts to become a major issue later (Bamford *et al.*, 2004) and should focus on critical success factors at each level of management (Rockart, 1979).

2) Governance system

Governance system should neither stifle entrepreneurship nor create dysfunctional bureaucracy for a child CBA. However, organizational mechanisms are needed for parent companies to have control such as Capital allocation, Risk management, Disclosure and Performance tracking to protect critical shareholders' interest in the child CBA (Bamford *et al.*, 2004).

3) Economic dependencies

Settling economic issues is not only a time consuming process but also can be a contagious issue later, if not properly defined. The process is to sort out who will provide what resources (such as intangible and tangible assets, employees, funds, etc) to the CBA and the associated transfer price (Bamford *et al.*, 2004).

4) Building Alliance Organization Structure

Forming the right organizational structure across the cultural barriers of the parents with proper ownership, responsibility and control are the hallmark of successful ventures. The form of the organization, the extent of independency of CBA, conflict resolving mechanisms, communication channels and a strong CEO with necessary supporting staff (Bamford *et al.*, 2004) etc. are the basic elements for building alliance organization structure.

5) Trust-based Relationship

The partner–specific learning involves the process of learning from and about an individual partner. This is very critical when there is an exchange of tacit, specialized and complex knowledge (Parise and Henderson, 2001). Transparency brings opportunity to learn more about the practices of world class organizations that they ally (Doz and Hamel, 1998). Haque *et al.* (2004) reported that supportive and open behaviour with honesty can create successful alliances. Kauser and Shaw

(2004) have found empirically higher level of trust in successful alliances than in less successful counterparts. The trust-based relationship, therefore, aids alliance success.

6) Staffing – Getting the right people

Skills are transferred by people, not by processes and contracts. Getting the right people committed for the alliance, with parent companies not losing the service of their top performers for themselves, is the challenge of staffing (Cascio and Serapio, 1991). Lajara *et al.* (2003) provide an excellent review on the HR issues for the success of alliances. Based on these, we have identified critical HR elements for success of the CBA as identifying the right people, securing commitment from the key staff, ensuring proper incentives and providing for their career aspirations.

e.   Measuring success

Defining success

Defining success for both partners and for the cross-border alliance requires careful evaluation. Apart from financial and marketing achievements, partners gain a lot more out of alliance that is deemed as success of their partnership.

Objectives of alliances

Several empirical studies have been carried out on performance of international alliances on different financial and objective indicators. The other set of studies looked whether the alliance has achieved the underlining aim or motives of its formation. Because there is no commonly accepted definition, there is no single adequate measure of alliance success. Therefore, in alignment with several researchers in the field (Johnson, 1999; Kauser and Shaw, 2004, etc.), subjective performance measures were employed through interviews and questionnaire-filling by *the respective CEOs and Top level Managers*. The use of such measures does not imply that financial indicators are inadequate to evaluate alliance performance, but rather that financial data are difficult to obtain (Schumacher, 2006).

Value appropriation for global business

The hallmark of successful alliances is their ability to evolve beyond initial expectations and objectives (Bleeke and Ernst, 1991). Beyond the immediate reasons of partnership, the alliance should offer the parties an option on the future, opening new doors and unforeseen opportunities (Kanter, 1994). Alliance should be viewed as an occasion to learn (Intent to Learn) for capturing long term benefits and make conscious effort to identify the value of new information, assimilate and apply to *commercial purposes* (absorptive capacity – Cohen and Levinthal, 1990). The alliance management capability equips firms with the art of entering, maintaining and capturing value from allying with different firms simultaneously (Parise and Henderson, 2001). The development of this capability is, therefore, essential for global business operations.

World class leading organizations are focussing on their core business and downsizing by outsourcing non-core activities (Hayes *et al.*, 2005). This new environment offers opportunities for IMEs to partner with such firms and enter into the realm of globalization. Secondly, new models of SME-SME collaboration create virtual organizations based on Information and Communication

Technologies (ICT) (Noori and Lee, 2006). This widens their scope of operations by imbibing strength based on cohesion as against being "annexure" to big players. Both situations require providing higher customer value in terms of cost, quality, services, shorter delivery time, and flexibility and alliance management capability. Value appropriation is the promotion of IMEs into global business as a consequence of and by the application of value captured as defined in sub-section 'a' of Critical Success Factors.

Termination

The termination of an alliance need not be a sign of failure, but it is to be made as a part of the agreement. The average life of a CBA is 7 years. More than 80 percent of CBA are purchased by one partner while the rest were either sold to a third party or dissolved. Exit terms are to be negotiated in advance as how to end the relationship and divide the assets since the bargaining power will decrease over time.

CASE STUDY – FINDINGS

a. The rationale for collaborating

Value Creation (VR) – *analyzing from the case studies*

Through various case studies, it was found that Indian Partners sought for superior technology and got customer acceptance from the foreign partners. In turn, foreign partners co-opt the Indian partners for accessing Indian customers, their local resources, and leverage the unique skills of the Indian partner in handling local people and government officials, etc. On the other hand, it also opened a way for the Indian partner to learn about world class manufacturing best practices, techniques and technology from the foreign counterpart.

A case is considered where the important question is *"Why does our Japanese partner want to collaborate?"* A clear understanding of this question is the beginning of a successful alliance, then General Manager, Finance & Strategic Planning of company **B** succinctly answered to our query about success in their alliance. Similar sentiments were expressed by other companies also. **Table-1** below is helpful in analyzing the rationale. It shows that *there was continuous value capture in terms of internalization of superior work culture, enhanced process capability and product design competence.*

Table 1: Tacit knowledge: Challenges and methods of transferring (Collins and Hitt, 2006) with some examples from Case Studies

Transfer challenges	Methods for overcoming	Some examples of overcoming transfer challenges in the case studies
Difficult to articulate	Learn-by-observing & -by-doing for individuals directly involved in utilizing the knowledge	General Manager (Finance & Strategic Planning) of company **B** recalled Japanese obsession for accuracy of processes or activities. **An attitude of** *absolute clarity "without any assumption" to the last detail*, **a culture that is difficult to emulate for many Indians**. Japanese are excellent trainers. Initially 250 disassembled products were brought and Japanese managers themselves trained personals at the shop floor as how to assemble. *Proper training and imparting a new working culture to Indian employees were the hallmark of association with Japanese.*
Difficult to diffuse	In-person contact between key executives and employees of partner firms	"We deliberately delayed the transfer of technology in three phases through seven years **for allowing the proper assimilation** (*diffusion*) **of technology and the process by our people**" the managing partner of company **D** replied to our query of value capture from their alliance. Now the Indian company has enhanced process capabilities and could design better and customized products.
Difficult to integrate with existing knowledge	Develop common understanding of how to utilize knowledge	Company **A** realized the fact that TQM will be the foundation for their future and became totally committed for its implementation, *a tribute to their alliance with Japanese firms*. Four companies in the group have won the Deming Prize in 2003, 2005 and 2007. **Their approach has been marked by a continual acquiring and applying of global technologies and cutting-edge strategies.**
Inter-firm differences	Firm-level social capital; intentionally work to develop trust between partners	"We have contributed to the alliance by providing knowledge about customers, government regulations, supply of inputs, low wage labour and most importantly **managerial personnel**" claimed the managing director of company **C**. The superior technologies for product, R&D and process capabilities were learned from the foreign partner, with which market network was developed further. Foreign partners have gained a clear insight of operating in India and market access. **This mutual learning creates interest in both partners in developing and cementing the CBA further**

Table – 1 Contd…

Table – 1 Contd…

Cultural differences	Focus on frequent communication, on-site meetings and partner visits	Company **A:** Implementing TQM means a radical shift in the mindset of the people. Company **B:** Installing a new work culture in the Indian workforce and managers is a major reason for the success of the alliance Company **D:** This prolonged transfer (*of technology and process in a span of 7 years*) enabled the effective training of the company's personnel until their employees learnt the soft and technical skills and able to apply. *Grooming Indian workforce/managers into a new working culture is of greater concern and considered as important item for success. This was expected as Indian firms look for world class manufacturing practices, which needs an equally "transformed" HR.*

b. Forms of Alliance Organizations: Based on analysing the case studies.

Various types of alliances of four companies based on company reports and secondary sources are described in **Table 2**. The classification of the alliances is based on Jagersma (2005). All companies took particular care in choosing right type of organization for CBA.

c.   Partner selection – analyzing the case studies

Trust-ability (TA)

Indian partners looked for similarity in size, business, objectives and what is called "feel good factor", which they called as cultural similarity. They looked for reputation, past performances and the number of previous successful alliances of the international partners. While Company A insists for clearly laid down documents and other formal way rating the firms, other firms found to have greater propensity to trust. Development of a social network facilitates communication, provides social norms to guide behavior, minimizes opportunistic activities and institutionalizes a framework for trust. However, this aspect has not been dealt in this study

Table 2: Types of Alliances of the Four Companies Studied. Classification is based on Jagersma (2005). Source – Company annual reports, news reports & websites

Objective of the alliance	Type of alliance	Purpose	Alliances of companies under study
For combining compleme ntary resources	*Cross-border joint ventures (JV) would be preferable*	*Entering a new market or starting a new business or developing a new project.*	*Companies A, B & C (in the 80's) had started JV for developing new markets or products. Recently Co. C has a JV for new business with Australian Co. (specialized ceramic products to power plants and Coal washeries) and south African company (bio-ceramic range of wound dressing products) & another JV with Chinese company to cater to the diamond tool and bonded abrasive markets (new market for C))*
For acquiring new technolog y	*either JV or direct parent interaction, often combined with technology licensing agreement is preferred*	*To take advantage of synergy from complementary strengths or resources such as the technology of one partner Vs the market access of the other*	*Company D has technology licensing from its first alliance. Company B has entered into JV with Australian company to develop fuel injection technology to widen its product profile and to escape from obsolete carburetor business. The beginning tripartite alliance of company C is a strategic alliance of this nature*
For managing industry rivalry and market share expansion	*parent- to- parent cooperation is typically best suited*	*To develop technical or long -term standards. It may be with component parts of two or more businesses being merged to face a strong competitor or possible takeover by the latter, or to overcome provisions of monopoly / merger laws, or sometimes for a takeover of their competitor firm.*	*Company B has entered with its first alliance partner (Japanese) for new product development and R&D in 2003 at Chennai in India since both are in fuel management business.*
For improving vertical linkages	*Non-equity arrangement such as long-terContract are usually best because of conflicts inherent between suppliers & customers*	*Specific agreement between manufacturers and their suppliers (supplier contract) or international trading partnerships*	*Company A has supplier contracts with leading Automobile OEMs (e.g. Volkswagen of Germany) and D has trading partnership with GE digital. All companies have supplier collaborations with Indian OEM companies in their respective sector.*
Besides these, Co.'s B & C have gone for acquisitions in North America to expand operations			

Capability (CA)

While Indian firms look for technology and techniques (process capability), foreign partners mainly look at sound financial position and capabilities such as whether partner can comply with rules and regulations of the land, able to manage local scenario, have market access and human resources availability.

Commitment (CO)

All firms consider commitment as an important partner selection criterion. They have indicated the amount of interest and availability of capability of their partner for alliance is directly depends on commitment. All four firms indicated the amount of investment that partner is ready to invest as a pointer towards the commitment. 50:50 or equal partnership is prerequisite for three firms interviewed. Ownership structure and attitude to the investment (whether for strategic or short gain) are other factors considered as indicators for commitment by the Indian firms.

d. Going with Alliance – *from case study*

The items for success during "Going with Alliance" are summarized in the following **Table-3**.

Table 3: Items for Critical Success Factors during "Going with Alliance" Phase

Align Strategically	Governance System	Economic Dependencies	Building Alliance Organization Structure	Staffing	Trust Building
Align Strategically **(AS)**	Performance focus **(PF)**	Pricing **(PR)**	Organization structure **(OS)**	Developing staff **(DS)**	Building Trust **(BT)**
Performance targets	*Being definite on the performance metrics to focus*	*Uniform and proper auditing practices*	*Type and Independence*	*Targeted trainings and working procedures*	*Being vigilant over the major barrier to integration*
Detailed plan of action and resource requirements	*Focusing to produce results on the performance matrices*	*Dealing with exchange rate fluctuations*	*Leadership*	*Timing of assimilation*	*Transparency and fair dealing*
Assigning to local management and appropriate team of people	*Performance reporting*	*Clarity in the inputs (by the parent organizations) and its quality levels*	*Mechanism for conflict resolution*	*Incentives to Employees to new organization set up*	-
-	-	*Need for localization of inputs*	-	-	-

e.   **Measuring Success** – *from case studies*

Value Appropriation (VP) *for globalization – from case studies*
It was found that all these companies have not only captured value, but also moved up in the value chain through proper value appropriation.

- ***Created superior customer value***
- ***Moving higher in the value chain through alliance, as time passes***
    - ○ *Company **A***
    - • *Becomes tier -1 supplier to leading OEM automobile companies of world, meeting stringent quality standards and time limits (e.g. supplier to Volkswagen of Germany)*
    - • *becomes product developer of specific automotive parts for them*
    - ○ *Company **B***
    - • *Alliance moves to product development & firm goes for related product diversification (e.g. from carburetor, they moved fuel injection technology)*
    - • *"The courage" for the small firm to acquire a firm in the competitive US market (A Precision Products company based in Illinois, U.S. in 2005)*
    - ○ *Company **C***
    - • *"Going global" strategy through collaboration and acquisition across the world (e.g. acquisition to expand its operation into the large North American market and CBA (JV) in China)*
    - • *Thrusts into new markets of world and to access niche technologies (e.g. JV in Australia to cater a particular market segment and CBA with South African company to offer special product)*
    - ○ *Company **D***
    - • *Becomes a technological provider to other firms*
    - • *Manufacturer and exporter of other products in the power conditioning sector*

- ***Managing different alliances together*** (sign of alliance maturity – see table 2)

Value appropriation (VP) - Summary from case studies
Indian firms have appropriated the value captured by earning superior customer acceptance, moving higher in the value chain, learning alliance management capabilities and thrusting into global business.
Termination
The process of forging and developing alliances takes time and full capture of value and strategic potential happens after the elapse of several years. Indian companies looked alliance "with perpetuity in mind", once the trust is established. Therefore Longevity (duration) has been included as a measure for success (Harrigan, 1986). It requires transparent dealings and continuous value creation between partners.
Strategic, marketing and financial results have been classified as one group under Alliance Performance (AP). The Value Appropriation (VA) or degree of

MODEL

The Critical Success Factors (CSFs) for Cross Border Alliance (CBA) of Indian Manufacturing Enterprises (IMEs) and its elements are based on these case studies which are summarized in the model given in **Figure-2**. While value creation brings the two partners together initially, it is the value capture that makes sense in continuing the relationship. Strategic fit is looked at not just in terms of value creation alone, but the ability to capture value in sharpening the competencies of IMEs such as improved product design, process capabilities, new work culture, alliance learning capability such as going along with foreign organization, etc. Not paying due attention to critical success factors during alliance process (i.e. Governance Mechanisms and Economics of Operations) may result in not achieving the financial and market objectives which can make partnership fall apart. Finally, studies show that the successful IMEs appropriate what they have learnt from the alliance for global business. This is aligning with the export performance of this sector. All Indian partners see alliance "with perpetuity in mind". So longevity has been introduced as a measure of success.

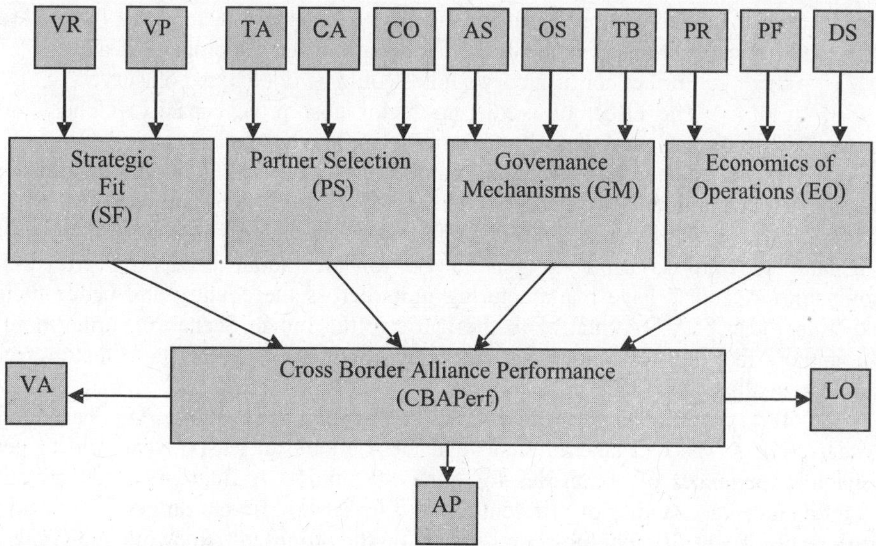

Figure 1: Proposed model for Critical Success Factors (CSFs) for Cross Border Alliance (CBAs) of Indian Manufacturing Enterprises (IMEs)

Figure 2 above and **Table-4** below present eleven identified critical success factors that enable the successful formation and operation of cross border alliances of IMEs, grouped into four structural and relational oriented factors. As observed, the way CBAs consider and integrate the proposed CSFs during its life cycle will impact the overall outputs which are also considered in the model as key performance indicators. The model serves as a reference guide for IMEs to look forward to create and manage successfully new potential CBAs.

Table 4: Critical Success Factors for Cross Border Alliance of IMEs

SF:STRATEGIC FIT	PA:PARTNER SELECTION	GM:GOVERNING MECHANISMS	EO:ECONOMICS OF OPERATION
1) VR: Value Creation	3) TA: Trust-ability	6) AS: Aligning Strategically	9) PR: Pricing
2) VP: Value Capture	4) CA: Capability	7) OS: Organization Structure	10) PF: Performance Focus
-	5) CO: Commitment	8) TB: Trust Building	11) DS: Developing Staff
Key Indicators for to measure success in CBAs of IME alliances			
VA: Value Appropriation	**AP: Alliance Performance**	**LO: Longevity**	

LIMITATIONS

Some limitations of this study are the following:

a) Theoretical replication (poor performance or absence of the factors (here-*CSFs)* when phenomenon *(successful CBA)* is not likely to occur (Yin, 2003 a, b) is not done. It would have been confirmatory if some unsuccessful alliances of IMEs are also studied and reviewed for the absence of these factors. All factors are affected once conflict arises in one of the factors and when not properly dealt.

b) Further confirmatory studies could be done based on survey.

c) The effect of mediating factor absorptive capacity (Cohen and Levinthal, 1990) of these organizations is not taken into account.

d) The effect of other factors such as learning intention, alliance management capability (Parise and Henderson, 2001) needs to be addressed

e) This paper is built on four case studies of Indian companies in Chennai, so findings can't be generalized for all Indian firms.. Nevertheless, companies A and C have manufacturing units across the country and hence their experience can be representative to the IMEs in the Indian Scenario. Furthermore, the authors feel that for a very fast emerging country like India, these factors can summarize alliances of IMEs.

f) Another identified issue is that the case studies are based on "older" CBAs. We had taken a stand that CBA should at least 5 years old to get reliable experiences of companies for our case studies. A future research project could include case studies of different CBAs formed in different ranges of time and analyze how their different life cycles impact on the proposed framework and CSFs.

g) Firms were dealt in their own individual setting. The effects of clusters and associated social network relationships on the alliance were not considered.

CONCLUSION

Indian Manufacturing Enterprises (IMEs) have benefited from Cross Border Alliances (CBAs) in sharpening their competences to become part of supply chains of global OEM companies. The case studies of four companies from South India show that critical success factors (CSFs) for successful CBAs include both structural and relational oriented elements. Eleven CSFs are identified *in IME alliance context* and are grouped into four structural and relational oriented factors. Further, the success of alliances is interpreted not only in terms of financial and market achievements, but also on continuous value creation of the alliance, value capture for sharpening its competence and appropriation of value for global business later. Future studies could be done to validate these CSFs and the nature and extent of value capture and appropriation process that benefits IME's transition from "people-cost arbitrage" to innovation.

ACKNOWLEDGEMENTS

The authors would like to thank the Swiss Innovation Promotion Agency – CTI International for the funding this research under the project SwissMAIN. Special gratitude is given to Mr. Duruz from Maillefer and to Mr. Voirol from Bosch Sapal, industrial partners of the project. We also sincerely thank Prof. L.S. Ganesh from the Indian Institute of Technology in Madras for supporting this Indo-Swiss research. A thank you note is also given for their important contributions to Luca Canetta and Michel Pouly from the Swiss Federal Institute of Technology, Lausanne (EPFL), institution leader of the SwissMAIN project, and to Prof. Claudio Boër, from the University of Applied Sciences of Southern Switzerland (SUPSI) for his important advises and support while Myrna Flores lead the Indian Pilot while working at the CIM Institute of Southern Switzerland (ICIMSI).

REFERENCES

1. http://www.krannert.purdue.edu/departments/gscmi/downloads/DR_ISB_NSF_NYU_Purdue-GlobalizingIndianManufacturing.pdf Based on "Globalizing Indian Manufacturing – Competing in Global Manufacturing and Service Networks": Report on the summit on Indian Manufacturing Competitiveness by Deloitte Research, the Indian School of Business, New York University and Purdue University with support from the National Science Foundation
2. Ahuja, G. (2000), "The duality of collaboration-inducements and opportunities in the formation of interfirm linkages", *Strategic Management Journal,* 21, pp. 317-43.
3. Anthony, R.N.; Dearden, J. and Vancil, R.F., (1972), "Key Economic Variables," *Management Controls Systems,* Homewood, Ill. Irwin, p 147.
4. Bacharach, S. B. and Lawler, E.J. (1981). "Power and Tactics in Bargaining" *Industrial & Labour Relations Review,* Volume 34, Issue 2, Jan. pp. 219-233.
5. Bamford J, Ernst D and Fubini D G., (2004) "Launching A World-Class Joint Venture" Harvard Business Review Feb.
6. Barney, J. B and Hansen, Mark H (1994) *"Trustworthiness as a source of competitive advantage"* Strategic Management Journal, Vol. 15, 175-190.
7. Barney, J. B. (1991), "Firm resources and sustained competitive advantage", *Journal of management,* Vol.17, pp. 99-120.
8. Bierly III P E and Gallagher S., (2007) "Explaining Alliance Partner Selection: Fit, Trust and Strategic Expediency" Long Range Planning 2007.
9. Cascio, W.F., Serapio, M.G. Jr. (1991), "Human resources systems in an international alliance: the undoing of a done deal?", *Organizational Dynamics*, Vol. 19 No.3, pp.63–74.

10. Chaston, I. and Mangles, T., (1997), "Core Capabilities as Predictors of Growth Potential in Small Manufacturing Firms". *Journal of Small Business Management,* Vol. 35, No.1, pp. 47-57.

11. Collins J D. and Hitt M A. (2006) *"Leveraging tacit knowledge in alliances: The importance of using relational capabilities to build and leverage relational capital"* Journal of Engineering and Technology Management, Vol. 23, Issue 3, pp 147-67.

12. Daniel, D.R. (1961) "Management Information Crisis," *Harvard Business Review,* Sep./Oct.

13. Doz Y.L. and Hamel G (1998) *"The Alliance Advantage: The Art of Creating Value through Partnering"* Harvard Business School Press, Boston, MA.

14. Doz, Y.L. (1996), "The evolution of cooperation in strategic alliances: initial conditions or learning processes?" *Strategic Management Journal,* Vol. 17 No. Summer Special Issue, pp.55-83.

15. Dyer, J.H and Singh, H (1998) "The Relational View: Cooperative Strategy and Sources of Interorganizational Competitive Advantage" *Academy of Management Review* Vol. 23, No.4, pp. 660-679.

16. Eisenhardt, K.M. and Schoonhoven, C.B., (1996). Resource-based view of strategic alliance formation: Strategic and social effects of entrepreneurial firms. *Organization Science* 7, pp. 136–150.

17. Geringer, J.M. (1991). "Strategic determinants of partner selection criteria in international joint ventures," *Journal of International Business Studies* 22 (1).

18. Grant, R.M. and Baden-Fuller, C. (1995) "A Knowledge-based theory of inter-firm collaboration, *Best Paper Academy of Management Proceedings,* Vancouver.

19. Haque, S.M. M.; Green, R.; Keogh, W. (2004), "Collaborative Relationships in the UK Upstream Oil and Gas Industry: Critical Success and Failure Factors" *Problems & Perspectives in Management,* Issue 1, pp. 44-51.

20. Harrigan, K.R., (1986) "Managing for joint venture success", Lexington Books, Lexington, MA (1986).

21. Hayes, Robert; Pisano, Gary; Upton, David; Wheelwright, Steven (2005), "Operations, Strategy, and Technology: Pursuing the Competitive Edge", John Wiley & Sons, Inc., Hoboken, NJ.

22. Hennart, J.-F. (1988) "A transaction cost theory of equity joint ventures", Strategic Management Journal 9 (1988) (4), pp. 361–374.

23. Huber, G.P. (1991), "Organizational learning: the contributing processes and the literatures", *Organization Science,* Vol. 2, pp.88-115.

24. Jagersma, P K (2005), *"Cross-border alliances: advice from the executive suite",* Journal of business Strategy, Vol. 26 No.1, Pages 44-50, ISSN 0275-6668.

25. Kauser, S. and Shaw, V. (2004), "The influence of behavioural and organisational characteristics on the success of international strategic alliances", *International Marketing Review;* Volume: 21 Issue: 1.

26. Khanna, T., Gulati, R. and Nohria, N. (1998), "The Dynamics of learning Alliances: Competition, Cooperation and Relative Scope. *Strategic Management Journal,* March. Vol. 19, Issue 3; p. 193.

27. Lajara, B. M.; Lillo, F. G. and Sempere V. S. (2003), "Human resources management: A success and failure factor in strategic alliances" Employee *Relations;* Volume: 25 Issue: 1.

28. Levin, M. (1997), "Technology transfer in organizational development: an investigation into the relationship between technology transfer organizational change", *International Journal of Technology Management, Vol.14 Nos.2-4, pp. 297-308.*

29. Levitt, B., March, J.G. (1996), "Organizational learning", in Cohen, M.D., Sproull, L.S. (Eds.), *Organizational Learning,* Sage Publications, Thousand Oaks, CA, pp.516-40.

30. Miles M.B., Huberman A.M. (1984), Quantitative Data Analysis: A Sourcebook of New Methods, Sage Publications, Beverley Hills, CA.

31. Nielsen, Bo Bernhard (2007), "Determining international strategic alliance performance: A multidimensional approach" *International Business Review* Volume: 16, Issue: 3, pp. 337-361.

32. Noori, H and Lee, W.D. (2006), "Dispersed network manufacturing: adapting SMEs to compete on the global scale" *Journal of Manufacturing Technology Management;* Volume: 17 Issue: 8.

33. Parise, S., Henderson, J.C. (2001), "Knowledge resource exchange in strategic alliances", *IBM Systems Journal*, Vol. 40 pp.908-24.

34. Ring. P.S and Van De Ven, A. H. (1994), "Developmental Processes of Cooperative Interorganizational Relationships" *Academy of Management Review*, Vol. 19 Iss.1, pp. 90-118.

35. Rockart, J.F. (1979) Chief executives define their own data needs, *Harvard Business Review* (March–April), pp. 81–93.

36. Saxena, N and Kumar, G.A (2007) "Complementary Strategic Motives for International Joint Venture Partners in Auto Component Sector in India" at *10th International Annual Strategic Management Forum Conference*, IIT Bombay.

37. Thierauf, R.J. (1982) "Decision Support Systems for Effective Planning and Control: A Case Study Approach", Prentice-Hall, Englewood Cliffs, NJ.

38. Vasconcellos e Sá, J (1988), "The impact of key success factors on company performance", *Long Range Planning*, Volume 21, Issue 6, pp. 56-64.

39. Williamson, O. E. (1975), *Markets and Hierarchies: Analysis and Antitrust Implications*, Free Press, NY.

40. Williamson, O.E. (1991), "Strategizing, economizing, and economic organization", *Strategic Management Journal* 12 (1991) (winter special issue), pp. 75–94.

41. Yin, R.K. (2003a), "Case study research: design and methods", Sage Publications, Thousand Oaks, CA.

42. Yin, R K (2003b), "Applications of case study research", Sage Publications, Thousand Oaks, CA.

PROFILE OF COMPANIES

Company A

Founded in 30's, company A is a leading auto component manufacturer based in South India city of Chennai. It is a group of 8 companies and 24 facilities across India, with supplies in almost every segment of the auto industry. The company embraces TQM as a way of life and pursues excellence in manufacturing through adoption of techniques like lean manufacturing, TPM. Four of the group companies have been conferred the coveted Deming Application Prize and has received number of other awards for its performances. With three major global partnerships for technology, it has supplier collaboration with world's leading OEM companies in India and abroad. Company exports to 20 countries and has a turnover of US$ 273 million.

Company B

Company B is part of a large group of companies situated in South India for over 75 years. Established as International Joint Venture with a leading company in Japan in 1985, the company provides holistic solutions in fuel management systems to two wheelers and passenger car. Its customers include leading automobile manufactures in India and abroad. After the exit of foreign partner in 2008, the company is totally under the Indian management.

It has two major tie-ups for technology, number supplier collaborations and acquired a precision company in US. Current turnover is US$ 100 million.

Company C

Headquartered in Chennai, company C is part of one leading business conglomerates of India that have business in wide range areas and annual turnover of US$ 3.14 billion. Started as tripartite venture with a UK and US companies in 1954, the company is in business of abrasives, ceramic and electrochemical. Current annual turnover is about US$ 147 million. Through its aggressive acquisitions and joint ventures, the company has its presence in Australia, Russia, China, South Africa, and North America. It has number of joint ventures and international collaborations. The strength of the company is in its strong market network and world class manufacturing facilities across the world, supported by its own R&D.

Company D

The company D is a small private limited firm. It has strong presence in the field of power conditioning by manufacturing and exporting products like Frequency Converters, UPSs, Voltage Stabilizers, K-Rated / Isolation Transformers, Energy Conservers for Lighting Applications and K-Rated Transformers. The company provides customized power solutions to meet the specific requirements of various industrial and commercial applications. It is GE Digital Energy's Indian business partner and national distributor for UPSs. Besides this, it has engaged in a few international alliances, particularly for Technology and many supplier collaborations with leading OEMs

****

ADVERTISING AND FIRM VALUE: MAPPING THE RELATIONSHIP BETWEEN ADVERTISING, PROFITABILITY AND BUSINESS STRATEGY IN INDIA

Anindita Kundu
Prashant Kulkarni
Anantha Murthy N.K.

Indian Business Academy, Bangalore

In today's competitive era one is constantly bombarded with advertisements. Empirical studies show that advertisements have an influence on the purchase behaviour of consumers. This behaviour is also influenced by the "value" they feel they would derive from purchasing that particular product or service. They expect a return on investment (price vis a vis value) i.e. value for each penny spent. At the other end of the spectrum the marketers expect a return on the investment they make (on advertising). This is natural given the fact that promotion activities do cost the firms a lot. The return may be in the form of increased profitability and an increase in the firm value. We find every year companies investing millions of rupees or dollars in marketing communication. A bulk of this obviously goes into advertising expenditure. Naturally, marketers expect a return on investment (RoI) on this. Their expectation stems from the likely impact, marketing investments have on the market performance and thus the profitability of the firm.

Raymond (1970) argues that the effectiveness of advertising conveys different meanings to different groups. To a general manager, it would obviously mean the impact that the advertising strategy has on the firm's profitability. This background makes it sufficiently on the trend in advertising research. With marketing communication used for creating awareness and building a long lasting relationship, many studies have focused on copy and media effects and awareness building about the product. Metrics have been developed to assess and measure consumer awareness and loyalty. Besides many studies use the AIDA or its adaptations that has been around from the early 20th century (Strong 1925). Few research studies also concentrate on measuring sales and profit effects (Gattignon 1993; Mantrala, 2002; Naik et al, 2007). A cursory glance at this suggests that these effects have been studied on the US consumers and markets. It is therefore imperative to study the impact of spending on advertisements on the profitability and firm value in case of Indian firms.

Moreover, questions arise whether advertising adds value to the firm. With little research focusing on this aspect we concentrate our study towards this end. Our objectives are:

- To determine whether advertising adds value to the firm
- Impact of advertising on profitability of the firm
- Differences between the impact both in degree and time across the industry
- Implications for the marketers

LITERATURE SURVEY

There is increasing awareness over the need to measure the impact of marketing activities on firm performance. Practitioners are increasingly under pressure to report their contribution to the overall firm performance. The inherent complexity in quantifying the marketing activities has often become a barrier in developing metrics for marketing measurement. O'Sullivan and Abela (2007) report that the ability to measure the internal marketing performance causes a significant impact on firm performance, profitability; stock return and marketing's stature within the firm.

In recent years a number of studies suggest that a firm's advertising (Frieder and Subrahmanyam 2005; Grullon, Kanatas, and Weston 2004; Joshi and Hanssens 2007) directly affects stock returns. This is in addition to the indirect effect of advertising through increase in sales revenues and profits. Srinivasan and Hansens (2007) carry out an extensive literature survey on the impact of advertisement on market and firm value.

The effect of advertising on consumers rests on the theory of message repetition. It can be classified into three main effects: a current effect on behaviour, a carryover effect on behaviour and a non behavioural effect on attitude and memory (Pechmann and Stewart 1988; Sawyer 1981; Sawyer and Ward 1976).

Researchers have tried to estimate the effects of advertising on brand sales using field data (Leone and Schultz 1980; Vakratsas and Ambler 1996). Most of these studies focus on technical issues involved in efficiently capturing the unbiased effects of advertising, given the limitations of field data (Hanssens, Parsons, and Schultz 1990). Deeper analysis of these studies finds that the effects of advertising are significantly greater than zero but do vary by market and product characteristics (Assmus, Farley, and Lehmann 1984; Sethuraman and Tellis 1991).

Few studies have addressed the effect of advertising effects on sales. Little has been researched on capturing the impact of how the effects vary by creative medium or vehicle, and time of the day for broadcast advertising (e.g., Bhattacharya and Lodish 1994). In particular, no study has researched the effects of advertising by these three factors simultaneously. While marketers know that consumer behaviour is influenced by multiple factors, yet little research has been done on understanding the impact using the integrated marketing mix model (Sethi 1977, Feichtinger, Hartl and Sethi, 1994). This is attributed to the fragility of advertising effects and the complexities involved in getting bias-free estimates.

Naik and Raman (2003) present an insight as to how a marketer or a shareholder is keen on measuring the impact of marketing (advertising investment) on market performance. To assess these effects marketers often use regression analysis. Arguing that OLS models introduce biasing effects, they put forward the Weiner Kalman Filter(WKF) that provides estimates that are closer to the true parameters.

The effectiveness of advertising lies in its capability to help stimulate or maintain sales (Eachambadi 1994; Mantrala, Sinha, and Zoltners 1992; Naik, Mantrala, and Sawyer Sethi 1998; Vidale and Wolfe 1957). Thus, advertising is frequently used as an independent variable in explaining changes in sales (Lilien 1994). Abraham and Lodish (1990) believe that advertising effectiveness has to be captured by the additional sales of a product over and above those that would have happened in absence of any advertising or promotion. Although advertising managers have long believed that advertising's impact on sales can persist longer than the current period (Clarke 1976), the tendency to assume that advertising's effect on sales is short-term is yet prevalent. They further argue that long term uses of advertising are better than its short term uses, irrespective of the nature of contribution of advertisement to sales (Jones 1992, 1995). The inability of measures to differentiate the impact of advertisement between its short term and long term effects have resulted in wastage of advertising expenditure (Abraham and Lodish, 1990; Bass 1969).

Eechambadi (1994) uses the analogy of capital budgeting process to capture the effectiveness of ad spending on sales and profitability. He suggests that brand managers be allowed to spend as much as they want on advertising if the return they generate is able to beat an internally agreed hurdle. His belief rests on the premise that absolute size of the ad budget does not matter but the return on that budget is the criteria for ad effectiveness.

The basic duopoly model leads to an equilibrium which can be determined analytically (Dixit, 1979); this basic model does not demonstrate any dynamic behaviour. Introducing advertising into the model allows firms endogenously alter demand which does invoke dynamic behaviour but is analytically intractable. Graham and Ariza (2003) present a model that optimizes allocation of firm advertising expenditure using a simulated annealing approach. Sterman et al (2007) use an approach that combines duopoly theory with the behavioural theory of the firm.

Research on the response to advertising had primarily looked at the shape of the response function (Aaker and Carman 1982; Simon and Arndt 1980; Mesak 1999), the dynamics of advertising effects (Simon 1978), and the interaction of advertising with other promotional mix elements (Winder and Moore 1989; Wildt 1977).

Luo and Donthu (2001) apply DEA – Data Envelopment Analysis to measure the efficiency of advertising in traditional media. Further, Yunjae Cheong (2006) uses a similar model to carry out a study on the evaluation of ad media spending efficiency. This model focused on how one could measure, maximize and benchmark the effects of advertising media spending, thereby improving the effectiveness of advertising.

Yew, Keh and Ong (2005) report that intensive investment in advertising contributes positively to the one-year stock market performances of non-manufacturing firms. However their results were inconclusive whether manufacturing firms benefit from investment in advertising as measured by the three-year stock market performance.

Mathur and Mathur (1995) using event study methodology concluded that investors react positively to announcements of advertisement changes leading to higher market value for firms.

Graham and Frankenberger (2000) examined the asset value of advertising expenditures of 320 firms with reported advertising expenditure for each of the 10 consecutive years ending in 1994, seeking to determine the impact of advertising expenditures on the financial performance. They used the changes in year to year differences in advertising expenditure to measure the impact on asset value and subsequent market value of the publicly traded firms.

FRAMEWORK FOR THE STUDY

A research framework is constructed to examine the impact of advertising on profitability of the firm as measured by profit after tax and the firm value as measured by Tobin's Q (Wu and Bjornson, 1996). Q ratio has extensively been used as a measure of firm's intangible value. This has enabled studies to be carried out in assessing the relationship between various firm and industry characteristics and firms intangible value. Besides, the impact of ad spending on Tobin's Q can serve as a proxy for contribution of ad spending on intangible firm value. We use an adaptation of Chung and Pritt's method to arrive at Tobin's Q. Since replacement costs of assets are difficult to obtain we take book value of assets to be a reasonable proxy.
Specifically in this method,
Tobin's q = (MVE + PS + DEBT)/TA
MVE = (Closing price of share at the end of the financial year)*(Number of common shares outstanding);
PS = Liquidating value of the firm's outstanding preferred stock;
DEBT = (Current liabilities - Current assets) +(Book value of inventories) + (Long term debt), and
TA = Book value of total assets.

Drawing from empirical literature in economics, finance and marketing, two firm specific variables that could potentially impact Tobin's Q were included in the study. Firm size as measured by the assets of the firm and leverage as measured by the Debt Equity Ratio (D-E ratio) were used as control variables to explain operating performance. Besides, finance text books have argued a positive relationship between leverage and profitability of the firm (eg. Brigham and Houston, Prasanna Chandra)

We ran a multiple regression equation to test our hypothesis. The following equation was framed for measuring the effect of advertising spending on profitability of firm as measured by PAT controlling for leverage:

- Profitability = α + β Advertising Expenses+ γ Dummy D/E Ratio +Error

We ran for the whole set of 172 firms. Further the same equation was run at the sectoral level. In multiple regressions we used ANOVA, coefficient of correlation in order to find out the impact of advertising on profitability and firm value. Besides, pie charts and graphs were used for the representation of data.

Further, we ran the following equation to test the impact of advertising spending on the firm value as measured by Tobin's Q controlling for firm size and leverage

- Firm Value=α+ β Assets + γD/E ratio +δ Advertising expenses +Error

Summarizing the above we state our propositions as follows:

Proposition I

H_0: There is no impact of advertisement spending on profitability of firm.

H_1: There is an impact of advertisement spending on profitability of firm.

Proposition II

H_0: There is no impact of advertisement spending on firm value.

H_1: There is an impact of advertisement spending on firm value.

DATA DESCRIPTION

The data for the study is obtained by CMIE-Prowess. The sample size was 200 companies. After accounting for the missing data, we got a sample size of 172 firms for a period 8 years (2000-2007). The variables which were included in data collection were sales, advertising expenses, PAT, Asset value of the firm (as a proxy for the size of the firm),and D/E Ratio (proxy for capital structure). Tobin's Q for each company was calculated using the given formula.

We further classified these firms into sectors as defined by the BSE Industry Classification. Some sectors were clubbed together. In some sectors, there were not enough firms to arrive at a robust conclusion necessitating their elimination for sectoral analysis. Results of our sectoral decomposition got clubbed under the following categories: Automobiles, Telecom, Fast Moving Consumer Goods (FMCG), Consumer Durables, Entertainment and Media, Pharmaceuticals and Health Care, Banking and Financial Services and Textiles.

RESULTS AND DISCUSSIONS

The following graph (Exhibit-1) illustrates advertisement spending, net profit and sales in different sectors.

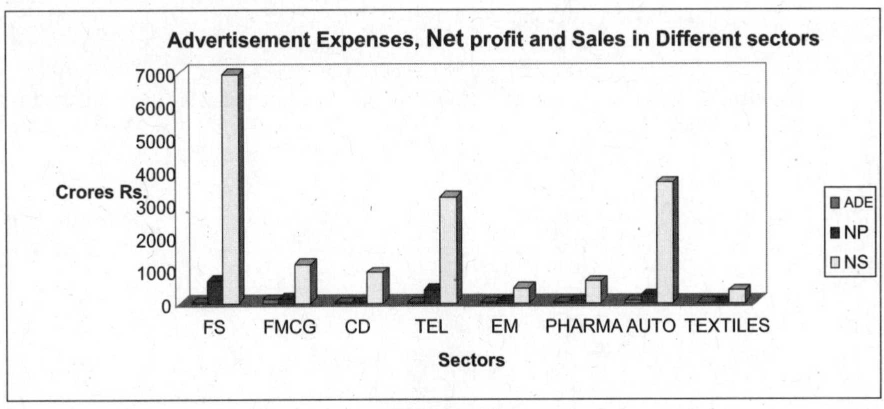

Exhibit-1

We proceed to test the correlation among the advertisement spending (ADE), Net Profit (NP) and Net Sales (NS) as represented in Table I.

It indicates a positive correlation between advertising spending and PAT and also between advertising spending and net sales. While results indicate that there is an increase in PAT and net sales following an increase in ad spending, the correlation is not strong enough to support a robust conclusion.

Table I
Table of Correlations

	ADE	NP	NS
ADE	1.000		
NP	0.166	1.000	
NS	0.172	0.809	1.000

The regression results on the impact of ad spending on profitability are shown in Table II. Table III shows the regression results for impact of ad spending on profitability on different sectors.

Table II

Sample Size	F value	Constt α	Ad. Coefficient β	Dummy DE-ratio Coefficient γ	R Square (Standard Error)
172	3.5351 **(0.0313)** **	17.4163 0.0313^{t} (0.0012)	2.1275 0.0012^{t} **(0.0358)****	1429.0836 -1.4836^{t} (0.1398)	0.0402 **(805.4751)**

  *   indicates Significant at 1% Level of significance
  **   indicates Significant at 5 % Level of significance
  ***   indicates Significant at 10 % Level of significance
The values inside the parenthesis are the p-values, and t indicates the computed t-statistic value.

<u>Table III</u>

Sample Size	F value	Constant α	Ad. Coefficient β	Dummy DE-ratio Coefficient γ	R-Square (and Standard Error)
Banking and Fin services (15 Samples)	5.7632 **(0.0176)** **	73.4163 0.3047^t (0.7658)	17.4334 2.1851^t **(0.0494)****	566.9134 1.6306^t (0.1289)	0.4899 **(614.8696)**
FMCG (18Samples)	189.1583 **(0.0000)***	-51.5167 2.6086^t (0.0198)	1.6506 14.9311^t **(0.0000)***	57.8048 1.0163^t (0.3256)	0.9619 **(71.9521)**
Consumer Durables (10 Samples)	24.8959 **(0.0004)***	3.9421 0.2088^t (0.8398)	0.2448 0.3150^t (0.7608)	239.5787 5.0502^t (0.0010)	0.8616 **(33.7502)**
Telecom (15Samples)	10.1375 **(0.0026)***	206.5603 0.4955^t (0.6292)	-7.1997 -0.9024^t (0.3846)	3473.3535 4.3283^t (0.0010)	0.6282 **(1053.3326)**
Entertainment & Media (7 Samples)	33.9175 **(0.0031)***	-36.6866 -1.7517^t (0.1547)	2.7325 3.2557^t **(0.0312)****	138.6127 4.3824^t (0.0119)	0.9443 **(31.1299)**
Automobile (10 Samples)	5.8247 **(0.0324)****	-0.3592 -0.0034^t (0.9974)	2.2474 1.6797^t (0.1369)	215.7577 1.2878^t (0.2388)	0.6247 **(203.5455)**
Textiles (10 Samples)	18.5949 **(0.0016)***	-14.1615 -1.5887^t (0.1562)	1.9968 3.6915^t **(0.0077)***	31.3119 1.7788^t (0.1185)	0.8416 **(18.0619)**
Pharmaceuticals (13 Samples)	12.1231 **(0.0021)***	8.5688 0.3835^t (0.7094)	1.6998 2.9324^t **(0.0150)****	56.4262 1.2673^t (0.2338)	0.7080 **(57.9580)**

*   indicates Significant at 1% Level of significance

**   indicates Significant at 5 % Level of significance

***   indicates Significant at 10 % Level of significance

The values inside the parenthesis are the p-values, and t indicates the computed t-statistic value.

The regression indicates a significant and positive relationship between advertisement spending and profitability as measured by PAT. However the elasticity is very small and this can be attributed to the fact that ad spending is given as the treatment of expense on the current revenue. The results show an aggressive impact of ad spending on PAT controlling for leverage in Banking and financial services (a one unit increase in ad spending results in 17.434 units of PAT). R and R^2 too show satisfactory results. Similar results albeit on a smaller scale are visible in FMCG (coefficient of 1.6506); Textile (1.99); Entertainment and Media (2.73) and Pharmaceuticals (1.70). In FMCG sector, R and R^2 approach near unity. We however find no significance in telecom, consumer durables and automobile sector.

FIRM VALUE AND AD SPENDING

Firm value has a tangible component and an intangible element. Tobin's Q is taken as the measure of firm value. We define the following function

Firm value= f(Assets, DE-ratio, Advertising expenses)

We then used the multiple regression model using the following equation.

Firm Value=α+ β Assets+ γ D/E ratio +δ Advertising expenses +Error

Regression results are given in Table IV. Table V gives the results of the multiple regressions when carried out on different sectors.

Table IV

Sample Size	F value	Constant α	Assets β	DE-ratio γ	Ad. Expenses δ	R Square (Standard Error
172	6.3536 **(0.0004)** *	1.5535 7.4849^t (0.0000)	0.0000 -2.0199^t (0.0451)	0.0435 0.9529^t (0.3421)	0.0082 3.8300^t **(0.0002)***	0.1095 **(2.0822)**

*   indicates Significant at 1% Level of significance
**   indicates Significant at 5 % Level of significance
***   indicates Significant at 10 % Level of significance
The values inside parenthesis are the p-values.
t indicates the computed t-statistic value.

<u>**Table V**</u>

Sector and Sample Size	F value (Overall)	Constant α	Assets β	DE-ratio γ	Ad. Expenses δ	R Square (& Stdd Error)
Banking& Financial Service (14 Samples)	10.3832 **(0.0020)** *	-0.0280 -0.3665^ت (0.7216)	0.0000 -2.2803^t (0.0458)	0.0860 2.1238^t (0.0596)	0.0094 4.1806^t **(0.0019)***	0.7570 **(0.1445)**
Automobile (10 Samples)	0.2639 (0.8492)	1.5977 2.7130^t (0.0350)	-0.0001 -0.7495^t (0.4819)	-0.0334 -0.4321^t (0.6808)	0.0037 0.6550^t (0.5368)	0.1166 **(0.8513)**
FMCG (16 Samples)	1.9716 (0.1721)	3.3703 3.8162^t (0.0025)	-0.0016 -0.8020^t (0.4382)	-1.6756 -1.1541^t (0.2709)	0.0172 1.1161^t (0.2862)	0.3302 **(2.0986)**
Telecom (13 Samples)	3.2585 **(0.0736)** *	1.2492 4.1893^t (0.0023)	0.0000 -1.9688^t (0.0805)	0.0727 1.4263^t (0.1875	0.0067 1.3283^t (0.2168	0.5207 **(0.6545)**
Entertainment and Media (5 Samples)	10.7212 (0.2200)	1.2303 2.9961^t (0.2051)	0.0007 4.9452^t (0.1270)	-2.0426 -1.8148^t (0.3206	0.0067 0.4210^t (0.7463)	0.9698 **(0.3789)**
Consumer Durables (10 Samples)	184.4977 **(0.0000)** *	1.0119 9.6686^t (0.0001)	-0.0001 -1.480^t (0.1892)	0.1656 23.1788^t (0.0000)	0.0081 1.9431^t **(0.1000)*** *	0.9893 **(0.1694)**
Textiles (10 Samples)	1.7754 (0.2516)	1.1546 6.5888^t (0.0006)	0.0005 2.0935^t (0.0812)	0.1086 1.6064^t (0.1593)	-0.0203 -1.7230^t (0.1357)	0.4703 **(0.3197)**
Pharmaceuticals (12 Samples)	4.4167 **(0.0413)** **	2.4515 6.3653^t (0.0002)	0.0008 1.7068^t (0.1262)	-2.1902 -2.4119^t (0.0424)	-0.0014 -0.1200^t (0.9074)	0.6235 **(0.7794)**

*   indicates Significant at 1% Level of significance
**   indicates Significant at 5 % Level of significance
***   indicates Significant at 10 % Level of significance
The values inside the parenthesis are the p-values.
t   indicates the computed t-statistic value.

Results present a mixed picture. We find a positive and significant relationship between ad spending and Tobin's Q accounting for firm size and leverage. However the weak coefficient (0.0082) coupled with R value of 33% and

R^2 of 10% do not present encouraging results. The effect e can sat at best is small. This is not surprising as ad spending has a time lag before creating an impact on the intangible. Moreover, we visualize a case of decreasing returns to scale. This gets reinforced when we analyze the results from different sectors. Only two sectors show a positive and significant relationship (Banking and Financial Services and Consumer Durables). However both the sectors tend to show a very high correlation coupled with a high coefficient of determination. This indicates that advertising does not influence firm value and that Tobin's Q is determined by other factors.

INFERENCES AND MANAGERIAL IMPLICATIONS

Taken together the results of regression in profitability and firm value provide indicators of ad spending influencing these factors. But this influence seems weak. The results therefore seem inconclusive. However this study which incorporates usage of metrics and attempts to establish a relationship between advertising (language of marketing) and firm value and profitability (language of finance) serves as an attempt to quantify the impact of marketing practices on valuations of the firm. The complexity of the relationships presents a challenge to researchers and managers alike. We believe that further investigation into these relationships is essential to uncover the influence of advertisement in building firm value. Besides, the study has sought to move away from the traditional approach of uncovering product-market demand effects of advertisement to uncovering financial effects of advertising. A major limitation of studies like the one here, is that the findings are only as good as the secondary data obtained. While some new and interesting insights on the effects of advertising on firm value could be garnered, the study can however be extended to include other elements of marketing mix that are likely to influence firm value and the linkages among these marketing mix activities particularly in the Indian context.

This study follows the current approach to the subject; we yet remain uncertain of the best way to value the effect on intangibles. However, we have attempted to use rational logic within the constraints of available data to uncover the relationship in the Indian context. We believe the study's attempt to explore the effects of firms' marketing activities on firm value is the first step in stimulating further studies on this subject.

REFERENCES

1. MacKenzie. Scott B. and Richard J. Lutz (1982), "Monitoring Advertising Effectiveness: A Structural Equation Analysis of the Mediating Role of Attitude Toward the Ad", unpublished manuscript, UCLA Center for Marketing
2. Aaker, D.A., Carman, J.M. (1982), "Are You Overadvertising?," *Journal of Advertising Research*
3. Naras V. Eechambadi(1994),"Does Advertising Work", The McKinsey Quarterly 1994
4. D. Epstein(1997), "The Valuation of a Firm Advertising Optimally", Mathematical Institute, Oxford University
5. Seiford, Lawrence, and Joe Zhu (1999), "Profitability and Marketability of the Top 55 U.S. Banks," *Management Science*
6. Vakratsas, D. & Ambler, T. (1999, January). "How advertising works: what do we really know?", *Journal of Marketing*

7. Bruce F. Hall(2001), "A New Approach to Measuring Advertising Effectiveness", Howard, Merrell and Partners

8. Luo, Xueming, and Naveen Donthu (2001), "Benchmarking Advertising Efficiency," *Journal of Advertising Research*

9. Amanda D.H. Smith,(2002), "Measuring Intangibles: The Asset Value of Advertising", Duke University

10. Yunjae Cheong (2006) "An evaluation of advertising media spending efficiency using data envelopment analysis" Conference of the American Academy of Advertising

11. Shuba Srinivasan Dominique M. Hanssens(2007), "Marketing and firm value"

12. Prasad Naik(2007), "Perils of Using OLS to Estimate Multimedia Communications Effects", Journal of Advertising Research

13. Max Kilger,(2007), "Do Measures of Media Engagement Correlate with Product Purchase Likelihood?", Journal of Advertising Research

DESIGNING SHOPPING MALL SERVICESCAPES: A PROBLEM STRUCTURING METHODS (PSMs) APPROACH

Masood H. Siddiqui
Shalini N. Tripathi

Jaipuria Institute of Management, Lucknow

INTRODUCTION

Service environments relate to the style and appearance of physical surroundings and other experience based elements encountered by customers at service delivery sites. Bitner (1992) coined the term **'Servicescapes'** in reference to the physical surroundings as fashioned by service organizations to facilitate the provision of service offered to customers, that is, the physical facilities of a company. Physical service environment plays an important role in shaping the service experience and providing customer satisfaction. In service organizations the same physical environment that communicates with and influences customers, may affect employees' satisfaction, performance, productivity, and motivation (Baker, Berry & Parasuraman, 1988). Both customers and employee groups may respond cognitively, emotionally and physiologically to the service environment. Designing this environment is an art that takes considerable time and effort and is expensive to implement especially for organizations delivering high contact services like shopping malls and retail stores because Servicescape can support positioning and segmentation strategies, secure strategic advantage and as such enhance strategic marketing objectives. Service environments are complex and have many design elements. In particular, if we consider design elements of a shopping mall/retail store service environment, then major dimensions will be exterior facilities, general interior, interior displays and social dimensions (attitude, behavior of staff etc.) (Berman & Evans, 2001; Turley & Milliman, 2000).

There is need for cross functional co-operation in decision making about service environment. Planning for facility and management is a problem solving activity that lies on the boundary between architecture, interior space planning and product design, organization (consumer) behavior, and planning and environment psychology. Designing, improving and managing service environment will have an impact on human resource, operations and marketing goals. So, planning should involve inputs from managers in these areas along with inputs from actual users, that is, customers and employees. So, larger the number of actors and stakeholders involved in planning more is the scope for conflicting agenda.

This kind of decision making takes place amidst conditions of uncertainties and complexities because all participants have varied perceptions about the "problem situation"; conflicting interests, different conventions and expectations and nature of social interactions. This kind of situations may be unpredictable, ill-structured and complex. Many variables have an impact on the situation, the linking and degree of interrelationship of these variables is uncertain. Business environment is dynamic and its rate of change is rather uncertain.

In the previous generation, emphasis was on analytic modeling (represented normally in quantitative analytic form), factors/alternatives and relationship among them in a decision situation are represented mathematically and then solved using software packages. Mostly these tools and techniques aim at finding the 'best' solution, considering a number of assumptions. Classical approaches to both planning and decision-making are inappropriate in theory, and have proved inadequate in practice for managing such ambiguous risks, which may fail in real life situations (Rosenhead & Mingers, 2001). Different people interpret problem situations from particular standpoints and in terms of distinctive interests. Fortune and Peters (1995) talk of 'complex discursive' networks frequently giving rise to contending interpretations of the system, problems and solutions to problems. Therefore problem situations in this area are ill-structured and management and performance improvement initiatives based either on 'rationally' predefined goals or spontaneous 'quick fixes' are likely to end in disappointment.

To be able to adequately handle such situations, analytical approaches to decision making must take into account differences in perception and conflict between participants. Companies find that traditional models of strategic planning suffer from serious shortcomings in the new business environment. So, companies now have to bring together the needs and expectations of diverse constituencies, each with unique and sometimes conflicting requirements. Additionally; social, economic and political factors; although difficult to predict; need to be reconciled. Therefore, time has come for alternative techniques and methodologies known as **Problem Structuring Methods** (PSMs). They certainly represent an emerging trend in business strategy research.

PSMs accept that the most demanding & troubling task in formative decision situations is to decide what the problem actually is. There are too many factors, many of the relationships are unclear, and do not reduce naturally to qualified form, different stakeholders/players have different priorities. PSMs use models to help group decision making. The aim of PSMs is both more modest and more ambitions than precious generation of optimizing methods; the solution provided by them may not be the best one but it will be for more general situations considering very few assumptions so it is more useful in the real business life (Rosenhead & Mingers, 2001). The principal PSMs are Strategic Options Development and Analysis (SODA), Soft System Methodology (SSM), Strategic

Choice Approach (SCA), Drama Theory etc., to assist strategic decision-making. This field is now generally referred to as 'Soft O.R.' as they are distinguished by the different assumptions these approaches make regarding problem definition, nature of organizations, use of models and the emphasis placed on organizational and individual learning.

All of the above PSMs take a process-oriented approach to model complex problems and have been developed through action research. Soft OR enables consultants to identify what particular information and knowledge might be structured in order to manage complex problems. These modeling techniques incorporate human dimensions and support transparency in conflict situations and therefore promote a 'beneficial' climate of conflict and confrontation (Liebl, 2002). This management of conflict and confrontation is an important feature of Soft OR process.

SOFT SYSTEMS METHODOLOGY (SSM)

The SSM, developed by Peter Checkland (1981; 95; 99), is a qualitative technique that can be used for applying Systems Thinking to non-systemic situations. It is a way of dealing with problem situations in which there is a high social, political and human activity component (Fortune & Peters, 1995), like dealing with the strategic issues of designing, improving and managing the physical service environment for organizations delivering high contact services like shopping malls and retail stores. This distinguishes SSM from other methodologies, which deal with HARD problems that are often more technology-oriented. SSM approaches issues of Servicescapes holistically so as to provide better understanding of complexities and vulnerabilities.

SSM provides a coherent approach to group and individual thinking about context, complexity and ambiguities of such organizations that have high level of human intervention (Checkland & Scholes, 1999). Stress is upon encouraging the involvement of system owners, actors and customers, collaborating with the analyst or consultant, in the process of situation improvement. Wider involvement is a crucial prerequisite for effective and sustainable improvement initiatives to achieve a broader perspective (Checkland & Holwell, 1998).

SSM operates by defining systems of purposeful activity (the root definition), building models of a number of relevant systems and comparing these models to the real world scenario, in order to structure a debate focusing on the differences. That debate should lead the people involved in the process to see their way to possible changes and motivate these people to carry out those changes. There are basically seven stages in the SSM process, not necessarily followed in a linear fashion (Checkland, 1981; 95):

Stages 1 and 2: Finding out- This stage entails entering the problem situation and identifying within it:

> *People-* all those with an interest in the system or likely to be affected by changes to it
> *Culture-* social roles, norms of behavior and values
> *Politics-*commodities of power and how they are obtained, used, preserved and transmitted

Checkland (1999) regards the 'finding out' about a problem situation through rich picture and analysis as critically important. A key feature of SSM is to keep the project vague and wide for as long as possible – neither jump to conclusions nor assume or ignore the current situation.

Stage 3: Developing root definitions- This intermediate stage, called 'systems thinking about the real world'; consists of 'developing root definitions' of associated purposeful activity systems. These are the sentences that describe the ideal system or sub system within it; the root definitions should specify CATWOE as following-

C: Customer/victim/beneficiaries of the system. **A**: Actors/ participants of the system. **T**: Transformation process. **W**: Weltanschauung, that is, worldview underlying the system. **O**: Owner of the system, having power to stop the system. **E**: Environmental constraints that cannot be altered and need to be considered.

The root definition and CATWOE have at their centre the transformation process, SSM centers upon these processes - upon the conversion of some input to some output. As each category of participants - designers, managers, users, or other beneficiaries may have different views of the organization's main goals or activities, many other transforming processes will be identified, and many other viewpoints will be elicited during an SSM investigation. Once these activities have been discussed and expressed, they can serve as the basis for formally expressed root definitions from which conceptual models of systems can be developed. By examining the most relevant of these, it is possible to develop an overall notion of a system in terms of some purposeful human activity. This process is accomplished by examining systems in terms of their owners, actors, beneficiaries, transformation processes, environments, and the world views or Weltanschauung of those involved. The investigation may help determine which activities are essential to the organization, and which are superfluous. As well, since many perceptions are elicited, potential conflicts may be uncovered, or potential areas of commonality revealed.

Stage 4: Building conceptual models- At this stage a model which is actually a diagram (map) of activities with links (arrows) connecting them, according to logical dependencies (Eden & Ackermann, 2004) is developed from the root definition (Checkland, 1999). It should be focused more on the 'softer' aspect of the client's requirement rather than 'harder' technical details (Howard, 1993).

Stage 5: Comparing- This stage is designed to provide structure and substance to an organized debate about improving the current situation .This stage involves comparing the models that have been developed with the real world situation.

Stage 6: Identifying changes- If the current system requires, then we have to agree on desirable changes. So, this stage involves identifying changes that could be made to the real-world system, changes that appear, to those participating in the SSM process, as worth trying. These changes need to be systematically desirable and culturally feasible (Pidd, 2003).

Stage 7: Taking action- The outcome of the previous stage is that there is some agreement - permission to move. So, this stage involves putting into practice the most appropriate changes identified in the previous stage.

So, the above seven stages SSM process can be summarized according to Figure 1 (Checkland,1999).

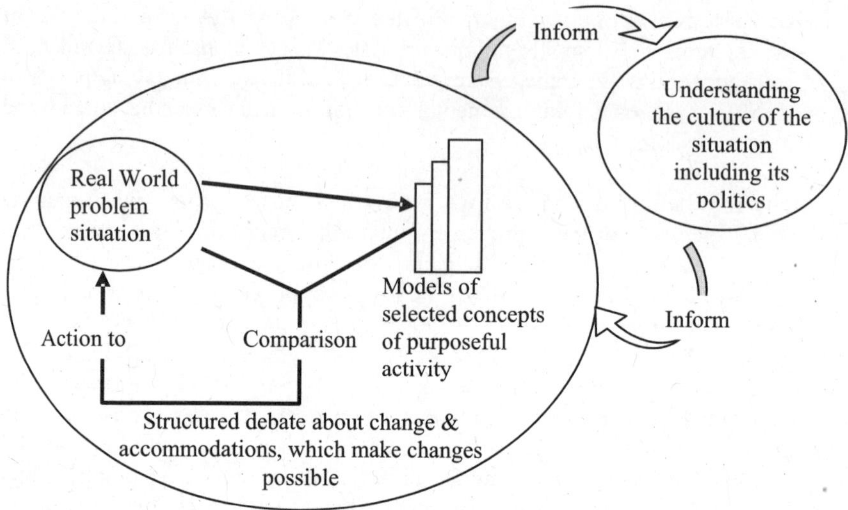

Figure 1: Representation of mature SSM

STRATEGIC CHOICE APPROACH (SCA)

SCA, developed by Friend and Hickling (1997) deals with the interconnectedness of the decision problems in an explicit yet selective way. The distinctive feature of this approach is that it helps people working together to make better progress towards decisions by focusing their attention on possible ways of managing uncertainty as to what they should do next (Rosenhead & Mingers, 2001). It combines concern for complexities with an emphasis on real time decision making. It works on the philosophy of managing uncertainty in a strategic way. SCA identifies four modes of decision making activities:

- **Shaping-** considering the structure of the decision problems.
- **Designing-** considering possible courses of action.
- **Comparing-** comparing possible courses of action.
- **Choosing-** choosing the most appropriate course of action.

A key theme underlying SCA is identifying **uncertainty areas,** having broad categories as:

- **UE:** uncertainty about working environment being reducible by technical response.
- **UV:** uncertainty about guiding values being reducible by political response.
- **UR:** uncertainty about related decision fields being reducible by exploring structural relationship (Figure 2) (Friend & Hickling, 1997).

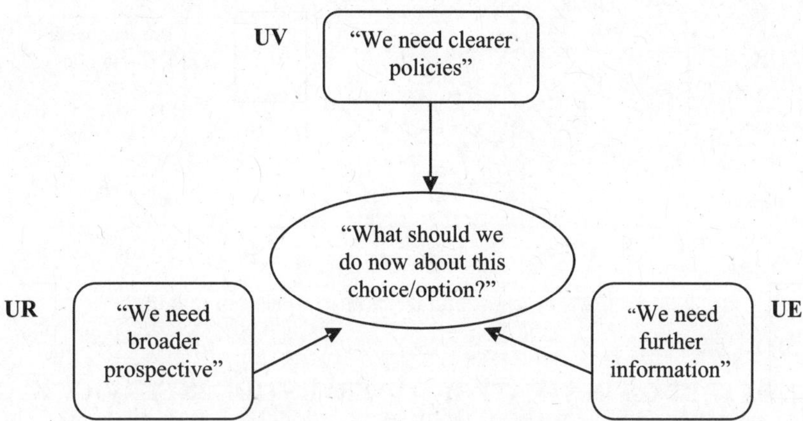

Figure 2: Structural Relationships

The shaping mode- When functioning in this mode, decision makers address concerns about the structure of the set of decision problems that they now face. They may be debating in what ways choices should be formulated, and how far one decision should be seen as linked to another.

The designing mode- Here, the decision makers address concerns about the courses of action that are feasible in their current view of problem shape. They may debate whether they have enough options before them, or whether there are design constraints of either a technical or policy nature that might restrict the scope for combining options.

The comparing mode- Here, the decision maker addresses concern about the ways in which the implications of different courses should be compared. It is in this mode that uncertainties of the three types come into sharpest focus (Figure3).

The choosing mode- In this mode, the focus of the decision makers is on agree on commitment to actions over time. It is in this mode that the dimension of time becomes critical, and strategies for managing uncertainty through time must be explored.

Figure 3 depicts a process in which opportunities exist to switch from working in any one of the four modes to work in any of the others for a while, with feedback loops it allows for possible recursion to earlier stages in a more fluid and adaptive way (Hickling, 1997).

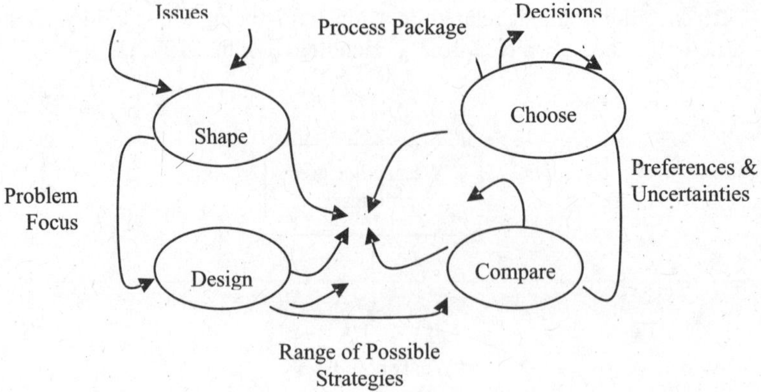

Figure 3: Three kinds of uncertainty in decision making

ROLE OF SOFT OR IN STRATEGIC INTERVENTION IN SERVICESCAPE DEVELOPMENT

Here, we apply selective mixing of two Soft OR methodologies- SSM and SCA for enhancing Servicescapes as a facilitator because this mixing can enhance and enrich the process of strategic decision making in complex problems. Rather than using one Soft OR approach from start to finish, the practitioner may use a component of methodology that best emphasizes the particular aspect of the problem in that given situation because while each methodology has something to offer to one of the identified challenges, it will equally prove inadequate on others (Lane, 1994). Ormerod (1995), Matthews and Bennett (1996) also demonstrated the value of this multi-methodology approach in complex problems. It is the high level of complexity and human element associated with this problem that recommended the possibility of linking Soft OR techniques to assist decision making. Bennett (1996) categorizes three forms of linkages: *comparison, enrichment* and *integration. Comparison*, questions how the approaches are theoretically or practically similar? Whether they are complementary or incompatible? *Enrichment* involves using theoretical or practical aspects of one method to improve another without producing a new approach. In *integration*, a new approach is developed as a consequence of linking principles of existing approaches. The approach we use for Servicescape development and management was one of *enrichment* and the rationale for this is described in Figure 4.

Root definition and *CATWOE* from SSM provide all base components to complete the understanding and definition of business (Servicescape) model. *Uncertainty Space* and *Commitment Package* tools from SCA are especially useful for handling risk and uncertainty inherent in it. With respect to dealing with conflicting situations in the business model both SSM and SCA may be equally useful (Figure 4) (Bennett, 1996; Gondal, 2004). So, this illustrates Bennett's assertion (1996) of mixing methodologies.

	Defining the business model	Handling risk/uncertainty	Dealing with conflict	Challenging mental model
SCA	◯ Low/None	● High/Large	◉ Medium	◯ Low/None
SSM	● High/Large	◯ Low/None	◉ Medium	● High/Large

◯ Low/None   ◉ Medium   ● High/Large

Figure 4: Rationale for selective mixing of Soft OR methodologies

Generally, a company can take two main approaches for strategy formulation and strategy implementation: *top-down change* or *bottom-up change*. With *top-down change*, top management analyzes how to alter strategy and structure, recommends a course of action, and then moves quickly to restructure and implement the change to achieve the desired change. The emphasis is on the speed of response and the management of problems as they occur. *Top-down approach* may be better for setting objectives that may ensure that the financial and strategic performance targets established for business units, divisions, functional departments, and operating units are directly connected to the achievement of overall objectives. *Bottom-up change* is much more gradual. Top management consults with managers at all levels in the organization. Then, over time, it develops a detailed plan for change, with timetable of events and stages that the company will go through. The emphasis in the *bottom-up change* is on participation and on keeping people informed about the situation, so that uncertainty is minimized. The advantage of *bottom-up change* is that it removes some of the obstacles to change by including them in the strategy plan, through consultation at all levels to revel potential problems that may be difficult to resolve, if they emerge later. The disadvantage with this approach is its slowness and difficulty to overcome organizational inertia. The soft OR approach suggested here is essentially the *bottom-up change* because the emphasis is on participation of possibly all the players and stakeholders. By selectively mixing these methodologies (SSM and SCA) the drawbacks of bottom-up approach can be taken care of up to a satisfactory level. Here our objective is not to provide a new methodology, but rather to provide an alternative way in which an OR practitioner can selectively apply different components of methodologies and by mixing methods enriching the process of development and management of the Servicescape.

If we consider various traditional strategic management tools vis-à-vis different stages of the two Soft OR techniques used here in the Servicescape planning and management, we can summarize the comparison/similarity areas and the applicability rationale as Figure 5 & 6 (Gondal, 2004).

Soft System Methodology Stages	Finding Out	Developing Root Definition & Building Conceptual Model	Comparing Conceptual Model with the Real World	Identifying Changes & Commitment Package
Strategic Choice Approach Stages	Shaping	Designing	Comparing	Choosing
SWOT Analysis [Weihrich(1982)]		Understanding the firms internal environment	Evaluating risks & uncertainty associated with the internal environment	
PEST Analysis [Porter(1980,85)]		Understanding the firms external environment	Evaluating risks & uncertainty associated with the external environment	
Porter's Generic Strategies [Porter(1980,85)]		Focus the business model	Determine whether focus creates a viable opportunity	
Porter's Five Forces Model [Porter(1980,85)]		Identify market consequences of, and impact on, business concept	Determine whether market can be managed to create a more favorable scenario	
Critical Success Factors/ Scenario Modeling [Rockart,Hofman,1992]		Identify factors required for success	Quantify & understand impact of options	Determine likelihood of factors required for success

[Gondal (2004)]

Figure 5: Comparison/Similarity of Strategic Management Tools with SSM & SCA

	Defining the business model	Handling risk/uncertainty	Dealing with conflict	Challenging mental model
SWOT Analysis	Medium	Medium	Low/None	Medium
PEST Analysis	Medium	Medium	Low/None	Medium
Porter's Generic Strategies	Medium	Medium	Low/None	Medium
Porter's Five Forces Model	Medium	Medium	Low/None	Medium
Critical Success Factors/ Scenario Modeling	Low/None	Medium	High/Large	Medium

○ Low/None   ◉ Medium   ● High/Large

Figure 6: Applicability of Strategic Management tools (Gondal, 2004)

So, Soft OR techniques like Soft System Methodology and Strategic Choice Approach and the well known traditional strategic management tools are complementary rather than in conflict, having a number of components common among them and their applicability is also at par with each other. They are designed to offer support to decision-makers (management team) by providing them with an efficient and structured way of identifying and evaluating options. Soft OR techniques are just alternative approaches towards decision-making incorporating subjectivity along with the 'hard' optimization tools of operations research. Here focus is also on people rather than on process alone. They are tools to enhance participation in decision-making, organizing debate towards a common and acceptable goal (s), approaching consensus and finally extracting commitment towards the actions. They are used primarily to promote integration of knowledge and transparency in the process, to build trust and understanding between different groups, therefore, enhancing the quality of decision-making.

These kinds of problems like designing, improving and managing Servicescape are essentially unique on their own because of elements of multi-perceptivity, intangibility and dynamism   associated with the Servicescape so they require inventive/creative solutions and group efforts. The tools and techniques used here to enrich decision-making process were chosen with the audience and the circumstances in mind i.e. they are basically situation specific and they may not be generalized so they may be or may not be used again.

RESEARCH LIMITATIONS AND CRITICISM

Soft OR methodologies are valuable in terms of supporting problem structuring and finding alternatives in different stages of problem solving process. It is however also clear that this process is not always straight forward. Not being ready to think differently and lack of research work in India on application of Soft OR tools in marketing settings are major barriers. Quantification of qualitative features and high level of intangibility involved in services and physical service environment are other limitations.

Radical critics say that SSM and SCA assume that all members of the enterprise have a choice, in fact an equal choice. The idea that managers and workers can openly discuss their problems and needs is fanciful, that is, both the approaches ignore issues of power. Further, critics claim, these approaches impose values of openness and 'niceness', which are more suitable to middle class academics than to managers or workers. These criticisms do indicate that Soft OR approaches have a fairly simple understanding of problem and society.

PARTICIPATORY ACTION RESEARCH STUDY OF SERVICESCAPE USING SOFT OPERATIONS RESEARCH

We have applied selective mixing of two Soft OR methodologies SSM and SCA for designing, improving and managing service environment of shopping malls/retail stores. As discussed, SSM is the main methodology used because it is very well capable of understanding and defining the Servicescape model incorporating most of the diverse view-points, perceptions, expectations, requirements related to the service environment model. *'finding out'* stage of SSM incorporates all the ingredients of *'shaping'* mode of SCA. *'developing root definition'* and *'building conceptual model'* stages of SSM are very similar to *'designing'* mode of SCA. Main objective of using SCA is that it is probably the best Soft OR technique to identify uncertainties associated with each stage of the process.

As a qualitative OR tool, SSM is designed to analyze and model complex system that integrates technology with human and organizational system. The synergistic relationship of SSM with its focus on human system, consensus building and comparison is very suitable for intangible concepts like service environment. SSM looks at a human system like service environment, which is defined as a collection of activities in which people are purposefully engaged and there is some relationship between these activities.

Strategic service environment planning is a comprehensive and ongoing management process aimed at formulating and implementing an effective comprehensive plan for accomplishing management goal of increased level of customer satisfaction and repatronage. This planning should be on the premise that an analysis of internal and external factors must be conducted. Firm's external environment must include not only market (Competitors and customers) conditions but also environmental management issues. These environmental issues require the understanding of multiple and ever-changing threats and opportunities resulting from regulatory, social, local and technological factors. Internally, the requirements and priorities of managers and employees and other stakeholders change with time.

1ˢᵗ Phase-Empirical Research: In this phase, investigators were asked to do a preliminary survey of shopping malls situated in Lucknow. A detailed survey of customers was carried out to know and measure the level of satisfaction with the current service environment of the shopping malls, expectations from them and relative importance of different macro-dimensions and micro-aspects of these dimensions. The survey(for both 'hard' & 'soft' data) was in the form of a structured questionnaire and direct observations and information was collected from about 500 customers using quota sampling so to make the sample representative of the diverse views. Quota was constructed on various socio-economic demographic-profiles. This stage, labeled as 'client analysis', seeks to achieve an understanding of the social-aesthetical aspect of clients in terms of culture, values, style, behavior, priorities, requirements, expectations etc. Simultaneously, the survey of all other actors and stakeholders like managers, floor managers, employees etc. was also carried out in the form of focus groups and semi-structured interviews using repertory grid procedure techniques. A considerable amount of information was gathered from them, a part of the information is used for the stage labeled as 'strategic analysis' which seeks to identify how business and decision activities are organized by drawing corporate goals, objectives, strategies and procedures vis-à-vis service environment, different types of stakeholders and their perspectives, assumptions, concerns and difficulties; the second part is meant for the stage termed as 'facility analysis' which is more technical in nature and focuses on built facilities. Note that both SSM and SCA are implemented as a participative process (application of action research) where the facilitator (modeler) works with the problem stakeholders. The purpose of this analysis phase is simply to get some idea, though it may be unstructured, so that a range of possible & relevant choices can be made.

2ⁿᵈ Phase-Empirical Research: Detailed discussions were being carried out with different actors and stakeholders like managers both at policy-making level and at operational levels, employees and finally customers. Their total number was 25; comprising of managers, floor managers, employees and some selected customers belonging to different socio-economic background. The purpose of this 'problem expressing' stage is to depict (through 'rich picture') the structure and process of the service environment, incorporating the multi-perspective complexity of the real situation. The relation between structure and process should illustrate the problem, tasks, and elements of the environment in a way, which is easy to understand. Participants were divided into sub-groups of sizes 4 to 6, so as to allow comparable data between the sub-groups to be collected and being in a small group, each participant was more likely to contribute better. Each group was asked to examine the core purpose, activities and information needs of functions involved in a shopping mall. The process used was Oval Mapping Technique (OMT), because it would be a better option for surfacing and structuring the thinking and it would involve more people. Here the two consultants (modelers) worked both as 'process facilitator' as well as 'content facilitator'.

Rich Picture and Cluster Maps: In this phase, a 'rich picture' has been drawn to depict the problem-situation by summarizing the findings of the above phase for in-depth analysis of the problem situation. Here a 'rich picture' (Figure 7) has been

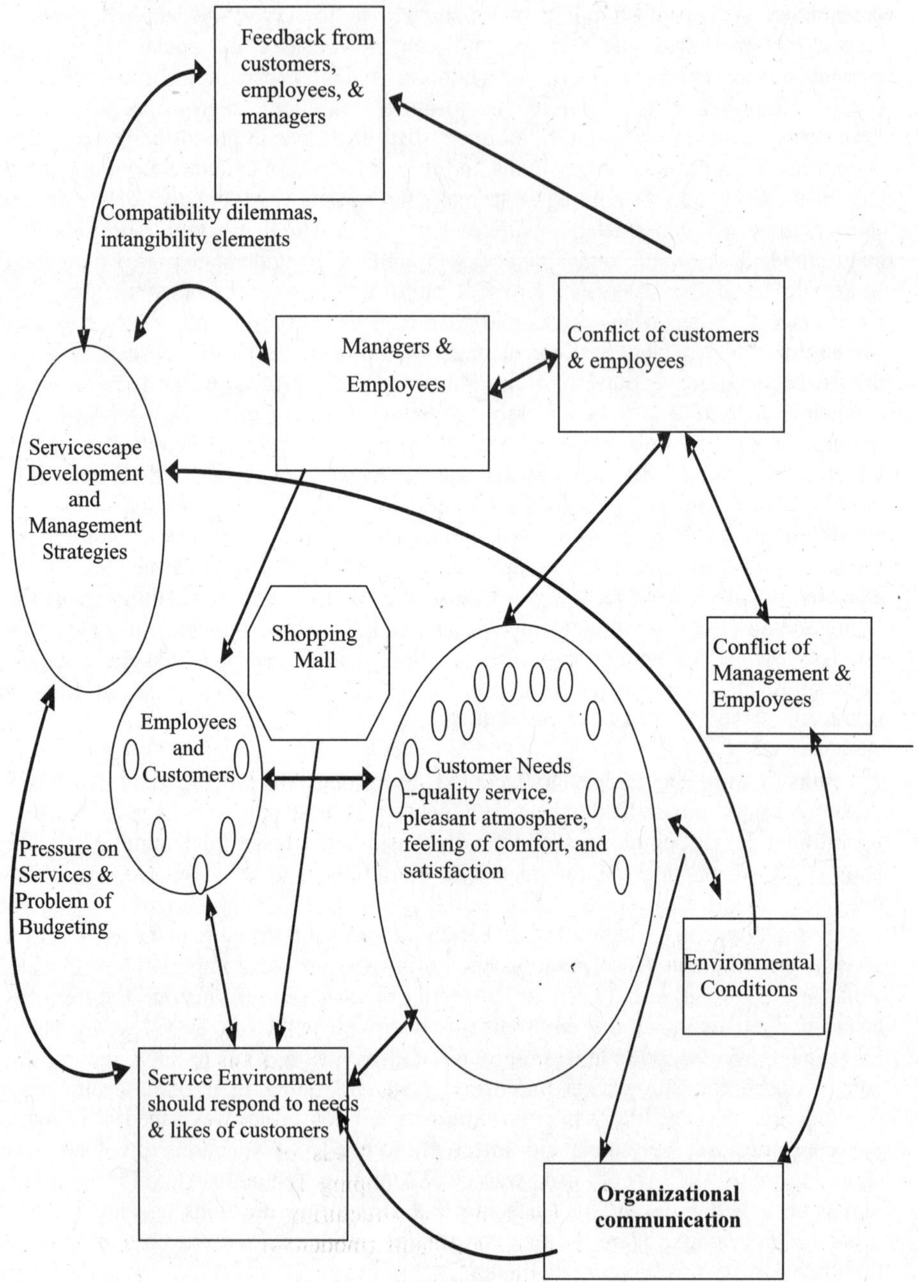

Figure 7: Rich Picture

drawn showing how they perceive the problem situation. After the detailed discussion with different groups, these groups were asked to formulate 'root definition,' and to 'draw' causal maps (*cognitive maps*) that would delineate the service environment situation according to the theme developed in discussions and represented. Here at least 12 sheets of flipchart papers were attached to the wall of the discussion room so that participants might be able to see the 'big picture' i.e. all the contributions at once.

This mapping was done by working with the concerned group to reach agreements about how to deal with strategic issues. Individual cognitive maps were merged into a single map (*cluster maps*) by consultants, where similar concepts were merged into clusters; concepts were discussed and negotiated in case of divergence and difference of views and a fine tune balance of concepts were tried. At this stage, the group was not much concerned with solving the problem; the emphasis was on to explore the problem and to understand the process.

Workshop: Merged overview cognitive maps and individual cluster maps served as focus for discussion at participative '*workshops*' involving analysis of its content and structure and identification of any '*emerging themes*' and '*core concepts*'. Participants invited to the 'workshop' were drawn from a wide cross-section of stakeholders, their total number being 12-14. In this way the workshop would provide participants with plenty of time and ensure that different perspectives could be fully expressed. Then a number of discussion rounds of key goals, inter-related problems, key options and assumptions were organized so as to achieve understanding, agreement and finally commitment for the service environment-management issue. Again all the results of different discussion rounds were displayed on the flipchart sheets attached to the wall of the room. Responses are analyzed by qualitative analysis tool, analytic hierarchy process (AHP), designed for situations in which ideas, feeling and emotions are to be quantified and decision alternatives based on them are prioritized. With respect to prioritization the major dimensions of service-environment, AHP (Using Expert-Choice Software), suggested that general interiors is the most important dimension (weight of 38%), and followed by social-dimension with 26%.

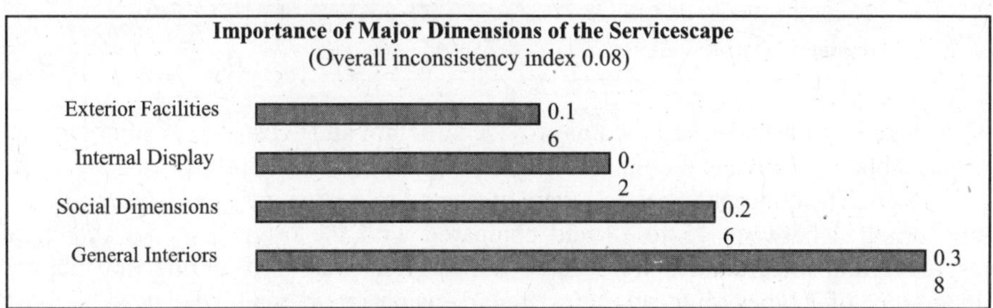

3rd Phase-Empirical Research: In the next phase namely 'building conceptual model', conceptual model of the problem situation was developed. It is simply an attempt to understand the activities needed to bring about necessary changes, and to conceptually construct a Servicescape that represents stakeholders' perspectives. A model was developed directly from 'root definition' using action statements describing activities. The idea was to better demonstrate and understand activities needed in transformation process, and to debate the different perspectives held about activities and their linkages and finally to develop a shared understanding of these perspectives. At this stage, a monitoring and control sub-system has also been constituted which would monitor: *Effectiveness* of the proposed system is determining if it is 'the right thing' to do, *Efficacy* of the system- 'does it work', *Efficiency* of the system-does it use minimum resources.

4th Phase-Empirical Research: The next phase consists of '*comparing conceptual model with the real world*'; it incorporates all the elements of '*comparing*' mode of SCA. The comparison reveals the differences between the models and the present reality by reflecting on the attitudinal, intangible, cultural and organizational barriers that need to be overcome for betterment. The systematic way of comparing *models* developed with the real world situation was by ordered questions like: Does this happen in the real situation? How? By what criteria is it judged? Is it a subject of concern in the current situation? etc. At this stage all participants of the different workshops were invited and a number of discussions were held by the two consultants. For comparisons, both qualitative and quantitative tools were used.
The broad comparison areas vis-à-vis Servicescape development and management are compatibility dilemmas, intangibility element associated with service, expansion potential (short-term), expansion potential (long-term), flexibility (different types of customers) and capital cost involved (both fixed and variable). AHP prioritized these comparison areas, thus indicating that intangibility element and capital costs are major concerns.

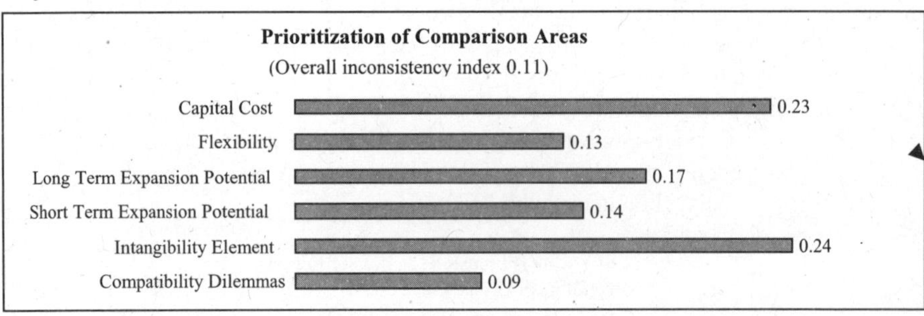

This stage was basically designed to provide structure and substance to an organized debate about improving the current situation. The process used was *interviews & workshops*. The conceptual models were presented to a large group of 'stakeholders', numbering in between 15 to 18 and compared with the original model and their responses and uncertainties were noted down. AHP was used to find out relative importance of 3 types of uncertainties, here decision-group perceived UE to be most important. To reduce *UE, technical response* was used in form of research investigations, surveys, and detailed estimation of costs or analytical analysis, ranging from informal conversation to elaborate mathematical modeling (using different optimization tools). To reduce *UR, structural relationship* with other sectors/areas was explored by adopting broader planning perspective, negotiating/collaborating with other decision makers.

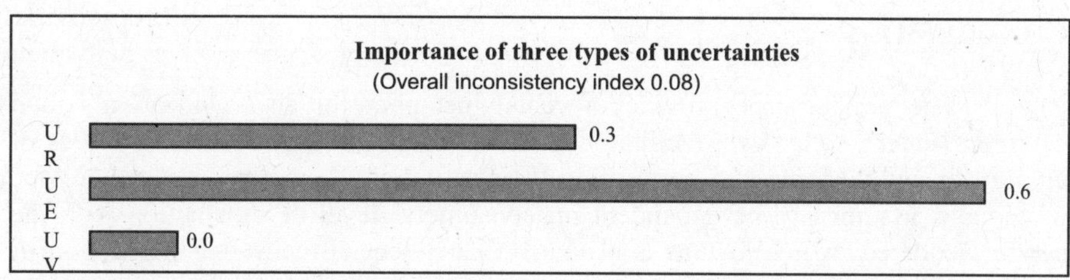

5th Phase-Empirical Research: In the next phase '*desirable and feasible changes*' were identified. They were the proposed changes in structure, in procedures and in attitudes. The conceptual model was revised through a process of iterations, always with the intention and focus to make it practically realizable. Thereafter a '*commitment package' (choosing mode)*, guided by preferred feasible decision scheme was decided upon. It consists of:

- Decision taken now.
- Exploration to reduce levels of uncertainty, estimates of resources needed and timescales.
- Decisions deferred until later.

The decisions and strategies emerged as the result of the empirical research study can't be divulged because of the confidentiality promised to the management of the shopping mall.

We have constructed the '*root definitions*' and mnemonic '*CATWOE*' as under-

Root definitions: A shopping mall is a marketplace amalgamating both tangible as well as intangible products and services. Servicescape can be used as a facilitator by providing an appropriate ambience to improve the overall shopping experience of the customers in particular and visitors in general hence ensuring repatronage of the shopping mall. At the same time it can also ensure greater employee productivity by providing them a sense of comfort, belonging and overall satisfaction.

CATWOE ANALYSIS ON THE ROOT DEFINITIONS:

C: Shoppers, visitors, employees, shop owners
A: Mall owner, shop owners, mall staff
T: Unsatisfied customers → Satisfied customer
　　Ordinary shopping experience → Exciting shopping experience
　　Low level of repatronage → High level of repatronage
　　Demotivated employees → Motivated employees
　　Difficulties in administration → Ease of administration
W: Rational & optimum actions for the improvement in the overall shopping experience
O: Mall owners, retail-store owner
E: Prevalent work culture & value system, facility-layout limitation, unruly behavior.

CONCLUSIONS

The Servicescape provides a visual metaphor for an organization's total offering. It can also act as a facilitator by either adding or hindering the abilities of employees and customers in performing their activities. Repatronage of the service provider is assumed to be dependent on consumers' level of satisfaction with the service rendered; which in turn is primarily dependent on consumer perception of quality of service rendered. Consumer perception of quality will be governed not only by tangible product offering but also by ambience created by the Servicescape in terms of internal facilities, display & décor of promotional material and various exterior facilities. All these put together ensure provision of a holistically enjoyable and satisfying experience for the customers and visitors. Through better creation and management of service-environment, shopping malls and retail stores may be able to contribute towards achieving both external strategic marketing goals and strategic internal organizational goals. To secure strategic advantage from the Servicescape, cross functional co-operation in decision making is of paramount importance. Soft OR techniques enable managers and others stakeholders to take account of the interrelationship between organizational contexts, activities, processes and structures, and therefore can add substantial value for policy makers and managers concerned with the improvement by enabling them to break away from narrow reductionism. They may be helpful in greater understanding of the situation approaching consensus and emotional and cognitive commitment to action and finally facilitate the group moving towards a common and agreeable solution. The desired solution will be more satisfying and committed one so it can be implementable and sustainable because it is a view of problems solving that focuses on the point at which people feel confident to take action that they believe to be appropriate So, success of Soft Operations Research techniques can't be measured by the optimality of the actions in terms of content alone, but rather also by the energy & commitment generated for delivering the agreements.

REFERENCES

1. Baker, J.; Berry L.& Parasuraman, A.(1988). The Marketing Impact of Branch Facility Design. Journal of Retail Banking, 10(2): 33-42.
2. Bennett, P.G. (1996). Mixing Methods. Combining Conflict Analysis, SODA & Strategic Choice, in Eden & Radford, Tackling Strategic Problems.
3. Bennett P.G. & Matthews, L.M. (1996). The Art of Course Planning: Soft O.R. in Action, Journal of Operational Research Society 67.
4. Berman B. & Evans J.R. (2001). Retail Management-A Strategic Approach, 8th ed., Prentice-Hall: 604.
5. Bitner, M.J. (1992). Service Environment: The Impact of Physical Surroundings on Customers and Employees. Journal of Marketing 56: 57-71.
6. Checkland, P. (1981). System Thinking: System Practice. Wiley, Chichester.
7. Checkland, P. (1995). Soft System Methodology and its relevance to the Development of Information systems. Information System Provision: the contribution of Soft System Methodology, Stowell (ed.). McGraw-Hill, London.
8. Checkland, P. (1999). Soft System Methodology: A thirty-year retrospective. System Research and Behavioral Science 17: A1-A66 and S11-S58.

9.   Checkland, P. & Holwell, S. (1998). Information, Systems and Information Systems: Making Sense of the Field. Wiley, Chichester.

10.   Checkland, P. & Scholes (1999). Soft System Methodology in Action. John Wiley & Sons, New York.

11.   Eden, C. & Ackermann, F. (2004). Cognitive Mapping views for Policy Analysis in the Public Sector. European Journal of Operational Research 152: 615-630.

12.   Expert Choice Software. Produced by Exper Choice Inc. 4922 Ellsworth Avenue, Pittsburgh.

13.   Fortune, J. & Peters, G. (1995). Learning from failures: The System Approach. Wiley, Chichester.

14.   Friend, J.K. & Hickling, A. (1997). Planning under Pressure: The Strategic Choice Approach, 2nd ed. Butterworth-Heinemann, Oxford.

15.   Gondal, S. (2004). Internet and Technology New Venture Development using Soft OR, European Journal of Operational Research 152: 571-585.

16.   Hickling, A. (2001). Gambling with Frozen Fire? Rational Analysis for a Problematic World Revisited, ed. Rosenhead, J. & Mingers, J. Wiley, Chichester.

17.   Howard, N. (1993). The Role of Emotions in Multi-Organizational Decision-Making,Journal of the Operational Research Society 44(6): 613-623.

18.   Lane, D.C. (1994). With a little help from our friends: How System Dynamics and Soft O.R. can learn from each other. System Dynamics Review 10(2-3): 101-134.

19.   Liebl, F. (2002). The Anatomy of Complex Societal Problems and its Implications for OR, Journal of the Operational Research Society 53:161-184.

20.   Ormerod, R. (1995). Putting Soft OR methods: Information Systems Strategy Development at Sainsbury. Journal of Operations Research 46: 277-293

21.   Pidd, M. (2003). Tools for Thinking. Modeling in Management Science. John Wiley, Chichester.

22.   Porter, M.E. (1980). Competitive Strategy: Techniques for Analyzing Industries and Competitors. The Free Press, New York.

23.   Porter, M.E. (1985). Competitive Advantage: Creating and Sustaining Superior Performance. The Free Press, New York.

24.   Rosenhead, J. & Mingers, J. (2001). Rational Analysis for a Problematic World Revisited. Wiley, Chichester.

25.   Rockart, J.F. & Hofman, J. (1992). System Delivery: Evolving New Strategies. Sloan Management Review 33(4): 21-31.

26.   Saaty, T.L. (1990). The Analytic Hierarchy Process, McGraw-Hill, RWS Publications, Pittsburgh,PA.

27.   Saaty, T.L. (2001). Decision Making with Dependence and Feedback the Analytic Network Process, 2nd ed. RWS Publications, Pittsburgh, PA.

28.   Turley, L.W. & Milliman, R. E. (2000). Atmospheric Effects on Shopping Behavior: A Review of the Experimental Literature, Journal of Business Research 49:193-211.

29.   Weihrich, H. (1982). The TOWS matrix: A Tool for Situational Analysis. Long Range Planning 15 (2): 54-66.

INORGANIC GROWTH STRATEGIES: AN EMPIRICAL ANALYSIS OF WHO BENEFITS FROM THEM

Latha Chari
Avani Mehta

ITM Institute of Financial Markets, Mumbai

INTRODUCTION

Today, business environment is rapidly changing, with competition, products, people, process of manufacture, markets, customers and technology being embedded in all functions. It is not enough for companies to keep pace with these changes; rather they are expected to beat competitors and innovate in order to continuously maximize the shareholder value. Inorganic growth strategies like mergers, acquisitions, takeovers and spinoffs are regarded as important engines that help companies to enter new markets, expand customer base, cut competition, consolidate and grow in size quickly, employ new technology with respect to products, people and processes. Thus inorganic strategies are regarded by companies as fast track strategies for growth and unlocking of value to shareholders.

Post liberalization and reforms, the Indian corporate sector had to restructure, reengineer, innovate to be competitive and to deliver value to stakeholders. This has led to increase in mergers and acquisitions in the Indian corporate sector. The acquisitions of late have been global in nature with big deals like Tata steel acquiring Corus, etc. and Indian companies going global.

The question of whether mergers and acquisitions pay, who gains more out of the deal, is of prime importance both to the management and investors. Finance literature consists of a number of studies conducted by researchers across the globe addressing this question. A review of these studies done with respect to mergers in UK and USA shows that M&A destroys value in most cases. With heightened M&A activity happening in the past decade in India, it is important to know about the profitability of M&A in India, which is the objective of this paper. In this paper we have looked at 12 cases of acquisitions during the period 2000-2006.

LITERATURE REVIEW

DEFINITION AND CLASSIFICATION OF INORGANIC GROWTH STRATEGIES

In finance literature the growth strategies followed by companies can be broadly classified into organic and inorganic. Organic strategies refer to internal growth strategies that focus on growth by the process of asset replication, exploitation of technology, better customer relationship, innovation of new technology and products to fill gaps in the market place. It is a gradual growth process spread over a few years (Bruner, 2004). Inorganic growth strategies refer to external growth by takeovers, mergers and acquisitions. It is fast and allows immediate utilization of acquired assets (Bruner,2004). It is less risky as it does not result in expansion of capacity. The classification of inorganic growth strategies is given in **Figure-1**.

A *merger* refers to the absorption of one firm by another; the acquiring firm retains its name and identity and acquires all of the assets and liabilities of the acquired firm. The acquired firm ceases to exist as a separate business entity. As opposed to this, in a consolidation, a new firm is created, both the acquiring and the acquired firm terminate their legal existence and become a part of the new firm. Here, the distinction between the acquirer and the target firm is not crucial.

Acquisition of stock refers to purchase of a firm's voting stock in exchange for cash, shares, or other securities; this may start as a private offer from the management of one firm to another. A tender offer is a public offer to buy shares of a target firm directly from its shareholders. Tender offers are usually unfriendly; they are used in an effort to circumvent the target firm's management, which usually actively resists acquisition.

Acquisition of assets refers to a method of acquisition where a firm can acquire another firm by buying all of its assets. Generally, a formal vote of the shareholders of the selling firm is required. Acquisition of assets avoids the potential problem of having resisting minority shareholders, which can occur in an acquisition of stock.

Proxy contests occur when a group of shareholders attempts to gain controlling seats on the board of directors by voting in new directors. A proxy authorizes the proxy holder to vote on all matters in a shareholder meeting. In going-private transactions, all the equity share of a public firm is purchased by a small group of investors (e.g., the incumbent management via an LBO). The shares are de-listed from stock exchanges.

Mergers can be further classified into:

- ***Horizontal merger:*** Takes place between two firms in the same line of business (e.g., Daimler-Benz and Chrysler, Hewlett-Packard and Compaq)
- ***Vertical merger:*** Involves companies at different stages of production (e.g., America Online and Time Warner)
- ***Conglomerate merger:*** Involves companies in unrelated lines of businesses (e.g., AT&T and NCR)

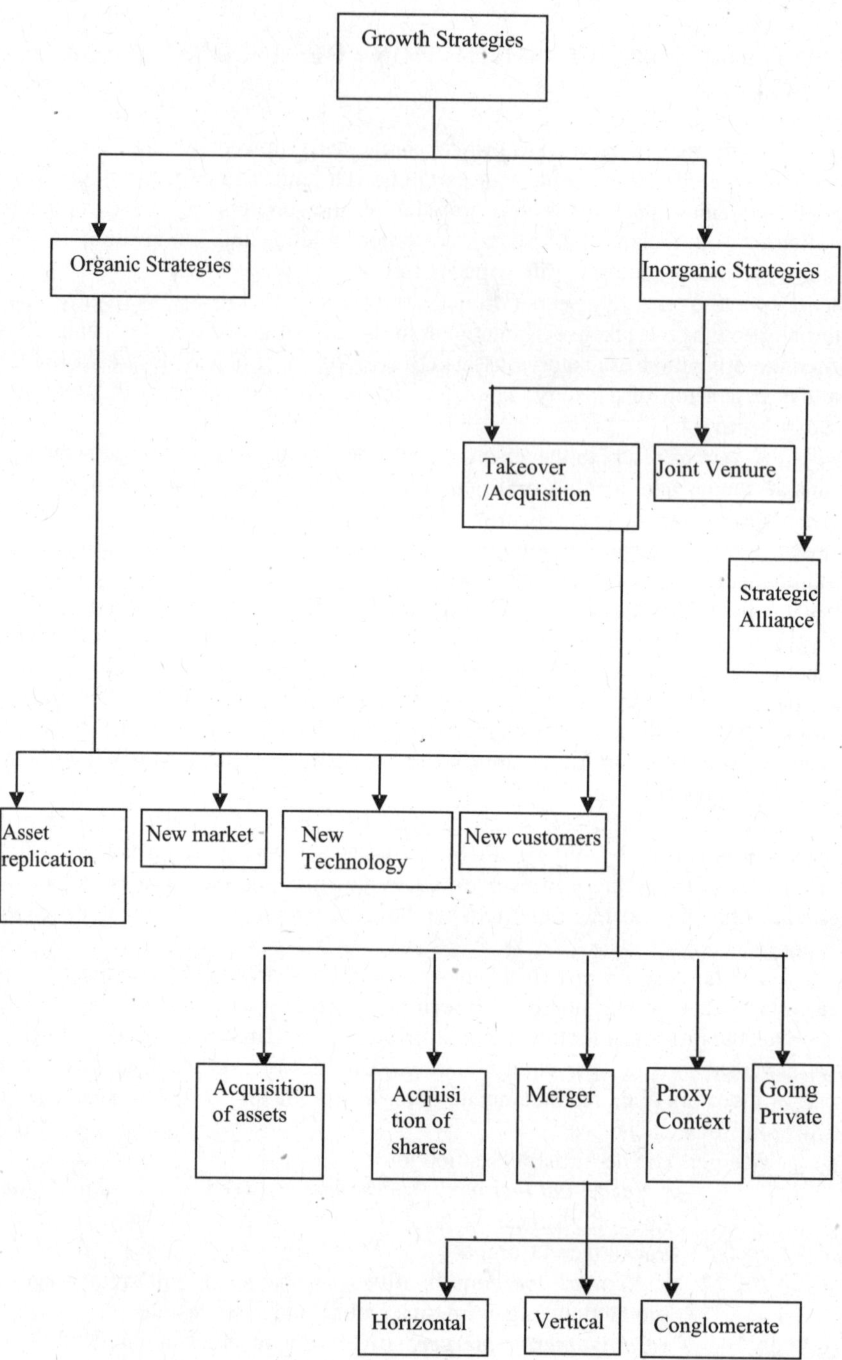

Figure 1: Growth strategies – Classification

196

In India these classifications are absent. The terms merger and amalgamations are used interchangeably. The Companies Act, 1956 does not define takeover, mergers and acquisitions. However as per the Indian Companies Act, 1956 amalgamation may take place in any of the following methods: *(Reference- Taxmann companies Act)*

- By amalgamation under a scheme under section 391-394.
- By way of acquisition of shares under a scheme as per section 395
- By an order of the central government in national interest under section 396
- By way of voluntary winding up scheme under section 494.

Review of literature with respect to studies on whether mergers and acquisitions pay, reveals that there are four approaches to the study (Bruner, 2004): Event studies, Accounting studies, survey of executives and clinical studies.

Event study method adopts market based returns to shareholders as a measure of value created. It has the advantage of using a leading measure of value creation as stock prices are supposed to reflect the expected future cash flows. However, the method suffers from the disadvantage that may result from inefficient and weak markets, where share prices may not reflect correctly the value of the company. Further, share prices may also react to other macro economic factors like exchange rates, interest rates, taxes etc. Findings using event studies have been mixed. Lang, Stulz, Walkling (1989), Berkovitch, Narayanan (1993), report significant positive cumulative abnormal returns to target firm shareholders in case of tender offers. Loughran, Vijh (1997) who study mergers, tender offers and combined returns have reported that all of them have returned significant positive returns to target firm shareholders. Houstan et.al (2001) and Beitel et al. (2002) who have studied deals which relate to banks have also reported that target firm shareholders gain and the acquirers' loose. A reason attributed to loss of value to buyer company's shareholders is the size effect. Asquith et. al(1983) have studied size effect and concluded that where the target's market value is greater than 10 percent of the market value of the buyer company, the buyer company shareholders gain significantly and wherever the target company's market value is less than 10 percent of the market value of the buyer company they do not have any significant gains because of the fact that the size of the buyer company is too large to actually make a material impact in value to shareholders.

Accounting studies use financial measures like return on equity, return on assets, earnings per share calculated from audited financial statements. These are compared for a time series before and after the event and also compared with peer group companies for the period in order to ascertain whether acquirers outperformed non acquirers. The method suffers from deficiencies that relate to accounting measures like being a lagging measure of value, does not consider intangibles and is subject to accounting bias. Healy, Palepu, Ruback (1997) studied 50 large mergers in the US using accounting based measures. They have reported that merged firms showed significant abnormal improvement in asset turnover. However, there was no improvement in operating cash flow margins. They also looked at market returns to shareholders and concluded that the net present value for the acquirer shareholders was zero as the cash flows did not improve. The target company shareholders gained significantly. Chatterjee, Meeks (1996) who studied mergers in UK concluded that the acquiring companies did not show any significant increase in profitability though they reported better accounting profits, which could be because of accounting policy changes. Sharma, Ho (2002) compared the ROE, profit margin and EPS of Australian companies for a period of 3 years before merger and three years after merger and concluded that buyers showed decline in these measures after merger. Revenscraft and Scherer [1987] conclude that, on average, acquiring firms have not been able to maintain the pre-merger levels of profitability of the targets. Ali and Gupta (1999) examine the potential motives and effects of corporate takeovers that occurred in Malaysia during the period 1980 through 1993 and find that the acquirer firms have achieved larger size at the expense of reduced profit both for themselves and the acquired firms. To sum up, most of the studies have concluded that based on accounting numbers the mergers have not resulted in significant benefits to the acquirers.

Survey of managers method is one where a questionnaire is administered across a sample of chief executive officers and findings are based on views given by them. The method has the advantage of looking at mergers from the point of view of managers and can reveal new insights into motives and achievements derived from such deals. However, the views of the officers may be biased or casual and need not be correct or based on scientific reasons. Hence, the findings can be distorted. Bruner (2004), initially conducted a survey of 50 executives, and found that only 37% of the respondents felt that the deals created value for the buyers and 21% of the deals achieved strategic goals. However, when he conducted the same survey among executives who were involved in the merger he found that 58% of the respondents believed that their own deals created value and 51% believed that they achieved their goals. Only 23% believed that they did not create value and 31% believed that they did not achieve their strategic goals.

Clinical studies are basically case studies that look into a specific merger deal and examine them with references to the goals of the deal and whether they were achieved from a strategic, financial and organizational perspective.

It can be seen that event studies have shown mixed findings with bias towards gains to target company, whereas most of the accounting based studies have shown that the buyers have not gained significantly post merger. The findings of clinical studies cannot be generalized and those of survey is mixed and highly influenced by the sample selected for the survey. Hence, we conclude that event based study and accounting study methods are superior and give better results.

RESEARCH METHODOLOGY

In this paper we have selected a sample list of 12 cases of acquisitions over the period from 1999 to 2005 in India. We have adopted both event based and accounting based methods to evaluate the success or failure of the merger. The listing of the sample and nature of study done is given vide annexure 1 enclosed.

Methodology – Event study: The method adopted for event based study is as follows:

We evaluated the performance of the merger/acquisition in terms of who benefits from the deal using market based share prices and only those cases where both target and acquirer are listed companies. Event study mechanism has been applied to 6 companies out of a total of 12 companies as only these cases suitable data required for event study was found. We have taken share prices of target company for a period of 12 months before the announcement date or effective date of merger. We have also provided for the noise prevailing during the announcement period by excluding the prices of shares for 1 month before and after the announcement date, thus eliminating the noise effect to a great extent. This methodology is discussed by Weston (1998). We have also taken the share prices of the target company for a period of 12 months after the said date to evaluate post merger impact on the company.

Similarly, we took the event window for the acquiring company as 1 year before the announcement date, and 1 year after the announcement date. The abnormal returns have been calculated using the Capital asset pricing model (CAPM).

Various inputs required by the CAPM for arriving at the expected return are the risk free rate, equity risk premium and beta, which have been calculated by us as follows:

Capital asset pricing model formula:

Expected return = Riskless return + Beta * (Market risk premium)

$$r = r_f + (\beta \times (r_m - r_f)) \tag{1}$$

where, r_f is the risk free rate,

r_m is the expected return on the market and

β is the beta of the cash flows or security being valued and beta of market will be 1.

The term $(r_m - r_f)$ is the market risk premium.

Equity Risk premium: - Equity risk premium is an important concept and its numerical value enters into many decisions made by financial managers, economist and analysts. It is widely used to forecast the growth of investment portfolios over long term. It is also used as an input to the cost of capital in project choice, and employed as a factor in the expected rate of return to stocks. Given the importance of equity risk premium, the estimation in practice is very haphazard mainly because of lack of reliable data. The total returns index needed for the estimation of the market return for Indian market is available only from 1999. Unavailability of long periods of historical data introduces noise and error in the estimation of risk premium. These issues have been addressed by J R Verma and S K Barua, (2006), where they have estimated equity risk premium after constructing their own total return index. The concept of estimating the premium for emerging markets using country risk premium have also been introduced by Aswath Damodaran where the issues of differing time frames and choosing between arithmetic and geometric means have also been considered. We estimated the risk free rate using 10 year G-Sec and 91 days Treasury bills. For the market return we took the total returns index(S&P CNX NIFTY). Details are as given below:

Estimating risk free rate

Return given by risk free investments: It is the interest rate that it is assured and can be obtained by investing in financial instruments with no default risk.

However, the instrument can carry other types of risk, e.g. market risk, liquidity risk etc. For truly riskless investments, the instrument must be free from default and market (interest rate) risks. Instruments issued by government, do not have any default risk. The 10 year Government security (G-sec) has an in-built reinvestment risk. For dealing with that problem, we calculated the historic 10 year rate and subtracted from it historic 91 days treasury bill rate, thus arriving at a better estimate for the risk free rate.

Estimating the Market return (Rm)

For estimating the market return we took the index values of total return index(S&P CNX NIFTY) which were available from 1999. We considered the S&P CNX NIFTY and not SENSEX mainly because SENSEX is price index and not the total return index. Price index clearly understates the return in the stock market because it omits the dividend payments. Thus the total return index becomes a more correct measure for estimation of market return. For calculating the Rm, we have taken the month end values of the nifty and noted the percentage change over the previous month. We have then annualized it and calculated the arithmetic mean, thus getting market return for each year starting from 1999 to 2007. (Data Source- The data on the total return index values from 1999 to 2007, was available from the nseindia website.)

Estimating the Beta

We have estimated the beta of the sample companies by following the regression method. We have regressed the share price data available for the relevant year of the study with the market return for the respective year. For this we have used excel sheet function SLOPE which regresses the share prices of the company and the market return for the relevant year.

Estimating the equity risk premium (Rm-Rf)

After estimating the risk free rate and the market return, market premium is simply the difference between the two. The premium so calculated is not real, it has inflation too built into it. For calculating the real equity premium we need to calculate the real risk free rate and real return index values. For that we take help of Fisher's equation:

$$(1+n)= (1+i)(1+r) \tag{2}$$

where,
N=nominal interest rate
i=inflation rate
r=real interest rate

The inflation rate can be calculated using the WPI index

$$\text{WPI } (i+1) = \text{WPI } (i)(1+i) \tag{3}$$

Methodology – Accounting study

For accounting based studies we have used accounting ratios as a tool for evaluating whether the mergers have benefited acquirers in terms of profitability, operational costs, asset utilization with respect to fixed and working capital assets and market share. Further, we also looked at whether the merger has resulted in creating more wealth for the shareholders. These ratios have been calculated for the period of 1 year before and 3 years after merger. We benchmarked them against the performance of the industry in order to evaluate whether they have succeeded or not. The benchmarking was done with a view to assess whether the acquisitions have created more value for the acquirers than in comparison with cases where no acquisitions have been done. Financial data for different companies is taken from the Capital line database.

RESULTS OF THE STUDY

a) Event study

Event study examines the gains to the target and the acquirer company taking into account only those transactions which were all cash deals. Further, in these cases the target company continued to operate after the sale of a specific percentage of stock to the acquirers till further stake was acquired and control transferred to the acquirer. Results of the event study are enclosed vide **Annexure-2** and **Annexure-3.** From annexure 2 it can be seen that most of the target company shareholders other than shareholders of Grasim and L&T have gained an acquisition premium ranging from 30% to 152%. Those shareholders who held on to the company shares for a period of 12 months from the date closure of the deal have not gained much. The excess abnormal returns on the shares over a period of 12 months post deal, is less than the immediate premium gained by the shareholders of the target company.

The results of gains to acquirer company shareholders as shown by **Annexure-3**, shows that over a period of 12 months after the acquisition date only 2 out of the 6 cases give a positive abnormal return. The results over a period of 2 years post acquisition are however encouraging for the acquirer company shareholders. 5 out of 6 cases show a positive abnormal excess returns.

b) Accounting study

The results of accounting study are given vide **Annexure-4**. The question of whether the profitability of the acquiring company has improved subsequent to the acquisition has been evaluated using the Cash Profit Margin % (CPM) and profit margin before interest and taxes % (PBITM). The sales growth of the two individual companies before merger has been compared with the sales growth of the combined firm post merger. The efficiency of utilization of assets has been assessed using the fixed asset turnover ratio. Similarly, the debtors and inventory turnover ratios are used to measure efficiency with respect to working capital management. Value to shareholders has been measured using the return on capital employed % (ROCE) and return on net worth % (RONW).

From annexure 4 it can be seen that the sales growth of the combined entity was negative in the first year after the acquisition in case of 3 out of a total of 8 cases and positive for the others. However, all cases reveal a positive growtUrmil Shah <urmilishere@gmail.com>h in sales from the second year onwards. 4 cases show a high growth in sales in the second year after the acquisition. The PBITM and CPM percentages compared with the pre-acquisition % and the benchmark of the industry shows that only in 4 cases the profits margins have improved. In the balance cases the profit margins have fallen both against the benchmark and the pre acquisition margins in the first year following the acquisition. The results with respect to margins do not undergo any changes in the subsequent years also.

Hence it can be concluded that companies do not gain any significant cost advantage due to acquisitions. The fixed asset turnover ratio of the cases show that 5 companies had a fixed asset utilization ratio that was better than the bench mark before the acquisition, whereas in case of 4 companies the asset turnover has improved significantly in the first year after acquisition and the years following it. In case of ITC Badrachalam and ITC the asset turnover has fallen and has not shown any improvement. Surprisingly, all cases of acquisitions have shown improvement in working capital management subsequent to the acquisition. The value to the shareholder, as measured by ROCE and RONW, shows that in 7 out of 8 cases the returns to shareholders were better than the benchmark and improved in the years after the acquisition.

CONCLUSIONS AND LIMITATIONS

Based on results from the event study it can be concluded that the target company shareholders gain immediately on the basis of the high premium they receive from the acquirer on acquisition. However, the acquirer company's shareholders gain abnormal returns over a period of 2 years. The accounting study results however vary from the event study results. As per the accounting study, it can be seen that though the returns to shareholders based on the ROCE and RONW show improvements, only about 50% of the companies show significant improvement in fixed asset utilization and cost reduction due to acquisition for the acquirer. Most acquirers have however shown significant improvement in working capital management. Overall the improvements achieved by Indian M&A's as compared to those in other nations seem to be better over a period of 2 years post acquisition. The limitation of the study is that the sample size is small and can be increased. Further, a statistical inference based on paired t test can be conducted over a larger sample to conclude better.

REFERENCES

1. Bruner (2004), Applied Mergers and Acquisitions. Published by John Wiley & Sons, Inc., Hoboken, New Jersey.
2. Lang, Stulz, Walkling (1989). Managerial performance, Tobin's Q, and the gains from successful tender offers. Journal of Finance Economics 24:137 – 154.
3. Berkovitch, Narayanan (1993). Motives for takeovers: An empirical investigation. Journal of Financial and Quantitative Analysis 28(3): 347 - 362

4.   Loughran, Vijh (1997). Do long-term shareholders benefit from corporate acquisitions? Journal of finance 52(5,December):1765-1790

5.   Houstan et.al (2001) .Whose do merger gains come from? Bank mergers from the perspective of insiders and outsiders. Journal of Financial Economics 60(2/3, may/June):285-331.

6.   Beitel et al. (2002) Explaining the M & A- success in European bank merger and acquisitions. Working paper, University of Written/Herdecke, Germany (January).

7.   Asquith et. al.(1983) Merger bids, Uncertainty, and stockholder returns,. Journal of Financial Economics 11(1, April):51-83.

8.   Healy, Palepu, and Ruback (1997).Which takeovers are profitable: Strategic of financial? Sloan Management Review 38(4, summer):45-57.

9.   Chatterjee, Meeks (1996). The Financial effects of takeover: Accounting rates of return and accounting regulation. Journal of Business Finance & Accounting. 23(5/6, July):851-868.

10. Sharma, Ho (2002). The impact of acquisitions on operating performance: Some Australian evidence. Journal of Business Finance and Accounting 29(1, January, March):155-200.

11. Ali, R. and G.S.Gupta, "Motivation and Outcome of Malaysian Takeovers: An International Perspective," Vikalpa, 24(3), 1999, 41-49.

12. Damodaran (2001) Corporate Finance: Theory and Practice, Second Edition, published by John Wiley & Sons, Inc.

13. Damodaran (2002) Investment Valuation, Tools and Techniques for determining the Value of Any Asset, Second Edition, published by John Wiley & Sons, Inc.

14. JR Verma and S K Barua, of IIM Ahmedabad(2006) , A First Cut Estimate of Equity Risk Premium in India (IIMA, Working Paper 2006-06-04, June 2006)

15. Aswath Damodaran (1999) Unpublished working paper, Equity risk premium, New York University, New York, NY, 1999 - stern.nyu.edu

16. Weston J Fred (2005) Chung Kwang S, Merger, Restructuring and Corporate Control-Publisher Prentice Hall New Delhi

17. Taxmann Companies Act: As amended by companies Act 2006: Company Law and guide, 3rd edition publisher taxmann.

Annexure-1 : List of Cases used for the study and nature of study done

1	2	3	4	5	6	7	8*	9 Rs.	10 %	11 %	12 #
CADILA HEALTH	GERMAN REMEDIES,RECON HEALTH	1-Aug-01	18-Jul-01	16-Aug-01	7:04	1649179	C	650	20	47	B
ASAHI INDIA GLASSLTD	FLOATGLASS INDIA Ltd	22-Sep-01	15-Nov-01	14-Dec-01	NA	19507008	C	11	25	100	B
COSMO FILMS LTD	GUJARAT PROPACK LTD	1-Apr-02	15-Nov 01	14-Dec-01	NA		C	29.25	50		A
GULF OIL CORPORATION	GULF OIL INDIA LTD	1-Jan-02			1:02	58,70,000	S			61.7	A
ITC LTD	ITC BHADRACHALAM PAPER	1-Apr-01			1:16	20,96,982	S				A
AARTI INDUSTRIES LTD	ALCHEMIE ORGANICS LTD	1-Apr-01			1:04	5,12,525					A
JK INDUSTRIES LTD	VIKRANT TYRES LTD	1-Apr-02			9:20	28,94,244	C				A

Notes: 1 = Acquirer company, 2 = Target company, 3 = Date of announcement, 4 = the date of offer, 5= Date of closure, 6 = Swap rate where payment is not by cash, 7 = No. of shares acquired, 8 = mode of payment, 9 =Price of deal, Col. 10 gives % stake acquired & 11 gives total stake in company after acquisition, Col.10 denotes nature of study done.

* C denotes all cash payment and S denotes payment by shares and cash

A denotes accounting study is done for the specific case and   B denots that both accounting and event study is done for the case

Annexure 2: Event study gains to the target company (all cash deals)

Sl. No	Acquirer	TARGET	% Stake Acquired	Price Paid Rs.	Market Price Rs.	Premium Rs.	Premium %	12 months Pre announcement *	12 months Post announcement *
1	CADILA HEALTH	GERMAN REMEDIES,RECON HEALTH CARE (WINTAC LTD),	20%	650	400.3	249.7	62%	-22%	-1%
2	ASAHI INDIA GLASSLTD	FLOAT GLASS INDIA LTD	25%	11	8.45	2.55	30%	0%	16%
3	GRASIM (ULTRATECH)	L & T	20%	190	173.9	16.05	9%	-41%	25%
4	SOFTWARE SOLUTIONS INTEGRATED LTD	APTECH	20%	49.8	23.75	26	109%	-46%	-35%
5	COROMANDAL	GODAVARI FERTILIZERS	20%	124	49.2	74.8	152%	88%	-8%
6	WEST COAST	RAMA NEWS PRINT & PAPERS LTD	20%	8.13	8.05	0.08	1%	73%	34%

Annexure 3 : Event study gains to the acquirer.

No	Acquirer	TARGET	Market price before 1 Month	Market price after 1 Month	% profit or loss	% Stake Acquired	12 months Pre announcement*	12 months Post announcement*	2 year post acquisition*
1	CADILA HEALTH	GERMAN REMEDIES,RECON HEALTH CARE(WINTAC LTD),	96.5	92.85	3	20%	-46%	-4%	
2	ASAHI INDIA GLASSLTD	FLOATGLASS INDIA LTD	295	204.05	-31	25%	-69%	-92%	166%
3	GRASIM (ULTRATECH)	L & T	302.2	305.5	1	20%	-10	51%	321%
4	SOFTWARE SOLUTIONS INTEGRATED LTD	APTECH	62.85	112.1	78	20%	-81	47%	71%
5	COROMANDAL	GODAVARI FERTILIZERS	94.6	118.1	25	20	-75%	-5%	-54%
6	WEST COAST	RAMA NEWS PRINT & PAPERS LTD	180.2	208.4	16	20	60%	-33%	108%

*** Represents abnormal excess returns calculated before and after 12 months from the date of acquisition**

Annexure 4 : Accounting study summary of results

Key Ratios	Before merger			After Merger			Benchmark			Comments
	TGT	ACQ	BMK	Target			Industry			
1. Gulf oil and gulf oil India	2001	2001	2001	2004	2003	2002	2004	2003	2002	
Sales Growth -%	-7.92	13.3		3.55	60.79	-44				falls in year 1 following M&A, then picks up
LTD to Equity Ratio	0.13	0.59	0.57	0.27	0.35	0.34	0.09	0.17	0.37	More than benchmark
Fixed Assets	7.69	2.43	8.17	2.85	2.84	2.27	7.97	7.35	6.87	Less than benchmark, improved two years after merger
Inventory	5.1	6.55	14.79	6.48	5.69	4.89	16.52	15.55	14.3	Less than benchmark improved two years after merger
Debtors	2.33	4	20.43	4.82	3.94	3.12	31.38	25.49	20.46	Bad, as compared to benchmark
PBITM (%)	3.89	-1.81	2.92	3.17	5.73	7.94	4.42	3.56	5.7	was bad earlier, but improved after merger
CPM (%)	1.54	-5.69	1.88	2.42	4.73	4.51	3.48	3.01	3.88	more than doubled
ROCE (%)	8.44	-2.88	16.3	6.37	9.8	9.95	39.05	27.73	33.7	negative before, but improved after merger
RONW (%)	1.83	18.75	11.01	1.69	8.71	5.25	28.02	21.33	26.78	

Note : TGT means Target company, ACQ represents acquiring company, and BMK is the benchmark

Annexure 4(Contd)

Key Ratios	Before merger			After Merger			Benchmark			Comments
	TGT	ACQ	BMK	Target			Industry			
2. Godavari & Coromandal	2003	2003	2003	2006	2005	2004	2006	2005	2004	
Sales Growth %	25.75	11.06		23.88	28.6	-9				falls in year 1 following M&A, then picks up
LTD to Equity Ratio	1.62	0.31	0	0.72	1.515	1.685	0	0	0	< bench, borrowings have increased
Fixed Assets	4.01	1.82		5.295	4.205	3.515	1.09	1.01	0.87	improved significantly
Inventory	4.34	5.23	0.82	8.16	7.82	6.4	7.92	7.57	6.21	improved significantly
Debtors	5.05	5.82	5.1	15.38	10.165	7.02	6.62	6.91	5.23	improved significantly
PBITM (%)	-0.14	10.01	9.5	5.63	5.015	5.455	6.66	7.55	7.98	fallen
CPM (%)	-0.78	7.19	-6.36	4.28	4.125	3.74	1.73	1.71	1.95	fallen but better than benchmark
ROCE (%)	-0.45	16.17	12.22	16.1	14.01	14.23	0	0	0	
RONW (%)	20.02	12.16		24.53	18.055	12.39	0	0	0	

Annexure 4(Contd)

Key Ratios	Before merger			After Merger			Benchmark			Comments
	TGT	ACQ	BMK	Target			Industry			
3. Aarti and alchemie	2001	2001	2001	2004	2003	2002	2004	2003	2002	
Sales Growth	12.5	16.98		6.4	38.86	6				falls in year 1 following M&A, then picks up
LTD to Equity Ratio	0.61	0.51	1.31	0.48	0.47	0.52	1.46	1.86	1.71	same as before but better than benchmark
Fixed Assets	1.4	2.11	1.43	1.97	2:17	1.94	1.46	1.4	1.42	fallen but betterchmark
Inventory	4.37	9.97	3.68	7.13	8.63	8.66	4.81	5.1	4.04	improved
Debtors	8.02	4.22	5.51	4.64	5.3	4.77	6.07	5.57	4.99	improved
PBITM (%)	3.11	11.29	6.34	12.38	11.91	14.38	9.93	7.1	5.69	improved
CPM (%)	0.27	9.92	2.81	10.57	9.96	12.58	8.62	4.71	2.14	improved
ROCE (%)	4.18	16.11	8.4	18.29	20.39	21.38	12.7	9.41	6.87	better than benchmark
RONW (%)	-8.97	16.92	-5.73	22.46	21.88	24.01	15.52	3.19	10.61	better than benchmark

Annexure 4(Contd)

Key Ratios	Before merger			After Merger			Benchmark			Comments
	TGT	ACQ	BMK	Target			Industry			
4 Spic and Manali	2000	2000	2000	2003	2002	2001	2003	2002	2001	
Sales Growth	22.29	23		6.71	1.45	2.23				falls in year 1 following M&A, then picks up
LTD to Equity Ratio	1.79	0.53	1.18	0.86	1.25	1.08	0.66	0.93	1.09	reveals consolidated debt, > benchmark
Fixed Assets	1.14	1.17	0.9	1.1	1.04	1.36	1.18	1.05	1.1	improved in the first year after merger, later, same as benchmark
Inventory	5.08	5.77	5.5	6.57	4.87	5.77	6.82	5.6	5.72	not materially different from the benchmark
Debtors	5.8	4.66	5	5.4	4.98	6.13	6.33	5.23	5.64	better after merger, but not better than benchmark
PBITM (%)	3.3	1.38	5.23	-1.58	0.28	-1.19	6.79	6.27	6.46	
CPM (%)	3.11	1.82	2.99	0.53	2.08	0.07	7.17	5.17	5.12	lower than the benchmark both before and after the merger
ROCE (%)	0	0	0	0	0	0	8.98	6.65	7.47	
RONW (%)	0	0	0	0	0	0	6.44	0.3	0.61	

Annexure 4(Contd)

Key Ratios	Before merger			After Merger			Benchmark			Comments
	TGT	ACQ	BMK	Target			Industry			
5. Float glass and asahi	2002	2002	2002	2005	2004	2003	2005	2004	2003	
Sales Growth	29.33	5.24		20.17	21.49	9.22				high growth in sales after merger
LTD to Equity Ratio	7.83	1.35	1.33	1.44	2.22	2.56	1.06	1.65	2.1	Deteriorated post merger
Fixed Assets	0.55	1.34	1.22	0.92	0.85	1.1	0.96	0.89	1.09	ATO has fallen but better than the benchmark
Inventory	4.45	6.64	6.66	6.01	5.63	7.28	5.99	5.8	7.31	as good as before
Debtors	13.07	17.96	14.28	9.91	10.44	13.74	10.15	10.8	13.42	better than benchmark
PBITM (%)	8.33	9.6	5.01	13.17	14.43	10.2	12.01	13.55	9.69	
CPM (%)	13.18	12.47	8.53	17.54	21.63	17.58	16.51	20.44	17.25	better & continues to be better than benchmark
ROCE (%)	5.62	16.3	6.57	17.12	19.41	16.12	14.89	17.37	13.32	
RONW (%)	20.25	31.61	3	50.98	68.92	62.7	32.23	41.26	32.51	

Annexure 4(Contd)

Key Ratios	Before merger			After Merger			Benchmark			Comments
	TGT	ACQ	BMK	Target			Industry			
6. Jk Tyres and Vikranth	**2002**	**2002**	**2002**	**2005**	**2004**	**2003**	**2005**	**2004**	**2003**	
Sales Growth	29.97	1		17.76	9.9	-27				falls in year 1 following M&A, then picks up
LTD to Equity Ratio	1.49	0.74	0.7	1.41	1.33	0.84	0.68	0.68	0.67	was higher than benchmark, post merger same as benchmark
Fixed Assets	1.5	1.23	1.96	1.59	1.57	1.26	2.26	2.25	2.08	was below benchmark, has improved after merger but < benchmark
Inventory	9.25	7.24	8.23	11.29	11.49	10.13	8.58	8.57	8.8	was below benchmark, has improved after merger
Debtors	5.58	6.73	6.83	5.54	5.19	5.35	8.15	7.75	7.18	"
PBITM (%)	3.01	8.61	6.49	2.64	4.56	6.96	3.95	5.28	6.86	was better but noe below
CPM (%)	0.76	3.72	4.18	3.04	3.29	4.02	3.93	4.38	5.06	was below contn to be below
ROCE (%)	5.05	8.77	11.88	5.34	8.42	9.31	9.43	12.1	14.28	improved in 1 year and then started decline
RONW (%)	-11.1	2.69	5.62	2.21	2.83	3.27	7.37	9.28	10.96	

Annexure 4(Contd)

Key Ratios	Before merger			After Merger			Benchmark			Comments
	TGT	ACQ	BMK	Target			Industry			
7. G. Propack and Cosmo	2002	2002	2002	2005	2004	2003	2005	2004	2003	
Sales Growth	-20.4	23.74		24.71	-0.63	35				significant improvement in 1st year
LTD to Equity Ratio	2.59	0.67	0.33	1.3	1.62	1.37	0.44	0.4	0.33	was as good as benchmark, but then on started falling
Fixed Assets	1.05	1.17	0.95	1.1	0.99	1.48	0.96	0.97	1.01	was better, now as good as benchmark
Inventory	9.23	8.21	7.44	8.81	8.76	10.87	8.24	7.91	8.27	improved, better than benchmark
Debtors	7.97	6.55	10.1	8.29	7.45	9.11	10.87	11.93	11.04	improved but still below benchmark
PBITM (%)	10.12	18.82	10.73	4.96	13.9	22.24	11.18	13.79	8.82	
CPM (%)	4.62	18.08	11.78	11.3	17.92	17.72	12.98	14.02	7.16	better than benchmark
ROCE (%)	14.84	22.88	7.06	6.52	16.21	37.84	8.75	10.55	6.61	
RONW (%)	0.73	25.54	5.17	9.45	30.56	50.05	8.6	9.9	1.05	

Annexure 4(Contd)

Key Ratios	Before merger			After Merger			Benchmark			Comments
	TGT	ACQ	BMK	Target			Industry			
8. Badra.paper & ITC	2001	2001	2001	2004	2003	2002	2004	2003	2002	
Sales Growth	36.04	9.18		9.05	16.99	5.4				falls in year 1 following M&A, then picks up
LTD to Equity Ratio	0.75	0.12	0.16	0.01	0.03	0.06	0.03	0.05	0.09	im
Fixed Assets	0.77	4.07	4.68	2.66	2.82	3.23	2.92	3.11	3.58	was better, has fallen after merger
Inventory	6.92	8.36	8.51	8.48	9.06	8.46	8.8	9.33	8.43	same as before
Debtors	11.17	77.8	54.89	51.28	53.35	65.56	47.35	46.45	50.72	improved
PBITM (%)	11.85	19.6	16.23	19.92	19.02	18.88	17.84	16.79	16.78	
CPM (%)	11.01	13.2	10.83	15.53	14.59	14.11	13.74	12.8	12.3	better throughout
ROCE (%)	8.66	44.1	41.58	39.58	41.69	41.44	39.25	40.62	40.35	
RONW (%)	6.86	32.43	32.18	27.34	28.41	30.43	27.32	28.44	30.59	

Note : TGT means Target company, ACQ represents acquiring company, and BMK is the benchmark

Section 6

EPILOGUE

Arun P. Sinha

Professor of Management
Indian Institute of Technology Kanpur

It has been our intention in this volume to track some *milestones-in-making* that recent strategy discourse appears to herald. Papers and cases in this volume have brought attention to these possible milestones, spread over four sections of this book -- emergent Missions, organizational Forms, Resources, and Geographic Locus. Each section was an amalgam of pieces that may point to one or more emergent directions. Let us now assess whether all these or any of them would qualify being anointed as possible milestones-in-making.

Emergent Missions

For one, do we see "new missions" emerging? Is the paper by Subhash Sharma a compelling statement of a difference of the emergent enterprise from earlier stories? Or, is it merely a re-statement of what organizations were doing anyway under their CSR? Sharma approaches the issue from the angle of control, which is, what actions may be prescribed, and how the resulting performance may be assessed. He posits that organizations should move from using a "balanced scorecard" to using a "holistic performance scorecard". This latter reflects the need to have not only commercial business concerns but also environmental concerns, social concerns, concern for good governance, as well as for the betterment of spiritual environment. Firms in many industrialized nations profess to taking care of some of these concerns. Many corporate leaders have been reassuring their stakeholders about this. Their 'CSR' firstly includes governance-ethical principles. It also reflects their 'social' concern; which however is entirely about the material needs of society. There is a persistent gap which is not addressed by CSR. This is about "spiritual needs". Some firms address their spiritual concerns by, for example, not doing business with some entities, maintaining vegetarianism or kosher, or avoiding the earning or payment of interest on capital, etcetera. Sharma's paper touches on some of these. More significant is his suggestion that "social good" is the primary, or even sole, mission for firms – a view that is attributed to traditional Indian basis of business. Despite its overlap with CSR, a 'spiritual' angle does seem to be evolving in business strategy.

215

Two other strategic missions have also been suggested in this section as emergent, which again seems appropriate. Both arise through the splitting of value-chains, exhibited by the two cases in this section. In one case, help-services to consumers are outsourced to agencies across the world. This is leading to the fast growing and internationalizing bpo industry. Another emergent transformation of mission, shown in the case 'IWM Project by IOCW', is the business model of an NGO run by a multi-lateral international agency which funds and manages a social initiative that would normally be run by the local government. Both types of emergent missions have been proliferating. Business Process Outsourcing has begun to pervade more and more sectors of business and more and more segments of value-chain. The NGO-in-government-sector is progressively helping many governments to deliver services like education and sanitation, and doing it far more efficiently.

Organizational Form

The second section - on emergent organizational forms - presented the rising relevance of the 'small' organization. It is perhaps a truism that small enterprise is the backbone of economic growth. The small enterprise is not however a recent phenomenon. Technologies have earlier too helped in the performance of the small enterprise. In recent times, the developments in ICT and in manufacturing flexibility have made it further possible for the small enterprise to be viable. While this has created new business models in some sectors that can work at small scale, the utility of small enterprise is hardly a new phenomenon. To refer to the small enterprise as 'emergent' would therefore be an exaggeration.

The small spin-off, where managers have to seek support from multiple organizations, is a more distinct emergence for strategy. Very large bureaucracies, like the government or large private enterprise, have begun to spin off smaller missions to small entities. The case of a small institution is displayed in this volume that has to seek resources from multiple stakeholders, public and private, individual and institutional. The other case in this section exhibits dysfunctional consequences in a situation when parts of the very large government organization function as if they were unconnected. Despite being owned by the government, or perhaps due to being so owned, the different arms exhibit adversarial behavior. The organization stuck in the middle has to adopt a uniquely different strategy for performance.

Resources

Two resources have been identified as possible emergent ones. One is the use of Innovation – the incremental knowledge that results in changed value. Amongst the many new business models that are evolving through splitting of value-chains, there is one essential process – the use of technology and the process of innovation. It is no doubt true that the technological environment and innovation has always been the critical change agent for society and economics. In recent times however, innovation and technology as a resource is affecting society far more frequently and in far more substantial ways. This is why it is important to view the paper on innovation in auto and other industries and see the emergent effects on strategy of the enterprise.

Another resource brought to our attention in a paper is 'organizational social capital'. The paper develops a dependency based index of power to measure structural social capital, looks into aspects of 'reputation capital', and shows the long term effect of 'reputation capital' on organizations. It is not that 'reputation capital' has not been there earlier. What is significant is a planned consideration of such resource for the strategy of organizations. It is therefore an emergent resource in the sense that it enters more formal consideration in the strategizing process.

Geographic Locus

There is, in the final section, an emergence of a new kind of 'geographic locus' in business. This is exhibited by the fast pace of globalization - of consumers as well as suppliers - and is reflected in the issues analyzed in the paper on 'Cross Border Alliance'. While the other papers on firm promotion, value, growth and the use of growth oriented methodologies for decision making are significant, it is the *coming together of the villages on the globe* that may be seen as an accelerating phenomenon. This movement in the geographic locus is clearly an emergent factor for strategy of the future.

Note that amongst the above four types, and their multiple examples, of emergent changes in strategic ideas, there are some that have appeared in the economic process to deal with 'local' issues, a response to some pressing need, and are therefore more easily tractable from an implementation point of view. New missions like BPO and the NGO-in-Government are such changing ideas. There are also, on the other hand, ideas that have a very wide-ranging impact, such as the inclusion of 'spiritual concern' in the mission of a firm. These are also changing ideas in strategy, with the difference that they are a long time in coming!

Arun P. Sinha
Editor
asinha@iitk.ac.in